P9-CKS-675

ALSO BY THE AMERICAN HEART ASSOCIATION

American Heart Association Cookbook, 5th Edition

American Heart Association Low-Fat, Low-Cholesterol Cookbook

American Heart Association Kids' Cookbook

American Heart Association Family Guide to Stroke

American Heart Association Brand Name Fat and Cholesterol Counter

American Heart Association Quick and Easy Cookbook

Living Well, Staying Well
(coauthored with the American Cancer Society)

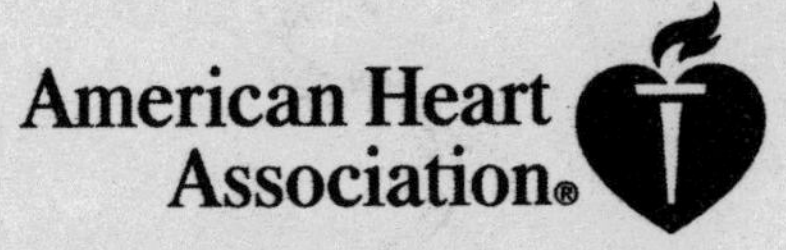

Fighting Heart Disease and Stroke

The American Heart Association LOW-SALT COOKBOOK

LOW-SALT COOKBOOK

A Complete Guide to Reducing Sodium and Fat in the Diet

Editors
Rodman D. Starke, M.D.
Mary Winston, Ed.D., R.D.

Illustrations by
Regina Scudellari

Clarkson Potter/Publishers
New York

Your contribution to the American Heart Association supports research that helps make publications like this possible. For more information, call 1-800-AHA-USA1.

Note to Doctor and Dietitian: This cookbook is designed for those who wish to restrict their salt or sodium intake mildly, to approximately 2,000 milligrams per day. If further restrictions are necessary, the recipes here can easily be adapted to a lower level of sodium.

Published by Clarkson Potter/Publishers, New York, New York.
Member of the Crown Publishing Group.

Random House, Inc. New York, Toronto, London, Sydney, Auckland
www.randomhouse.com

Printed in the United States of America

Art direction by Naomi Osnos
Book design by MM Design 2000

Library of Congress Cataloging-in-Publication Data
The American Heart Association low-salt cookbook: a complete guide to reducing sodium and fat in the diet / by the American Heart Association.
1. Salt-free diet—Recipes. I. American Heart Association.
II. Title: Low-salt cookbook.
RM237.8.A45 1990
641.5'632—dc20 90-10823

ISBN 0-8129-2476-2

20 19 18 17 16 15 14

Preface

Cutting down on sodium in your diet is a good idea for a lot of reasons. But most people make this change only when they have to, when advised to by their doctor, to help treat high blood pressure, also known as hypertension.

About 60 million Americans have high blood pressure. Many of them follow medical treatment their doctors have recommended. But over the past decade, concern over the potential danger of lifelong drug therapy for all hypertensives has grown. Shouldn't there be ways to reduce high blood pressure in some cases without resorting to drugs?

Fortunately, there are. Two of the best treatments today seem to be reducing the amount of sodium in the diet and controlling weight.

While it may be impossible to know how effective a sodium-restricted diet would be for *all* hypertensive patients, it does appear that a sizable group of them could benefit greatly from this approach. We wrote this cookbook for those patients.

Actually, research is beginning to show that *most* of us—not just hypertensives—would benefit from reducing the sodium in our diets. Studies of people around the world have indicated that habitual high sodium intake may "set the stage" for hypertension in certain people who are genetically prone to it. Many Americans want to reduce their sodium intake—either as a preventive measure or because their doctors have advised them to do so. If you are one of these people, this book can help you do just that.

It is well established that the chance of developing cardiovascular disease increases if you have high blood pressure. Sometimes people with high blood pressure are also fighting high blood cholesterol. In *The American Heart Association Low-Salt Cookbook,* we've acknowledged and addressed that problem; all the recipes are not only low-sodium, but low-modified-fat and low-cholesterol, too. Without extra effort, you can help control both high blood pressure and high blood cholesterol with the recipes here and cut your risks of cardiovascular disease even further.

You'll also find in this book a nutrient analysis of each recipe, its calorie count per serving, tips on buying and preparing foods and two easy-to-follow eating plans, the Step-One and Step-Two diets (see Appendix A, pages 313–361).

Best of all are our newly created and revised recipes. If your idea of low-sodium cooking has been "cardboard on a plate," you're in for a wonderful surprise! Featuring fresh ingredients, herbs, spices and spirits, these recipes pack flavor into each dish. You'll be so dazzled by these taste sensations, salt may seem almost bland by comparison.

Most of us know from experience that change—any change—is hard. Changing longtime eating habits is no exception. So take it slowly, one step at a time. In a few months, you'll wonder why you didn't start eating this way years ago.

To health and happiness.

RODMAN D. STARKE, M.D.
Senior Vice President
Office of Scientific Affairs
American Heart Association
National Center
Dallas, Texas

Acknowledgments

The credit for recognizing the need for a low-sodium, low-modified-fat, low-cholesterol cookbook—and for the hard work and dedication that goes into developing such a book—goes to the American Heart Association Northeast Ohio Affiliate's Low Sodium Cookbook Task Force.

The teamwork and expertise of those volunteers resulted in the publication of *Cooking Without Your Salt Shaker,* the first edition of this book, in 1978. The Task Force members and significant contributors were: Sharon Reichman, R.D., chairperson; Charlene Krejci, R.D.; Karen Wilcoxon Izso, R.D.; Grace Petot, R.D.; Sally Gleason, R.D.; Tab Forgac, R.D.; Rosemary Manni, R.D.; Auretha Pettigrew, R.D.; Robert Post, M.D.; Mary Ann Weber, R.D.; and Cleveland Dietetic Association, Diet Therapy Section.

That cookbook was available only through the American Heart Association. But its popularity convinced us to offer it to a wider audience. At the same time, changes in science and trends in food preparation prompted us to update and expand the book significantly.

Kudos to Mike Semon for creating delicious new recipes and modifying existing ones for more flavor and variety. Thanks also to the Nutrition Coordinating Center, University of Minnesota, for nutrient analyses.

Sincere thank-yous go to Jane Ruehl for the excellent but tedious task of copyediting and to Pat Covington for copywriting.

Thanks also go to Lynne Scott, M.S., R.D., for her expertise and undying efforts in developing the diet plan.

Finally, without Ann Yanosky's untiring efforts to keep all of us on schedule and attention to every detail, this book would never have been published.

MARY WINSTON, Ed.D., R.D.
Senior Science Consultant
Office of Scientific Affairs
American Heart Association
National Center
Dallas, Texas

Contents

Fighting Heart Disease and Stroke

THE AMERICAN HEART ASSOCIATION LOW-SALT COOKBOOK

Introduction

Congratulations.

You are about to do something exciting: learn to cook without salt. Maybe you picked up this book because your doctor recommended reducing your sodium intake to control your high blood pressure. Or maybe you decided on your own that you'd like to cut down on salt. Whatever the reason, this cookbook will help you do just that.

THEY SAID IT COULDN'T BE DONE

People often claim that food cooked without salt is boring, flat and tasteless. Well, they're wrong.

With no-salt cooking you'll learn to use your imagination. You'll try spices and herb combinations you've never heard of . . . and be glad you did. You'll create new taste sensations with wines and spirits and with exotic spices and oils. Cooking without salt may be as easy or as elaborate as you wish to make it, but it can always be deliciously flavorful.

SALT, FAT AND HEART DISEASE

At the American Heart Association, we've learned a lot about the many possible causes of heart attack and stroke—and what can be done to try to prevent them.

The top three ways to help prevent these and other cardiovascular diseases are: avoid smoking, try to achieve a desirable blood cholesterol level and control high blood pressure.

By the millions, Americans have stopped smoking. Millions more are cutting down on total fat, saturated fat and cholesterol in their diets. Now, Americans in record numbers are helping control their high blood pressure by reducing—or eliminating—the salt in their diets.

WHAT IS HIGH BLOOD PRESSURE?

Blood pressure describes the pressure exerted by the blood against the artery walls. The heart creates this pressure as it pumps blood. A blood pressure measurement is written in two numbers, such as 120/80. It is read as "one-twenty over eighty."

The first, or upper, number represents systolic pressure —the blood pressure in the arteries when the heart is pumping blood. The second, or lower, number represents diastolic pressure—the pressure in the arteries when the heart is at rest between beats.

As a general rule, any blood pressure greater than 140/90 is considered to be high. And the higher your blood pressure above this point, the greater your risk of stroke, heart attack, kidney failure and other cardiovascular complications. That's why treating high blood pressure is so important.

The cause of 90 percent of all high blood pressure is unknown. All the same, it has been found that too much salty food may contribute to high blood pressure in certain "genetically susceptible" people. Occasionally, high blood pressure is caused by another medical problem and will disappear once the problem is corrected.

IS THERE A CURE?

Unfortunately, there is no cure for hypertension. But there are many things you can do to help bring your blood pressure under control. You can keep your weight at a normal level, get regular exercise and use this cookbook to help you reduce your sodium intake. Hypertension and high blood cholesterol are both risk factors for heart attack. This cookbook will show you how to help reduce both of these risks by limiting your intake of sodium, saturated fat and cholesterol.

Too much sodium in your system holds water in your body and puts an extra burden on your heart and blood vessels. That's why low-sodium diets are often effective for treating high blood pressure. Eating more foods that contain potassium or calcium may help lower blood pressure in some people. (See the list of these foods in "Potassium Sources" on page 298.)

THE SALT-SODIUM CONNECTION

Many people use the words *salt* and *sodium* as if they were the same thing. Not quite. Salt is actually sodium chloride, a chemical compound that is about half sodium.

Sodium is a mineral found in nature and in almost all the food we eat. Everyone needs some sodium to live, but this need can be met easily without adding even a pinch of salt to food. The foods themselves contain all we need.

The average American eats an estimated ten times more sodium than he or she actually needs for good health. One way to reduce that intake is to cut down on ordinary table salt even if you have no health problem. If you have high blood pressure, your doctor will probably advise you to do that. It's one way to help keep your blood pressure under control to reduce your risk of stroke, heart attack and kidney failure.

WATCHING YOUR HEART—AND YOUR WAISTLINE

This low-sodium cookbook was also designed with fat in mind. "Low" fat, to be exact. Each recipe and recommended serving size was created to be low in total fat, saturated fat and cholesterol.

Watching your fat intake does more than just help your heart. It helps your waistline, too. If you're counting calories, look for the calorie content of each serving size listed in the analysis of each recipe.

In this cookbook, we use "acceptable" margarines and vegetable oils wherever fats are called for. Acceptable margarine is unsaturated and unsalted. Acceptable vegetable oils include polyunsaturated cooking oils such as corn and safflower, or monounsaturated oils such as canola and olive. You'll learn more about these oils later in the cookbook. (See the list of recommended oils on page 16.) Just remember that they provide flavor—with the added benefit of contributing to a cholesterol-lowering eating plan.

WHEN YOU ARE FOLLOWING SPECIAL DIET INSTRUCTIONS

If your doctor or dietitian has given you a low-sodium diet instruction sheet, check it against the ingredients in these recipes. If there is a difference, follow the instructions on your instruction sheet. If, for example, your instructions tell you to use only unsalted bread, use that in place of the regular bread listed in the ingredients list of our recipes. Such substitutions will result in slightly different values from those listed in our nutrient analysis for that particular recipe.

If you have not received a diet instruction sheet from your doctor or dietitian, we offer our own low-sodium diets to help you reach your goal. (See pages 313–361 in the Appendix.) Follow the recipes in the book closely, and be sure to use the ingredients specified.

EATING WITH YOUR HEART IN MIND

When you reduce the amount of sodium in your foods and change the kind and amount of fat in your diet, you can help lower your risk of heart and blood vessel disease.

It's never easy to change old cooking habits. You may find it difficult at first. But when you savor the exotic taste of our Lamb Curry or a light but flavor-filled bite of Herbed Fillet of Sole, you'll realize that it is worth the effort. Creative, help-your-heart cooking can be "just what the doctor ordered" for you and your family.

So go ahead. Take the salt shaker off the table. Then pick up this cookbook. Consider it the beginning of a great culinary adventure. If you have questions, ask your doctor or call your American Heart Association. We're here to help.

Bon appétit!

When You Go Shopping

Shopping for a low-sodium menu is easier than you might think, now that many familiar items are available in no-salt or low-salt varieties.

With a little effort, you can learn to cut the sodium, change the kind of fat and reduce the amount of fat and cholesterol in your diet. As part of that effort, you'll have to start reading the product labels on prepared foods to make sure they're really low in sodium, total fat, saturated fat and cholesterol.

CHECK FOR SODIUM

Check ingredient lists for salt and other high-sodium additives. Be alert to any food label that has the word *sodium* on it. Watch especially for these sources of "hidden salt" in foods:

- Monosodium glutamate (MSG) (flavor enhancer)
- Sodium bicarbonate (leavening agent)
- Sodium nitrite (meat curing agent)
- Sodium benzoate (preservative)
- Sodium propionate (mold inhibitor)
- Sodium citrate (acidity controller)

When you see the phrase *sodium-free* on a label, it means the item has less than 5 milligrams of sodium per serving. *Very low sodium* means less than 35 milligrams per serving. *Low sodium* means less than 140 milligrams per serving, and *reduced sodium* means the product was processed to reduce the usual sodium level by 75 percent.

Unsalted, no salt added and *without added salt* mean the product is made without the salt that is normally used in processing, but the product still contains the sodium that is a natural part of the food.

DOWN WITH CHOLESTEROL

When you see the phrase *no cholesterol* on a label, it means the product does not contain any cholesterol. But it may still contain saturated fat, which raises blood cholesterol. Basically, any product that does not contain ingredients from an animal source is naturally cholesterol-free. But coconut, palm and palm kernel oil—the "tropical oils"—are three plant sources that contain saturated fat.

A few product labels will give you the percent of calories derived from fat. Peanut butter and margarine labels often give this information, alerting you to the fact that these products contain primarily fat.

Most of the recipe ingredients called for in this cookbook are readily available in your local grocery store. Some, such as no-salt-added tomato paste and sauce, will be found in the usual section of the grocery store. Other unsalted foods can be found in the special diet section. If the items you want are not in stock, ask your grocer to order them for you.

COUNTING CALORIES

The words *low-calorie* mean the product contains no more than 40 calories per serving. *Reduced calorie* means the product has at least one-third fewer calories than the product for which this food is substituted.

When you shop, be sure to compare labels. Some premixed, frozen or prepared foods have a lower sodium, saturated fatty acid or cholesterol content than others. Now that many products list their sodium, fat and cholesterol content, shopping for low-sodium, low-saturated-fatty-acid, low-cholesterol foods is easier than ever before.

HOW TO READ A LABEL

This is important. First, look at the ingredients listed. All food labels list the product's ingredients in order by weight. The ingredient present in the greatest amount is listed first. The ingredient present in the least amount is listed last.

As a rule, if salt and several sodium compounds are listed as ingredients, the product contains more salt than is advisable on a low-sodium diet. To avoid too much total fat or saturated fatty acids, limit your use of products that list a fat or oil first, or that list many fat and oil ingredients.

The nutrition label also tells you what types of nutrients the product provides, the relative proportions of those nutrients and their contributions to the U.S. Recommended Daily Allowances for protein, vitamins and minerals.

WHAT TO SHOP FOR

Now make your shopping list. The key to a healthful diet is to make sure you eat a variety of foods. Your daily food choices should include:

- No more than 6 ounces of lean meat, fish or poultry
- Dried beans, peas, lentils or soybean curd (tofu) in place of meat a few times a week
- Whole-grain or enriched bread or low-sodium cereal products
- 3 or more servings of fruit and 3 or more servings of vegetables (include 1 serving of citrus fruit or vegetable high in vitamin C and 1 serving of dark green, leafy or deep yellow vegetables)
- 2 or more servings of skim milk or low-sodium, low-fat milk products for adults; 3 to 4 servings for children or adolescents
- 5 to 8 teaspoons of polyunsaturated and monounsaturated fats and oils in the form of unsalted margarine, cook-

ing oil and unsalted salad dressing (this amount may vary according to caloric needs)

DAIRY PRODUCTS

For a balanced diet, include two or more servings of skim milk (0 to 1 percent milk fat) or low-sodium, low-fat milk products every day.

With the exception of buttermilk and cheese, most milk and milk products do not contain added salt—but do watch out for the cholesterol and saturated fats found in whole milk and whole milk products. Try to make your dairy selections from the wide variety of low-fat dairy products on the market instead.

It's amazing how much fat and cholesterol you can eliminate from your diet by using low-fat or nonfat milk products. One ounce of plain, low-fat yogurt, for example, has 0.28 grams of saturated fat and 1.70 milligrams of cholesterol, while the same amount of plain, nonfat yogurt has just 0.03 grams of saturated fat and 0.57 milligrams of cholesterol.

The comparison can become even more dramatic. Look at regular sour cream: It has 3.41 grams of saturated fat and 18.71 milligrams of cholesterol per ounce, compared with low-fat sour cream, with just 1.15 grams of saturated fat and 6.39 milligrams of cholesterol per ounce.

Whole-milk products can be replaced with the following:

- Skim milk, evaporated skim milk, nonfat dry milk
- Dry-curd cottage cheese that has no salt added
- Cheese made from skim or partially skim milk with no salt added (no more than 5 grams of fat and 150 milligrams of sodium per ounce)
- Low-fat yogurt or low-fat frozen yogurt
- Ice milk and sherbets
- Polyunsaturated nondairy creamers or whiteners

Note: Imitation sour cream, nondairy whipped toppings

and nondairy coffee whiteners that contain saturated fat are not recommended.

EGGS

One large egg yolk contains almost the entire daily allowance for cholesterol, approximately 213 to 220 milligrams. It's a good idea to limit your egg yolk consumption to three per week.

On the other hand, egg whites contain no cholesterol and are an excellent source of protein. You often can use egg whites in place of whole eggs. In fact, in most recipes two egg whites and a little acceptable vegetable oil will substitute nicely for a whole egg. (See our recipe for No-Cholesterol Egg Substitute on page 164.)

Be sure to eat only cooked eggs and egg whites—not raw.

MEAT PRODUCTS

A balanced diet requires some protein foods every day. With meats, keep your sodium intake to a minimum by buying only unsalted fresh or frozen lean meat. And because meats contain cholesterol and saturated fat, you'll want to limit yourself to six ounces per day.

The best meats for you are lean cuts with less fat around the outside and less marbled fat throughout. Some of the leanest cuts are round steak, sirloin tip, tenderloin and extra-lean ground beef. All cuts of veal are lean except cutlets. Look for lean pork, such as low-sodium fresh center-cut ham, tenderloin and loin chops.

Pay particular attention to ground beef. It's best to select a lean cut of meat and ask the butcher to trim and grind it for you. This is usually done at no extra charge.

Fresh poultry pieces cooked without skin are an excellent protein choice. When using whole chickens and turkeys, roast them with the skin on. This will help prevent the meat from drying out. Be sure to remove the skin before eating. Stay away from self-basting turkeys, because commercial basting fats are highly saturated. Even when the turkey is basted in broth, the broth is usually high in sodium. It's much better to baste your own turkey with an unsalted broth.

In general, steer clear of the following meats, which contain large amounts of one or more of the things we are trying to limit (sodium, fat and cholesterol): luncheon meats; frankfurters; sausage; spareribs; corned beef; salt pork; liver and other organ meats; smoked, cured or dried meats such as ham and bacon; and canned meat or poultry, unless packed without salt.

FISH

Fish is a versatile low-sodium favorite. While not free of cholesterol, fish generally contains less than red meat. For a cholesterol-lowering diet, this gives fish a slight edge over lean red meat and a definite edge over fatty red meat. For this reason, many authorities recommend that fish be eaten two or three times a week.

Fish itself can be either fatty or lean. Omega-3 fatty acids, found in some varieties of fatty fish, are currently being studied for potential lipid (blood fat)-lowering benefits. Some fish high in Omega-3 fatty acids are: Atlantic and coho salmon, albacore tuna, mackerel, carp, lake whitefish, sweet smelt, and lake and brook trout.

Shrimp, lobster, crab, crayfish and most other shellfish are very low in fat. However, ounce for ounce, some varieties contain more sodium and cholesterol than do poultry, meat or other fish. Even these, however, can be eaten occasionally within the recommended guidelines of 300 milligrams of cholesterol per day.

FRUITS, VEGETABLES, GRAINS AND LEGUMES

With few exceptions, fresh foods in these categories have no cholesterol, tend to be low in sodium and fat and, in many cases, are high in fiber and vitamins.

The exceptions include coconut meat, avocados and olives. Coconut meat is high in saturated fatty acids. Both avocados and olives are high in fat, although the fat is largely unsaturated. Green olives are high in sodium (800 milligrams in 10 small), and ripe olives are moderately high in sodium (250 milligrams in 5 extra-large). Stay away from vegetables that have been packed in brine, such as pickles and sauerkraut, because they're loaded with sodium.

In this category, always read the labels on frozen and processed foods. Many of them contain added salt, butter or sauces.

Also note that fruits that are fresh or canned in water are lower in calories than fruits canned in juice or in syrup.

NUTS AND SEEDS

These are tasty snacks and most kinds are available in their natural state: unsalted. But remember that although the fat in nuts and seeds is mostly unsaturated, there's lots of it, so the calorie count is higher than most people realize. Nuts and seeds are good sources of incomplete proteins and can replace other high-protein foods to some degree—especially when eaten with beans, legumes and grains, which are also incomplete proteins. Together, they provide complete protein.

BREADS, CEREALS AND PASTA

Whole-grain or enriched breads, cereals and pastas are an important part of a balanced diet. They provide plenty of nutrients and relatively few calories. (But avoid the high-fat or salty sauces and condiments that often accompany them.)

Go ahead and experiment with different kinds of breads, such as whole or cracked wheat, rye, French, Italian and pumpernickel. They do contain some sodium and a small amount of fat, but not enough to outweigh their natural goodness for you.

Check the labels on crackers for sodium, fats and oils. Look for soda crackers without salt, or try matzo, melba toast or bread sticks if you want something crunchy. Scandinavian-style rye crackers and other whole-grain crackers are often made without fats or oils and with little or no salt. Also look for unsalted popcorn, pretzels and bread sticks.

Be wary of commercially baked goods and mixes such as muffins, biscuits, sweet rolls, cakes, cookies and pastries. They contain significant amounts of sodium and/or cholesterol and saturated fat. It's 100 percent better to bake your own: Just use the recipes in this book or adjust your own favorites by omitting the salt and using the ingredient substitutions listed on pages 26–29.

Cereals are great for anyone on a low-sodium, low-modified-fat diet. Most cereals don't have saturated fat or cholesterol. (One of the few exceptions is granola.) Most do, however, contain sodium. Be sure to read the label and choose those that are low in sodium and are made with the kinds of fats recommended in the following section on fats and oils. Look for the word *sodium* on the label, because it appears disguised in many different sodium compounds. (These are listed in the Appendix, on page 305.)

Hot cereals, rice and pastas contain almost no sodium—just remember to leave the salt out of the cooking water when you prepare these foods.

FATS AND OILS

Polyunsaturated and monounsaturated fats and oils are the kinds of fats you'll want to include in your daily diet. In fact, 5 to 8 teaspoons of these fats and oils daily is a reasonable amount.

You can use them in the form of unsalted salad dressing, unsalted margarine or oil used in cooking. Oils are cholesterol-free and do not contain sodium. Mayonnaise and most margarines, on the other hand, do contain some salt, but they're still okay to use occasionally. Most commercial salad dressings contain large amounts of salt and should be avoided.

WHAT KIND OF FAT IS IT?

When reading the labels on packaged goods, pay particular attention to the kinds of fats and oils present.

Saturated Fat. Fats and oils high in saturated fatty acids tend to become hard at room temperature. Butter, lard and tallow from animals, and coconut, palm and palm kernel oils from plants are common examples. These saturated fats raise blood cholesterol and should be avoided.

Monounsaturated and Polyunsaturated Fat. Oils that stay liquid at room temperature are high in unsaturated fats. They include corn, safflower, soybean, sunflower, olive and canola (rapeseed) oils. All are low in saturated fatty acids and can be used to help lower blood cholesterol. They do not contain sodium, either.

Hydrogenated Oils. These are ordinarily found in liquid form at room temperature but have been artificially hardened to produce margarines and shortenings. Their effect on blood cholesterol depends on how much they are hydrogenated. It's best to look for margarines that have the hydrogenated oil listed as the second ingredient.

As a rule, keep your total fat intake to no more than 30 percent of your total diet, and use the following lists to help you identify recommended fats and oils.

FATS AND OILS

Recommended:	***Not recommended/ saturated:***
Safflower oil	Butter
Sunflower oil	Vegetable shortening
Corn oil	Vegetable fat
Soybean oil	Bacon, salt pork
Sesame seed oil	Suet, lard
Canola oil	Chicken fat, meat fat
Olive oil	Coconut oil
Polyunsaturated margarine	Palm kernel oil
Unsalted oil-based salad dressing (using recommended oils)	Palm oil
	For occasional use only:
	Peanut oil

BEVERAGES

When you're thirsty, look for beverages that are not high in sodium, fat or cholesterol. These include skim milk and low-sodium fruit juices, fruit drinks and carbonated beverages. Some diet soft drinks and mineral waters are high in sodium. Be sure to read the label before selecting your beverage. The sodium content of tap water varies widely from one location to another. If your water supply is high in sodium, use low-sodium bottled water for drinking and for making drinks such as tea and coffee.

If you're trying to lose weight, steer clear of sugared carbonated beverages, fruit drinks, beer, wine and alcohol.

Alcohol has been erroneously credited with preventing heart disease. In moderation, alcohol does not appear to be harmful. But the ill effects of excessive alcohol consumption are well established. If you drink, it's smart to limit your alcohol intake to one ounce per day.

MISCELLANEOUS FOODS AND FLAVORINGS

On a low-sodium eating plan, be careful of the many commonly used commercial seasonings and sauces containing large amounts of sodium or salt. These include: soy sauce, Worcestershire sauce, steak sauce, ketchup, chili sauce, monosodium glutamate, meat tenderizer, flavored seasoning salts and bouillon cubes. Look for low-sodium versions of these items, or use the recipes we've included in this cookbook to make your own.

Try making your own salad dressings from herbs, oil and vinegar. Cook with spices, flavorings, freshly ground horseradish, hot pepper sauce, garlic, herbs and fruit juices.

Many snack foods, commercial soups, green olives, relishes and pickles contain lots of salt. Some of them are available commercially in no-salt varieties. Try the recipes in this cookbook for soups and sauces—and even pickles.

You'll want to substitute unsweetened cocoa powder for baking chocolate and chocolate chips. Chocolate and cocoa butter contain lots of saturated fat, but most of the fat has been removed from cocoa powder.

SNACKS

Many snack products, such as chips and rich crackers, are high in sodium and saturated fatty acids. However, some chips are cooked in unsaturated oil. Choose only those labeled as having lower salt and more polyunsaturated than saturated fatty acids. Better yet, make your own cookies, cakes and snack foods without salt and with acceptable oils or margarines.

Food Preparation Ideas

Now you know what kinds of foods are part of a low-salt, low-modified-fat, low-cholesterol eating plan. That's great, but it's just the beginning. It's not enough just to *buy* healthful foods. You also need to know how to prepare them so that they *stay* that way.

All cooking methods are not created equal. Some are better than others for retaining vitamins and minerals and for cutting cholesterol, fat and calories. Basically, stay away from cooking techniques that add fat or allow food to cook in its own fat, such as deep-fat frying or pan frying.

Instead, look for cooking techniques that enhance flavor, preserve basic nutrients, and keep added fat and sodium to a minimum. To get you started, here are a few examples of cooking methods that will help you help your heart.

Roasting. Always place a rack on the bottom of the roasting pan so the meat or poultry doesn't sit in its own fat drippings. Be sure to roast at a low temperature, about 350° F., to avoid searing the meat or poultry and sealing in the fat. For basting, use low-sodium, fat-free liquids such as table wine, no-salt-added tomato juice or fresh lemon juice.

Baking. Poultry, fish and meat can be baked in covered cookware with a little additional liquid. The moisture that the liquid adds makes this method particularly good for fish or chicken breasts, which tend to be a little dry.

Braising or Stewing. This method uses a little more liquid than baking does. Try it in a covered container on top of the stove (using low heat) or in the oven (using medium temperatures, 300°–325° F.). If you're braising or stewing meat or poultry, begin a day ahead of time and refrigerate the dish overnight. The next day, when the chilled fat has congealed, you can remove it easily before reheating. Braising is also an excellent way to cook vegetables.

Poaching. To poach chicken or fish, immerse it in a pan of simmering liquid on top of the stove. This method works especially well when you serve the food with a sauce made of pureed vegetables and herbs.

Grilling or Broiling. Placing food on a rack and cooking with either of these methods allows the fat to drip away from meat or poultry. It's also a tasty way to cook fish steaks or whole fish. For extra flavor, try marinating food before putting it over the coals or under the broiler. Skewered vegetables also taste great browned over an open flame.

Sautéing. Fish, poultry and vegetable dishes can be sautéed in an open skillet with little or no fat; the high temperature and motion keep food from sticking. Try sautéing with a tiny bit of unsaturated oil rubbed onto the pan with a paper towel. Better still, use vegetable oil spray or sauté in a small amount of low-sodium broth or table wine.

Steaming. Cooking food in a basket over simmering water leaves the natural flavor, color and nutritional value of vegetables intact. Try adding herbs to the steaming water or using low-sodium broth instead of water to add even more flavor to the finished dish.

Stir-frying. Done in a Chinese wok, this method relies on the same principle as sautéing. The high temperature and the constant movement of the food keep it from sticking and burning. Try stir-frying vegetables and diced poultry or seafood with a tiny bit of peanut oil. Use the low-sodium version when your recipe calls for soy sauce.

Microwave Cooking. This is a fast, easy cooking method that requires no added fat. You don't have to add fat to keep the food from sticking to the pan because foods don't tend to stick in the moist heat of microwaving. In fact, you can drain food of fat as it cooks by placing it in the microwave between two paper towels.

If you want to adapt a recipe for microwaving, try cutting the cooking time to one-fourth to one-third of the conventional time. If the food needs more cooking, increase it a little at a time. You might also look for a microwave recipe similar to the one you're trying to adapt. Keep the following in mind when microwave cooking:

- Choose foods that cook well in moist heat: chicken, fish, ground meat, vegetables, sauces and soups.
- Pieces that are about equal in size and shape will cook uniformly.
- You can reduce the liquid used in cooking beverages, soups, vegetables, fruits and main dishes by about one-third because less evaporates in microwave cooking.
- Choose a microwave-safe container slightly larger than the dish required for cooking the recipe in a conventional oven.
- Use a high setting (100 percent power) for soups, beverages, fruits, vegetables, fish, ground meat and poultry. Use a medium-high setting (70 percent power) for simmering stews. And use a medium setting (50 percent power) for baking breads, cakes and muffins and for cooking less tender cuts of meat.
- To create a crusty look on baked items, grease pans with an acceptable vegetable oil and add ground nuts or crumbs. (Be sure to calculate the values for the fat and/or sodium in these added nuts when deciding how these foods fit into your dietary plans.)
- Add low-fat, low-sodium cheese and other toppings near the end of cooking to keep them from becoming tough or soggy.
- Don't try coating meat with flour if you will be adding liquid for cooking. The coating only becomes soggy.
- Use quick-cooking instead of long-grain rice.

COOKING TIPS

Keep the taste, but trim the fat and salt. That's the challenge you'll face cooking for a low-sodium, low-modified-fat, low-cholesterol eating plan. Here are a few helpful hints.

- Use a nonstick skillet so that you can cook with a minimum of oil, or cook with vegetable oil spray, another good fat-cutting technique.
- Trim all visible fat from meat before cooking.
- After you roast meat or poultry, chill the drippings in the refrigerator. Once they are cooled, the fat will rise to the top and harden; it can be removed easily and the broth saved to use in stews, sauces and soups.
- Buy only the leanest ground beef, pork and turkey (no more than 15 percent fat). After browning it, put ground meat into a strainer or colander lined with paper towels. Allow fat to drain out. "Ground" meat is generally higher in fat than nonground meat. Even the leanest ground beef contains more fat than is recommended for those on the Step-Two Diet (see pages 339–361). Instead of buying packaged ground beef, have your butcher grind a sirloin steak for you. Be sure to have him remove all visible fat and clean the grinder to remove any fat from previous grindings.
- When figuring serving sizes, remember that meat loses about 25 percent of its weight during cooking. (For example, 4 ounces of raw meat will be about 3 ounces cooked.)
- To make gravy without fat, blend a teaspoon of cornstarch with a cup of room-temperature, low-sodium broth by shaking the two together in a jar with a tight-fitting lid. Then heat the rest of the defatted broth in a saucepan and add the blended liquid. Simmer until thickened.
- Make a habit of skinning chickens before cooking and removing all visible fat below the skin. The skin will be easier to remove if you use paper towels or a clean cloth to take hold of it. Be certain to scrub the cutting surface and utensils well with hot sudsy water after preparing poultry for cooking.
- Fresh fish should be cooked for 10 minutes per inch of thickness. Add 5 minutes if it's wrapped in foil. Frozen fish requires 20 minutes per inch of thickness, plus 10

minutes if it's wrapped in foil. Cooking time may vary, depending on the cooking method used, but fish is done when the flesh is opaque and it flakes easily.

- Prepare scrambled eggs or omelettes so that only one egg yolk per portion is used. Add a few extra egg whites to the mixing bowl to make more generous servings.
- Seal natural juices into foods by wrapping them in foil before cooking. Or try wrapping foods in edible pouches made of large steamed lettuce or cabbage leaves and placing them seam-side down in the baking dish before cooking.
- Cook vegetables just long enough to make them tender-crisp. Overcooked vegetables lose both flavor and important nutrients.
- Clean mushrooms as you use them by wiping them with a damp cloth. A quick rinse in cold water is fine, but never soak them or they'll get soggy.
- Be sure to wear rubber gloves when handling hot peppers or wash hands thoroughly after handling. Skin, especially around the eyes, is very sensitive to the oil from peppers.
- Cut down on cholesterol by using more vegetables and less poultry or meats in soups, stews and casseroles. Finely chopped vegetables are great for stretching ground poultry or meat, too.
- Cut down on fat in creamy salad dressing by mixing it with plain, low-fat or nonfat yogurt.
- Sweeten plain, low-fat or nonfat yogurt with pureed fruit or applesauce instead of buying prepared fruit yogurt.

ENHANCING FLAVORS WITHOUT USING SALT

Spicing up low-salt cooking is easy when you know a few good tricks. The following ideas will help you enhance the flavor of a variety of foods without using salt. After trying a few of these techniques, you'll agree that the best things in life are salt-free.

- To remove oils and salty liquids, drain canned salmon, tuna or sardines. Then add water to the can and drain again to rinse.
- Toast seeds, nuts and whole spices to bring out their full flavor. Cook them in a dry skillet over moderate heat or on a baking sheet in a 400° F. oven.
- Roasting vegetables in a hot oven will caramelize their natural sugars.
- Pound garlic, chilies and fresh herbs and spices with a mortar and pestle to release their flavors.
- Use citrus zest. The zest is the part of the peel without the white pith; it holds the true flavor of the fruit. Either grate it with a flat, sheet-type grater or remove it with a vegetable peeler and then cut the piece into thin strips.
- Grate fresh ginger with a flat, sheet-type grater. Use a food processor to grate fresh horseradish, which packs more punch than the salted, bottled kind.
- Use fresh herbs instead of dried when possible. Chop and add them at the last moment for fresher, more "alive" taste.
- Add dried herbs such as thyme, rosemary and marjoram for more pungent flavor, but use them sparingly.
- Sprinkle vinegar or citrus juice for a wonderful flavor enhancer, but add it at the last moment. Vinegar is wonderful on vegetables such as greens, citrus on fruits such as cantaloupe. Either is great on fish.
- Use dry mustard or salt-free mustard. Mix the dry mustard with water to make a very sharp condiment. You can also find bottled, salt-free mustard that's just as powerful as the kind that contains salt.
- For a little more "bite," add fresh hot peppers to your dishes. Remove the membrane and seeds before finely chopping. They are fine raw, and a small amount goes a long way.
- Vegetables and fruits are easy to season without salt. Fill an herb shaker with a combination of fresh herbs and

spices. Use that in place of a salt shaker. One of our favorites can be found on pages 38–39.

- Some vegetables and fruits, such as mushrooms, tomatoes, chilies, cherries, cranberries and currants, impart a more intense flavor when dried than when fresh. And if they are soaked in water and reconstituted, you get as a bonus a natural "broth" to work with.
- Buy the best and the freshest whole spices and grind them in a spice grinder. You'll taste a big difference.

Ingredient Substitutions

No need to toss out old family recipes and holiday treats because you're watching your salt intake. You can keep many of your favorite recipes if you're willing to make a few simple ingredient substitutions. Just by making these few changes, you will reduce enough of the sodium and fat to make almost any recipe fit right into your new eating plan.

If your own recipe calls for:	**Use:**
Broth or bouillon	Unsalted bouillon cubes according to package directions; commercially prepared low-sodium broth; Chicken Broth (page 44); or Beef Broth (page 45).
Tomato juice	No-salt-added tomato juice; or dilute 1 6-ounce can of no-salt-added tomato paste with 3 cans of water.
Tomato sauce	Combine 1 6-ounce can of no-salt-added tomato paste with 1 can of water.
Salt	See "Seasoning Blends" (pages 38–40).
Flavor salts such as onion salt, garlic salt and celery salt	Onion powder, garlic powder, celery seed or flakes as indicated in the recipe or according to your preference.
Sour cream	Mock Sour Cream (page 194); plain low-fat or nonfat yogurt; unsalted low-fat cottage cheese plus low-fat yogurt for flavor; unsalted ricotta cheese made from part-skim milk (thinned with yogurt or low-fat buttermilk, if desired); 1 can of chilled evaporated skim milk whipped with 1 teaspoon of fresh lemon juice; or low-fat buttermilk. *Note:* When using yogurt in sauces, mix 1 tablespoon cornstarch with 1 tablespoon of

If your own recipe calls for:	Use:
Sour cream *(continued)*	yogurt and then mix into remainder of yogurt. This prevents the yogurt from separating.
Whipped cream	Mock Whipped Cream (page 195). Evaporated skim milk (thoroughly chilled before whipping).
Unsweetened baking chocolate	Unsweetened cocoa powder or carob powder blended with unsaturated oil or unsaturated, unsalted margarine (1 1-ounce square of chocolate = 3 tablespoons of cocoa or carob plus 1 tablespoon polyunsaturated oil or unsaturated, unsalted margarine). Because carob is sweeter than cocoa, reduce the sugar in the recipe by one-fourth.
Butter	Unsaturated, unsalted margarine or oil (1 tablespoon butter = 1 tablespoon unsaturated, unsalted margarine or ¾ tablespoon oil); if you wish to substitute margarine for oil, use 1¼ cups unsaturated, unsalted margarine for 1 cup of oil; use 1¼ tablespoons of unsaturated, unsalted margarine for 1 tablespoon of oil.
Melted butter or shortening	Vegetable oil or melted unsaturated, unsalted margarine.
Eggs	Commercially produced, cholesterol-free egg substitutes according to package directions; or use 1 egg white plus 2 teaspoons of unsaturated oil for each egg. For every 2 whole eggs requested in baking recipes, substitute 3 egg whites. For 1 whole large egg, substitute 2 egg whites. The table on page 319 shows the approximate whole egg content of various prepared foods.
Whole milk	Use 1 cup of skim or nonfat milk plus 1 tablespoon of unsaturated oil as a substitute for 1 cup of whole milk.

If your own recipe calls for:	Use:
Cream cheese	Blend 4 tablespoons of unsaturated, unsalted margarine with 1 cup dry, unsalted, low-fat cottage cheese. Add a small amount of skim milk if needed in blending mixture. Vegetables such as chopped herbs and seasonings may be added for variety.
Cream	Polyunsaturated coffee creams; undiluted evaporated skim milk; double-strength reconstituted nonfat dry milk powder; or skim milk.
Evaporated milk	Evaporated skim milk
Ice cream	Ice milk; fruit ice; sherbet; or low-fat frozen yogurt.

MORE SUBSTITUTION IDEAS

- Use low-fat buttermilk in place of sour cream in salad dressing recipes.
- Thicken soups, stews or sauces that have been defatted, with cornstarch or flour dissolved in cold liquid, or with pureed vegetables.
- Substitute chopped vegetables for some of the bread when you make poultry stuffing.
- Since most recipes include more sugar than necessary, you can usually reduce the amount of sugar by one-fourth to one-third.
- Reduce salt in nonyeast baking recipes.
- Add a drop of fresh lemon juice to the water you cook pasta in and eliminate the salt.
- Substitute brown rice for white rice to add whole-grain fiber.
- Use a blend of whole-wheat flour and all-purpose flour in recipes that call for regular flour.

- Use wheat germ, bran and whole-wheat bread crumbs in place of buttered crumbs to top casseroles.
- Using vegetable oil for shortening in cakes that require creaming will affect the texture, so use unsaturated, unsalted margarine instead. Do use vegetable oil in recipes calling for melted butter.

How to Use These Recipes

When planning menus, remember to read the analysis following each recipe to help you keep track of your sodium, fat, cholesterol and calorie intake. (Also calculated there are protein, carbohydrate and potassium values.) The recipes were all calculated by the University of Minnesota School of Public Health's Nutrition Coordinating Center. All values are rounded to whole numbers. Note that the values for saturated, monounsaturated and polyunsaturated fatty acids will not add up precisely to the total fat value in the recipe. That's because the total fat report includes not only fatty acids but other fatty substances and glycerol as well.

Each analysis is based on a single serving unless otherwise indicated. The analyses do not include the optional ingredients listed. They do not include ingredients listed as suggested accompaniments unless there's a note to that effect on the analysis.

When figuring portions, remember that the serving sizes are divided equally; they're not listed as a measured amount. All figures for the total amount made are approximate.

The calories in alcohol evaporate when heated, and this reduction is reflected in the calculations. When a marinade is used in a recipe, some of the liquid is discarded. This is also accounted for in our calculations.

All of the recipes were analyzed using mostly unsalted or low-sodium ingredients. We used unsalted margarine, no-salt-added tomato sauce, low-sodium soy sauce, etc. In a few instances where we used "regular" ingredients, you may wish to use the low-salt version. A few examples of these are baking powder, bread crumbs and mayonnaise.

Caloric values reflect physiological energy values. (This means they represent the energy values remaining after the losses in digestion and metabolism have been deducted from the total.) The caloric values are based on the Atwater system for determining energy values.

In recipes calling for vegetable oil, choose corn, safflower, soybean or sunflower oils because they contain polyunsaturated fat. Canola and olive oils are acceptable monounsaturated oils. You also may use peanut oil occasionally for variety.

Finally, although specific ingredients are listed for each recipe, feel free to experiment or substitute when necessary —as long as your ingredient substitutions do not add sodium or fat. Interchanging herbs, spices, spirits, vinegars and kinds of vegetables can give you variety and can customize the recipe to your taste and will not change the nutritional value of the dish substantially. Above all, remember the cardinal rule of cooking and eating: have fun!

RECIPES

SEASONING BLENDS

Herb Seasoning

Lemon Herb Seasoning

Salad Herb Blend

Chili Powder

So you've thrown away your salt shaker. "But what *else*," you ask, nervously rifling the kitchen shelves, "can make my food taste good?"

Don't panic. There are hundreds of alternatives to salt. You are limited only by your imagination. Start by borrowing from some exotic cuisines: use spices to create the taste of foods from India, Vietnam, China and Thailand; use wines for a European flavor. Consider the cornucopia of taste sensations you can create from ginger, sesame seeds, orange rind, horseradish and dozens of other things.

And that's only the beginning. Not only can you combine these tastes endlessly, your cooking methods can be varied also. Baked apples with cinnamon and margarine enhance the sweetness of the apples. Orange juice on chicken or apple juice concentrate on pork enhance the flavors of those meats beautifully. Using foods with a natural sweetness rounded out with herbs and spices is especially delicious. Also using foods with contrasting textures and presenting them beautifully can delight the senses—and the appetite!

Here's an easy way to keep your favorite seasonings on hand: place a mixture of herbs in an herb shaker. Use that instead of your salt shaker. You'll find three of our favorite combinations here, or invent an herb-shaker combination custom-made for your tastebuds.

And don't forget the possibilities of using wine, vinegar or unsalted salad dressings to create delicious marinades.

Although table wines contain no salt, "cooking wines" do. Read labels carefully and use only those without salt.

For meats, soups and vegetables, try fresh lemon juice, hot pepper sauce, vinegar or unsalted liquid smoke for a variety of flavors.

To get you started, try cooking with the herbs and other items suggested for certain foods on the chart in Appendix B. They're guaranteed to add spice to your life!

HERB SEASONING

MAKES APPROXIMATELY ⅓ CUP

½ teaspoon cayenne pepper
1 tablespoon garlic powder
1 teaspoon dried basil
1 teaspoon dried marjoram
1 teaspoon dried thyme
1 teaspoon dried parsley
1 teaspoon dried savory
1 teaspoon mace
1 teaspoon onion powder
1 teaspoon freshly ground black pepper
1 teaspoon powdered sage

Place all ingredients in a medium bowl. Toss gently with spoon until well blended. Store in an airtight container in a cool, dry, dark place for up to 6 months.

This mix is perfect for keeping on hand at the table as an all-purpose replacement for the salt shaker. It's good on casseroles, stews, fresh vegetables and meats.

LEMON HERB SEASONING

MAKES APPROXIMATELY 1 CUP

4½ tablespoons dried basil
3¾ tablespoons dried oregano
1½ tablespoons finely ground black pepper
1½ tablespoons dried onion flakes

1½ tablespoons whole celery seed
1¼ tablespoons powdered basil
½ teaspoon garlic powder
½ teaspoon grated lemon rind

Place all ingredients in a medium bowl. Toss gently with spoon until well blended just before using. (For a more lemony flavor, add a small amount of fresh lemon juice.) Store in an airtight container in a cool, dry, dark place for up to 6 months. This seasoning is good on fish, poultry and salads.

SALAD HERB BLEND

MAKES APPROXIMATELY 1 CUP

¼ cup dried parsley
¼ cup dried marjoram
2½ tablespoons dried basil
1½ tablespoons sesame seeds
1½ tablespoons chili pepper flakes
1½ tablespoons powdered rosemary
1¼ tablespoons powdered celery seed
2½ teaspoons dried savory
2½ teaspoons powdered sage
2¼ teaspoons dried thyme
2 teaspoons granulated onion
2 teaspoons dried dill weed
1¼ teaspoons fine ground black pepper
¾ teaspoon garlic powder

Place all ingredients in a medium bowl. Toss gently with spoon until well blended. Store in an airtight container in a cool, dry, dark place for up to 6 months.

CHILI POWDER

MAKES APPROXIMATELY 4 TABLESPOONS

3 tablespoons paprika
2 teaspoons finely crushed oregano
1 teaspoon ground cumin
1 teaspoon ground turmeric
1 teaspoon garlic powder
¼ teaspoon cayenne pepper

Place all ingredients in a medium bowl. Toss gently with spoon until well blended. Store in an airtight container in cool, dark, dry place for up to 6 months.

Use in place of packaged chili powder.

SOUPS

CHICKEN BROTH

BEEF BROTH

VEGETABLE SOUP

MINESTRONE

TURKEY VEGETABLE SOUP

ONION SOUP

SPLIT PEA SOUP

LENTIL SOUP WITH LEMON

GAZPACHO

NEW ENGLAND FISH CHOWDER WITH THYME

An old proverb says, "Of soup and love, the first is best." A strong sentiment understood by those of us who love good soup. Whether it's Vegetable Soup simmering on a winter's day or cold Gazpacho, soup is diversity in a bowl.

Your greatest challenge in cooking soups is to get the zest and flavor you want—without the salt you don't want. Steer clear of canned, dried or frozen soups and soup mixes always. They're among the saltiest foods available. Instead, make your soup just like Grandma did—from scratch.

It's easy, really. Just remember that soup is composed basically of three elements—liquids, solids and seasonings—and the sky's the limit on herb and spice combinations.

The liquid base or broth is critical. It is best prepared by cooking the protein source you plan to use: low-fat beef, poultry or fish. It may be tempting to use bouillon cubes or flavor packets, but they contain lots of salt. Instead, use our recipes for Beef or Chicken Broth, or, if you must, unsalted bouillon cubes or canned low-sodium broth.

Here's an easy trick for removing a lot of the fat in your soup: Just prepare the soup a day in advance and chill it overnight. The fat will rise to the top, and you can easily remove it. If you can't prepare the broth in advance, try to skim off as much fat as possible before adding your vegetables, grains, beans, pastas and seasonings. Some kitchenware stores carry inexpensive gadgets to help you with this.

Finally, inventive toppings can add further interest and flavor to your soups. Garnish them with lemon slices, low-fat yogurt, chopped onions, chives, a sprinkling of herbs or Seasoned Croutons (page 230). Team your soup with unsalted pretzels, toast strips or soda crackers made without salt sprinkled on top.

So, go ahead. Try Onion Soup as an appetizer at a dinner party. Serve Lentil Soup with Lemon for a deliciously different lunch. You'll love the variety of flavors soup can provide.

CHICKEN BROTH

MAKES 2½ QUARTS

3 pounds chicken, skinned, all visible fat removed
3 quarts cold water
1 medium onion, chopped
2 large carrots, chopped
2 stalks celery, chopped
5 or 6 peppercorns
1 bay leaf
1 teaspoon dried thyme

NUTRIENT ANALYSIS*	
Calories	243 kcal
Protein	27 g
Carbohydrate	13 g
Total Fat	9 g
Saturated	3 g
Polyunsaturated	2 g
Monounsaturated	4 g
Cholesterol	0 mg
Sodium	559 mg
Potassium	1239 mg
Calcium	97 mg

* For entire recipe.

Rinse chicken and pat dry.

In a large stockpot, combine all ingredients and bring to a boil. Reduce heat and simmer 1 to 2 hours for a lightly flavored soup. For a richer, more flavorful soup simmer the broth for 3 to 4 hours. Skim the froth off the top of broth. Remove chicken and strain broth. Refrigerate until the fat hardens on the surface. Remove fat and discard.

This dish may be served as a light soup or used in recipes calling for chicken broth.

BEEF BROTH

MAKES 2 QUARTS

4 pounds beef or veal bones (preferably shank or knuckle bones)
3 quarts water
1 medium onion, coarsely chopped
1 bay leaf
2 whole cloves
1 teaspoon dried thyme
5 or 6 peppercorns
8 sprigs fresh parsley

NUTRIENT ANALYSIS *	
Calories	194 kcal
Protein	22 g
Carbohydrate	11 g
Total Fat	7 g
Saturated	2 g
Polyunsaturated	2 g
Monounsaturated	3 g
Cholesterol	0 mg
Sodium	447 mg
Potassium	991 mg
Calcium	78 mg

* For entire recipe.

Preheat oven to 400° F.

Place bones in a roasting pan and bake 25 to 30 minutes, turning bones once. Pour off collected fat.

Transfer bones and remaining ingredients to a large stockpot. Simmer 4 to 6 hours; do not boil. Skim fat off the top. Strain through a fine strainer lined with cheesecloth. Refrigerate. Fat will harden on the surface when chilled. Skim fat from top.

This dish may be served as a light soup or used in recipes calling for beef broth.

VEGETABLE SOUP

SERVES 4; APPROXIMATELY 8 OUNCES PER SERVING

1 tablespoon olive oil
½ cup chopped onions
½ cup diced celery
½ cup sliced carrots
½ teaspoon oregano
½ teaspoon thyme
2 cloves garlic, minced
4 cups low-sodium beef broth
Freshly ground black pepper to taste
½ cup cut fresh green beans
½ cup chopped fresh tomatoes

NUTRIENT ANALYSIS	
Calories	73 kcal
Protein	3 g
Carbohydrate	6 g
Total Fat	4 g
Saturated	1 g
Polyunsaturated	1 g
Monounsaturated	3 g
Cholesterol	0 mg
Sodium	76 mg
Potassium	252 mg
Calcium	38 mg

Place oil in a medium stockpot over medium heat. Add onions, celery, carrots, oregano and thyme and sauté until soft, about 5 to 7 minutes. Add garlic and cook for another minute. Add beef broth, pepper and the rest of the vegetables. Simmer 30 to 45 minutes, or until vegetables are soft.

MINESTRONE

SERVES 6; 1 CUP PER SERVING

4 tablespoons olive oil
1/2 cup chopped onions
1/2 cup sliced carrots
1/2 cup diced celery
1 to 2 cloves garlic, minced
6 cups low-sodium chicken broth
1 cup canned no-salt-added tomatoes
1 cup cooked macaroni (no salt added)
1 cup cooked white beans (no salt added)
2 tablespoons chopped fresh parsley
1/2 teaspoon freshly ground black pepper
1/4 cup grated Parmesan cheese

NUTRIENT ANALYSIS

Calories	218 kcal
Protein	9 g
Carbohydrate	20 g
Total Fat	12 g
Saturated	2 g
Polyunsaturated	1 g
Monounsaturated	7 g
Cholesterol	4 mg
Sodium	161 mg
Potassium	480 mg
Calcium	125 mg

Heat olive oil in a large pot over low heat. Add onions, carrots, celery and garlic. Cook 5 to 7 minutes, or until soft. Next add the chicken broth, tomatoes, pasta, white beans, parsley and black pepper. Cook 5 minutes, or until thoroughly heated. Pour into individual bowls and garnish with Parmesan cheese.

TURKEY VEGETABLE SOUP

SERVES 6; 1 CUP PER SERVING

2 tablespoons acceptable margarine
½ cup chopped onions
¼ cup diced celery
6 cups low-sodium chicken broth
1 cup canned no-salt-added tomatoes
1 pound cooked and diced turkey meat
½ teaspoon freshly ground black pepper
¼ teaspoon hot pepper sauce
½ cup frozen peas, thawed

NUTRIENT ANALYSIS	
Calories	217 kcal
Protein	26 g
Carbohydrate	6 g
Total Fat	10 g
Saturated	3 g
Polyunsaturated	3 g
Monounsaturated	4 g
Cholesterol	63 mg
Sodium	139 mg
Potassium	477 mg
Calcium	45 mg

Melt margarine in a large pot over low heat. Add onions and celery and cook 5 minutes, or until soft. Add chicken broth and tomatoes. Cook 10 minutes, or until vegetables are soft. Add turkey, black pepper and hot pepper sauce. Cook 5 more minutes. Add the peas and cook another 5 minutes. Serve hot.

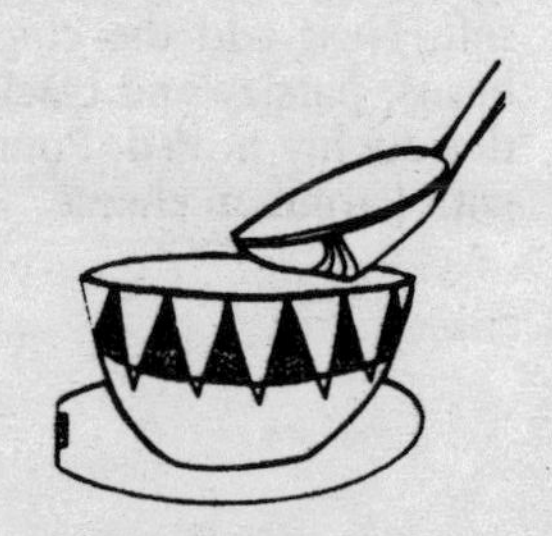

ONION SOUP

SERVES 3; APPROXIMATELY 1 CUP PER SERVING

2 tablespoons acceptable margarine, melted
1 tablespoon acceptable vegetable oil
2 medium onions, sliced
1/8 teaspoon sugar
2 teaspoons all-purpose flour
2 1/2 cups low-sodium beef broth
2 tablespoons vermouth or dry white table wine
1/8 teaspoon freshly ground black pepper
1/2 cup Seasoned Croutons (see recipe, page 230) or 1 slice bread, toasted and cut into cubes

NUTRIENT ANALYSIS	
Calories	211 kcal
Protein	4 g
Carbohydrate	11 g
Total Fat	17 g
Saturated	3 g
Polyunsaturated	7 g
Monounsaturated	7 g
Cholesterol	0 mg
Sodium	99 mg
Potassium	226 mg
Calcium	38 mg

Combine margarine, oil and onions in a saucepan. Cover and cook over low heat 15 minutes.

Add sugar and cook uncovered 10 minutes, stirring occasionally, until the onions are a deep, golden brown.

Add flour and mix thoroughly. Stir in broth. Add vermouth and pepper and simmer 15 to 30 minutes.

Place soup in cups and top with Seasoned Croutons or cubes of toast.

SPLIT PEA SOUP

SERVES 6; APPROXIMATELY 1½ CUPS PER SERVING

1 cup (½ pound) dried split peas
2 quarts water
1 carrot, chopped
2 stalks celery, chopped
1 medium onion, chopped
½ teaspoon unsalted liquid smoke
1 tablespoon chopped fresh parsley or 1½ teaspoons dried parsley flakes
¼ teaspoon onion powder
⅛ teaspoon garlic powder
⅛ teaspoon freshly ground black pepper

NUTRIENT ANALYSIS	
Calories	123 kcal
Protein	8 g
Carbohydrate	23 g
Total Fat	0 g
Saturated	0 g
Polyunsaturated	0 g
Monounsaturated	0 g
Cholesterol	0 mg
Sodium	22 mg
Potassium	436 mg
Calcium	33 mg

Place all ingredients in a large pan. Cover and simmer 2½ to 3 hours. If soup becomes too thick, add more water, stirring it in slowly.

If a smooth soup is desired, remove from heat and process in a blender or force through a sieve. Serve immediately.

LENTIL SOUP WITH LEMON

SERVES 8; APPROXIMATELY 1¼ CUPS PER SERVING

2 cups lentils, dry
½ yellow onion, diced
2 cloves garlic, minced
2 tablespoons olive oil
8 cups water or no-salt-added vegetable broth
1 medium potato, diced
½ teaspoon oregano (optional)
2 tablespoons fresh lemon juice
Freshly ground black pepper to taste

Rinse lentils and drain.

Place onion, garlic and oil in a medium stockpot over medium heat. Sauté until soft. Add all ingredients except lemon juice and pepper. Simmer 45 to 60 minutes, or until the lentils are soft. Stir in lemon juice and pepper and serve immediately.

NUTRIENT ANALYSIS

Calories	186 kcal
Protein	11 g
Carbohydrate	28 g
Total Fat	4 g
Saturated	1 g
Polyunsaturated	1 g
Monounsaturated	3 g
Cholesterol	0 mg
Sodium	6 mg
Potassium	509 mg
Calcium	34 mg

GAZPACHO

SERVES 8; APPROXIMATELY 1 CUP PER SERVING

1 medium fresh tomato
1 small green bell pepper
2 medium cucumbers
1 small zucchini
1/4 cup chopped onion
1/4 cup chopped green onions, with tops
1/4 cup chopped fresh parsley
2 cloves garlic, minced
1 teaspoon freshly ground black pepper
1 teaspoon Worcestershire sauce
4 cups no-salt-added tomato juice
1 tablespoon fresh lemon juice (optional)

NUTRIENT ANALYSIS	
Calories	40 kcal
Protein	2 g
Carbohydrate	9 g
Total Fat	0 g
Saturated	0 g
Polyunsaturated	0 g
Monounsaturated	0 g
Cholesterol	0 mg
Sodium	24 mg
Potassium	466 mg
Calcium	31 mg

Finely chop all vegetables. Place in a large bowl. Add remaining ingredients. Stir to mix well. Cover and refrigerate. Serve cold.

NEW ENGLAND FISH CHOWDER WITH THYME

SERVES 6; 1 CUP PER SERVING

4 tablespoons acceptable margarine
½ cup diced onions
4 tablespoons flour
6 cups low-sodium fish stock or chicken broth
2 medium potatoes, peeled and cut into small cubes
1 cup low-fat (2 percent) milk
1 teaspoon thyme leaves
⅛ teaspoon white pepper
1 pound boneless fish fillets (haddock, cod or other firm white fish) cut into ½-inch cubes

Melt margarine in a large pot over low heat. Add onions and cook 5 minutes, or until soft. Add flour and cook 2 minutes. Next, add fish stock, stirring vigorously. Add potatoes and simmer 20 to 25 minutes, or until potatoes are tender. Add milk, thyme leaves, white pepper and fish. Cook 10 more minutes. Serve immediately.

NUTRIENT ANALYSIS

Calories	228 kcal
Protein	20 g
Carbohydrate	14 g
Total Fat	10 g
Saturated	3 g
Polyunsaturated	3 g
Monounsaturated	4 g
Cholesterol	43 mg
Sodium	143 mg
Potassium	517 mg
Calcium	79 mg

SALADS

Three-Bean Salad

Texas Caviar (Black-eyed Pea Salad)

Spicy Marinated Vegetables

Summer Pasta Salad

Potato Salad

Macaroni Salad

Creamy Coleslaw

Pineapple Coleslaw

Cucumber Raita

Waldorf Salad

Ambrosia

Orange-Grapefruit Salad

Chicken Salad

Hawaiian Chicken Salad

Tuna Salad

Seafood Salad

If your picture of a salad is iceberg lettuce with a tomato, you'll be delighted with the variety of these recipes. From Texas Caviar (Black-eyed Pea Salad) to Hawaiian Chicken Salad or creamy Cucumber Raita, salads can mean exciting tastes and textures.

Of course, tossed green salads *are* a staple of healthful cuisine. But insiders know the trick to making them magnificent every time: using more than one variety of lettuce. Today your grocer probably offers a dozen kinds to choose from. Consider using romaine of Caesar Salad fame; or the soft, velvety leaves of Boston, bibb or endive; or green- or red-leaf lettuce with its curly, narrow leaves. And don't stop there! Experiment with beet, dandelion and mustard greens —even nasturtium leaves. Add watercress, chicory and spinach to your "standard" salad. With such a wealth of greens, a tossed salad need never be boring.

Upon this delicious foundation, you can add nearly endless varieties of vegetables, seeds, nuts and sprouts. Also consider chopped hard-cooked egg whites, cooked chicken or turkey, marinated fish and croutons. For even more variety, look for unusual toppings such as alfalfa sprouts or other fresh sprouts, jicama, fresh jalapeños, cilantro or fresh raw peas.

Virtually any food can be made into a salad. Just look at our Summer Pasta Salad, Orange-Grapefruit Salad and Spicy Marinated Vegetables. One of the nicest things about salads is that you can enjoy them as a side dish or, with soup and bread, make them an entire meal.

Best of all, salads with fresh ingredients are naturally low in salt. As long as you stay away from salt-filled accompaniments such as green olives, pickles, sardines, luncheon meats, cheeses and commercial dressings, salads can be one of the tastiest staples of your low-salt eating plan.

THREE-BEAN SALAD

SERVES 14

3/4 cup dried kidney beans
4 cups water
1 10-ounce package frozen or 1 pound fresh cut green beans
1 10-ounce package frozen or 1 pound fresh cut yellow beans
1/2 cup cider vinegar
3/4 cup sugar
1/3 cup acceptable vegetable oil
1/2 teaspoon freshly ground black pepper
1 clove garlic
1 medium onion, sliced
1/2 green bell pepper, chopped

Place kidney beans and water in a saucepan. Bring to a boil and cook for 2 minutes. Set aside for 1 hour without draining.

Return beans to heat and simmer for 1 hour or until beans are very tender. Drain, rinse and set aside.

Cook green and yellow beans until tender. Drain.

Heat vinegar and sugar together to dissolve sugar. Add oil, pepper and garlic and mix.

Toss vinegar mixture with beans, onion and green pepper. Cover and chill 6 hours or overnight. Remove garlic clove before serving.

Bean and Sprout Salad
Add 1 cup fresh bean sprouts to the cooked bean, onion and green pepper mixture.

THREE-BEAN SALAD NUTRIENT ANALYSIS

Calories	100 kcal
Protein	1 g
Carbohydrate	14 g
Total Fat	5 g
Saturated	1 g
Polyunsaturated	3 g
Monounsaturated	1 g
Cholesterol	0 mg
Sodium	6 mg
Potassium	68 mg
Calcium	21 mg

BEAN AND SPROUT SALAD NUTRIENT ANALYSIS

Calories	106 kcal
Protein	1 g
Carbohydrate	14 g
Total Fat	6 g
Saturated	1 g
Polyunsaturated	3 g
Monounsaturated	1 g
Cholesterol	0 mg
Sodium	6 mg
Potassium	92 mg
Calcium	24 mg

TEXAS CAVIAR (Black-eyed Pea Salad)

SERVES 6

2 cups black-eyed peas, dry
1/2 cup diced green bell pepper
1/4 cup diced white onion
2 tablespoons finely chopped canned jalapeño peppers
2 tablespoons acceptable vegetable oil
2 tablespoons red wine vinegar
1 clove garlic, minced
1/4 teaspoon freshly ground black pepper

Sort black-eyed peas and soak overnight in 6 cups of water. Drain. Cook peas in 4 cups of fresh water until done but still firm, about 1½ hours.

Rinse in cold water and drain. In a medium bowl, combine all remaining ingredients and mix well. Add peas and chill.

NUTRIENT ANALYSIS

Calories	172 kcal
Protein	9 g
Carbohydrate	24 g
Total Fat	5 g
Saturated	1 g
Polyunsaturated	3 g
Monounsaturated	1 g
Cholesterol	0 mg
Sodium	38 mg
Potassium	341 mg
Calcium	30 mg

SPICY MARINATED VEGETABLES

SERVES 4

½ cup julienned yellow onion
1½ cups diced raw broccoli
1½ cups diced raw cauliflower
1 cup sliced yellow squash
1 cup sliced carrots
½ cup red wine vinegar
2 tablespoons olive oil
1 teaspoon garlic powder
½ teaspoon cayenne pepper

Combine vegetables in a large glass or ceramic bowl.
In another bowl, mix remaining ingredients. Pour over vegetables and stir to mix thoroughly. Cover and refrigerate 6 to 8 hours. Serve cold.

NUTRIENT ANALYSIS

Calories	110 kcal
Protein	3 g
Carbohydrate	11 g
Total Fat	7 g
Saturated	1 g
Polyunsaturated	1 g
Monounsaturated	5 g
Cholesterol	0 mg
Sodium	27 mg
Potassium	493 mg
Calcium	48 mg

SUMMER PASTA SALAD

SERVES 4

3 cups pasta spirals
1½ cups broccoli florets
½ cup sliced carrots
1½ cups sliced zucchini
¾ cup plain nonfat yogurt
¼ cup cider vinegar
2 tablespoons Parmesan cheese
2 tablespoons mayonnaise
½ teaspoon garlic powder
½ teaspoon freshly ground black pepper

NUTRIENT ANALYSIS	
Calories	510 kcal
Protein	19 g
Carbohydrate	91 g
Total Fat	8 g
Saturated	2 g
Polyunsaturated	4 g
Monounsaturated	2 g
Cholesterol	7 mg
Sodium	142 mg
Potassium	532 mg
Calcium	193 mg

Cook pasta according to package directions, omitting salt. Drain and rinse under cold water and set aside.

Blanch vegetables in unsalted boiling water for 2 to 3 minutes, or just until tender crisp. Drain, rinse under cold water and set aside.

In a small bowl, mix yogurt, vinegar, Parmesan cheese, mayonnaise and seasonings. Set aside.

In a large bowl, combine pasta, yogurt mixture and vegetables. Mix well. Chill thoroughly and serve cold.

POTATO SALAD

SERVES 6

5 medium red potatoes, cooked, peeled and diced
3/4 cup chopped celery with leaves
1/2 cup sliced radishes
2 green onions, diced
2 tablespoons mayonnaise
2 tablespoons plain nonfat yogurt
1 teaspoon dry mustard powder
1 tablespoon sugar
1/4 teaspoon freshly ground black pepper
1/4 teaspoon turmeric
1/2 teaspoon celery seed (optional)
2 1/2 tablespoons white vinegar
3 tablespoons skim milk

NUTRIENT ANALYSIS	
Calories	121 kcal
Protein	2 g
Carbohydrate	20 g
Total Fat	4 g
Saturated	1 g
Polyunsaturated	2 g
Monounsaturated	1 g
Cholesterol	3 mg
Sodium	54 mg
Potassium	371 mg
Calcium	39 mg

Combine potatoes, celery, radishes and onions.

In a separate bowl, mix together mayonnaise, yogurt, mustard powder, sugar, pepper, turmeric and celery seed. Add vinegar and milk and stir until mixed.

Combine with potato mixture and stir to mix well. Chill before serving.

MACARONI SALAD

SERVES 4

1 cup uncooked macaroni
2 tablespoons mayonnaise
2 tablespoons plain nonfat yogurt
1 tablespoon sugar
2 teaspoons cider vinegar
1/8 teaspoon freshly ground black pepper
1/4 cup chopped cucumber
1/4 cup chopped celery
2 radishes, sliced
1 tablespoon finely chopped onion

NUTRIENT ANALYSIS	
Calories	201 kcal
Protein	5 g
Carbohydrate	31 g
Total Fat	6 g
Saturated	1 g
Polyunsaturated	3 g
Monounsaturated	2 g
Cholesterol	4 mg
Sodium	53 mg
Potassium	136 mg
Calcium	31 mg

Cook macaroni according to package directions, omitting salt. Drain and allow to cool.

Mix mayonnaise, yogurt, sugar, vinegar and pepper together to make a dressing.

Toss macaroni, dressing and remaining ingredients together. Chill and serve cold.

CREAMY COLESLAW

SERVES 4

2½ cups shredded red cabbage
1 cup grated carrots
⅓ cup plain nonfat yogurt
2 tablespoons mayonnaise
1 teaspoon mustard
½ teaspoon sugar
2 tablespoons cider vinegar
¼ teaspoon freshly ground black pepper

Place cabbage and carrots in a large bowl. Mix and set aside.

In a small bowl, combine yogurt, mayonnaise, mustard, sugar, vinegar and pepper. Mix well. Add yogurt mixture to cabbage-carrot mixture. Stir to mix thoroughly. Chill for 1 to 2 hours.

NUTRIENT ANALYSIS	
Calories	87 kcal
Protein	2 g
Carbohydrate	8 g
Total Fat	6 g
Saturated	1 g
Polyunsaturated	3 g
Monounsaturated	2 g
Cholesterol	4 mg
Sodium	88 mg
Potassium	262 mg
Calcium	72 mg

PINEAPPLE COLESLAW

SERVES 5

2 cups shredded cabbage
1/4 cup chopped green bell pepper
1 15 1/4-ounce can crushed pineapple, canned in natural juices, drained
3 tablespoons mayonnaise
1 1/2 teaspoons white vinegar
1/4 teaspoon dill weed
1/8 teaspoon freshly ground black pepper

In a large bowl, combine cabbage, green pepper and crushed pineapple. Toss lightly.

In a separate bowl, combine remaining ingredients. Mix well. Add to cabbage mixture and blend thoroughly.

Chill well before serving.

NUTRIENT ANALYSIS	
Calories	120 kcal
Protein	1 g
Carbohydrate	16 g
Total Fat	7 g
Saturated	1 g
Polyunsaturated	3 g
Monounsaturated	2 g
Cholesterol	5 mg
Sodium	53 mg
Potassium	191 mg
Calcium	28 mg

CUCUMBER RAITA

SERVES 4

3 cups plain nonfat yogurt
2 small cucumbers, peeled, seeded and finely diced (approximately 2 cups)
2 green onions with tops, finely chopped (approximately 4 tablespoons)
1/8 teaspoon cayenne pepper

In a bowl, whisk the yogurt until smooth. Add remaining ingredients. Stir well, cover and chill until ready to serve. Can be made up to 2 hours in advance.

NUTRIENT ANALYSIS

Calories	115 kcal
Protein	11 g
Carbohydrate	17 g
Total Fat	0 g
Saturated	0 g
Polyunsaturated	0 g
Monounsaturated	0 g
Cholesterol	4 mg
Sodium	142 mg
Potassium	607 mg
Calcium	381 mg

WALDORF SALAD

SERVES 6

3 tablespoons reduced-calorie mayonnaise
1 cup plain nonfat yogurt
2 tablespoons cider vinegar
4 medium apples, unpeeled, cored and diced
1/4 cup diced celery
1/4 cup chopped walnuts

In a medium bowl, combine mayonnaise, yogurt and vinegar. Mix until blended. Add apples, celery and walnuts and mix until well combined. Chill thoroughly before serving.

NUTRIENT ANALYSIS

Calories	133 kcal
Protein	3 g
Carbohydrate	19 g
Total Fat	6 g
Saturated	1 g
Polyunsaturated	3 g
Monounsaturated	2 g
Cholesterol	3 mg
Sodium	80 mg
Potassium	256 mg
Calcium	95 mg

AMBROSIA

SERVES 6

¼ recipe (½ cup) Mock Sour Cream (see recipe, page 194)
¼ cup powdered sugar
¼ teaspoon vanilla
1 15-ounce can pineapple chunks, canned in natural juices, drained
1 11-ounce can mandarin orange segments, canned in light syrup, drained
½ cup miniature marshmallows
6 lettuce leaves

Mix Mock Sour Cream, powdered sugar and vanilla. Add fruit and marshmallows and toss together lightly. Chill for at least 1 hour.

Serve on salad plates lined with lettuce leaves.

NUTRIENT ANALYSIS

Calories	119 kcal
Protein	2 g
Carbohydrate	29 g
Total Fat	0 g
Saturated	0 g
Polyunsaturated	0 g
Monounsaturated	0 g
Cholesterol	1 mg
Sodium	10 mg
Potassium	155 mg
Calcium	25 mg

ORANGE-GRAPEFRUIT SALAD

SERVES 4

1 large orange, preferably navel, peeled and sectioned
1 large grapefruit, peeled and sectioned
1 green onion and top, chopped
1 tablespoon acceptable vegetable oil
1 tablespoon white vinegar
4 large lettuce leaves

In a medium bowl, combine orange and grapefruit sections with onions. Cover and chill.

When ready to serve, mix oil and vinegar together with a fork and toss lightly with fruit.

Divide fruit mixture into 4 portions and serve on lettuce leaves.

NUTRIENT ANALYSIS	
Calories	88 kcal
Protein	1 g
Carbohydrate	14 g
Total Fat	4 g
Saturated	0 g
Polyunsaturated	2 g
Monounsaturated	1 g
Cholesterol	0 mg
Sodium	1 mg
Potassium	257 mg
Calcium	35 mg

CHICKEN SALAD

SERVES 6

2 cups unsalted, cooked and diced chicken
½ cup chopped celery
½ cup chopped fresh parsley
½ cup chopped fresh scallions
⅛ teaspoon dry mustard powder
¼ teaspoon freshly ground black pepper
1 teaspoon fresh lemon juice
½ cup mayonnaise

In a large bowl, toss chicken with celery, parsley and scallions. Combine dry mustard, pepper, lemon juice and mayonnaise and mix well. Pour over chicken mixture and stir until well mixed. Cover and chill.

Use as a sandwich filling or serve on lettuce leaves for a main dish salad. Garnish with any of the following: grapes, cut in half and seeded; pineapple chunks; fresh tomato wedges; toasted, unsalted almonds or pecans.

Turkey Salad
Use turkey in place of chicken.

CHICKEN SALAD NUTRIENT ANALYSIS

Calories	223 kcal
Protein	14 g
Carbohydrate	2 g
Total Fat	18 g
Saturated	3 g
Polyunsaturated	8 g
Monounsaturated	5 g
Cholesterol	50 mg
Sodium	153 mg
Potassium	213 mg
Calcium	29 mg

TURKEY SALAD NUTRIENT ANALYSIS

Calories	223 kcal
Protein	14 g
Carbohydrate	2 g
Total Fat	18 g
Saturated	3 g
Polyunsaturated	8 g
Monounsaturated	5 g
Cholesterol	50 mg
Sodium	153 mg
Potassium	213 mg
Calcium	29 mg

HAWAIIAN CHICKEN SALAD

SERVES 6

2 cups unsalted, cooked and diced chicken
1 8-ounce can crushed pineapple, canned in natural juices, drained
2 tablespoons finely chopped green bell pepper
1/4 cup mayonnaise

In a medium bowl, mix all ingredients together. Cover and chill.

Serve on bread as sandwiches or on lettuce leaves for a main-dish salad.

NUTRIENT ANALYSIS

Calories	174 kcal
Protein	14 g
Carbohydrate	6 g
Total Fat	10 g
Saturated	2 g
Polyunsaturated	5 g
Monounsaturated	3 g
Cholesterol	44 mg
Sodium	90 mg
Potassium	181 mg
Calcium	17 mg

TUNA SALAD

SERVES 3

1 6½-ounce can unsalted tuna, in spring water, drained, rinsed and flaked
½ cup chopped, unpeeled cucumber
3 tablespoons mayonnaise
⅛ teaspoon onion powder
⅛ teaspoon dry mustard powder

In a medium bowl, combine flaked tuna with cucumber. In a small bowl, combine mayonnaise, onion powder and mustard and mix well. Pour over tuna mixture and toss until well mixed. Chill.

Use as a sandwich filling or serve on lettuce leaves for a main-dish salad.

NUTRIENT ANALYSIS

Calories	174 kcal
Protein	17 g
Carbohydrate	1 g
Total Fat	11 g
Saturated	2 g
Polyunsaturated	6 g
Monounsaturated	3 g
Cholesterol	30 mg
Sodium	106 mg
Potassium	204 mg
Calcium	12 mg

SEAFOOD SALAD

SERVES 8

½ pound imitation crab
½ pound fresh cooked crabmeat
4 ounces cooked shrimp, without shells
¼ cup reduced-calorie mayonnaise
¼ cup low-fat sour cream
⅓ cup chopped green bell pepper
¼ cup chopped green onion
2 tablespoons fresh dill weed
2 tablespoons fresh lemon juice
¼ cup chopped fresh parsley
2 cloves garlic, minced
¼ teaspoon cayenne pepper
¼ teaspoon freshly ground black pepper
¼ teaspoon hot pepper sauce

NUTRIENT ANALYSIS	
Calories	108 kcal
Protein	14 g
Carbohydrate	5 g
Total Fat	4 g
Saturated	1 g
Polyunsaturated	1 g
Monounsaturated	1 g
Cholesterol	68 mg
Sodium	411 mg
Potassium	224 mg
Calcium	76 mg

Dice imitation crab, crabmeat and shrimp and place in a medium bowl. Set aside. In a small bowl, combine remaining ingredients and mix thoroughly. Add to diced seafood. Stir to mix thoroughly. Cover and refrigerate for 30 to 60 minutes. Serve cold.

SALAD DRESSINGS

The taste of homemade salad dressing prepared with fresh herbs, spices and oils is a little bit of heaven—vastly better than that of commercially prepared dressings.

When salad dressing ingredients are at their freshest and most piquant, what they do to a colorful variety of greens and vegetables—or fruit—is nothing short of amazing. Spicy Russian Dressing is a wonderful example. So is Lemon-Poppy Seed Dressing, with its crunchy texture and tangy taste. You'll even find that the make-your-own mayonnaise recipe here, Tofu Mayonnaise, is much smoother and richer than what you're used to.

Now, most people think that making their own salad dressing is complicated and time-consuming. Not true: You can make almost any salad dressing in this book in under five minutes.

Is it worth it? You bet! You can control your fat and salt intake and enjoy herbs and spices at their flavor-packed best. You can also avoid chemical stabilizers and other additives so often found in commercial brands of dressing.

And here's another place you can be really creative: Use oil bases such as corn, olive and sesame. Flavor a polyunsaturated oil with apple cider vinegar, garlic and mustard. Other possible bases for salad dressings include low-fat or nonfat yogurt, tahini and other nut and seed butters, or hummus, made from chick-peas. Flavored vinegars, from balsamic to raspberry to tarragon, can also change a salad dressing dramatically. The creations you like best can make thoughtful, tasty gifts for friends when presented in a pretty stoppered cruet. (Be sure to use only sterilized glass bottles or cruets for gifts or storing dressing.)

For a delicious taste treat, try using homemade dressings as marinades for vegetables and meats. Instead of basting a roast chicken with pan drippings, try using one of these salad dressings. You'll be glad you did.

BASIC SALAD DRESSING I

MAKES 1 CUP
SERVES 16;
1 TABLESPOON PER SERVING

¼ cup cider vinegar
¼ cup acceptable vegetable oil
½ cup water
1 teaspoon Dijon mustard
1 clove garlic, minced
¼ teaspoon freshly ground black pepper
¼ teaspoon sugar

In a jar with a tight-fitting lid, combine all ingredients. Shake well and refrigerate.

Note: Basic Salad Dressing I has a more robust flavor, while Basic Salad Dressing II has a more delicate citrus flavor.

NUTRIENT ANALYSIS

Calories	31 kcal
Protein	0 g
Carbohydrate	0 g
Total Fat	3 g
Saturated	0 g
Polyunsaturated	2 g
Monounsaturated	1 g
Cholesterol	0 mg
Sodium	4 mg
Potassium	5 mg
Calcium	1 mg

BASIC SALAD DRESSING II

MAKES 1 CUP
SERVES 16;
1 TABLESPOON PER SERVING

1/4 cup red wine vinegar
1/4 cup acceptable vegetable oil
1/2 cup water
1/4 teaspoon freshly ground black pepper
1/4 teaspoon garlic powder
1/4 teaspoon sugar
1 teaspoon fresh lemon juice

In a jar with a tight-fitting lid, combine all ingredients. Shake well and refrigerate.

NUTRIENT ANALYSIS

Calories	31 kcal
Protein	0 g
Carbohydrate	0 g
Total Fat	3 g
Saturated	0 g
Polyunsaturated	2 g
Monounsaturated	1 g
Cholesterol	0 mg
Sodium	0 mg
Potassium	5 mg
Calcium	0 mg

TOMATO FRENCH DRESSING

MAKES 1¼ CUPS
SERVES 20;
1 TABLESPOON PER SERVING

1 recipe Basic Salad Dressing I or II (see pages 80 and 81)
2 tablespoons no-salt-added tomato paste
2 teaspoons sugar
1 tablespoon minced onion

In a jar with a tight-fitting lid, combine all ingredients. Shake well and refrigerate.

NUTRIENT ANALYSIS

Calories	28 kcal
Protein	0 g
Carbohydrate	1 g
Total Fat	3 g
Saturated	0 g
Polyunsaturated	2 g
Monounsaturated	1 g
Cholesterol	0 mg
Sodium	4 mg
Potassium	20 mg
Calcium	2 mg

ITALIAN DRESSING

MAKES 1¼ CUPS
SERVES 20;
1 TABLESPOON PER SERVING

1 recipe Basic Salad Dressing I or II (see pages 80 and 81)
½ teaspoon basil, crumbled
½ teaspoon oregano, crumbled

In a jar with a tight-fitting lid, combine all ingredients. Shake well and refrigerate.

NUTRIENT ANALYSIS

Calories	25 kcal
Protein	0 g
Carbohydrate	0 g
Total Fat	3 g
Saturated	0 g
Polyunsaturated	2 g
Monounsaturated	1 g
Cholesterol	0 mg
Sodium	3 mg
Potassium	5 mg
Calcium	2 mg

RUSSIAN DRESSING

MAKES 1¼ CUPS
SERVES 20;
1 TABLESPOON PER SERVING

1 recipe Basic Salad Dressing I or II (see pages 80 and 81)
2 tablespoons no-salt-added tomato paste
1 tablespoon finely chopped green bell pepper
¼ teaspoon Chili Powder (see page 40)
⅛ teaspoon onion powder
Dash hot pepper sauce

In a jar with a tight-fitting lid, combine all ingredients. Shake well and refrigerate.

NUTRIENT ANALYSIS

Calories	27 kcal
Protein	0 g
Carbohydrate	1 g
Total Fat	3 g
Saturated	0 g
Polyunsaturated	2 g
Monounsaturated	1 g
Cholesterol	0 mg
Sodium	5 mg
Potassium	21 mg
Calcium	2 mg

THOUSAND ISLAND DRESSING

MAKES 1¼ CUPS
SERVES 20;
1 TABLESPOON PER SERVING

½ cup plain nonfat yogurt
2 tablespoons reduced-calorie mayonnaise
½ cup Chili Sauce (see recipe, page 200)
1 tablespoon finely chopped green bell pepper
1 tablespoon finely chopped celery
¼ teaspoon onion powder
Dash freshly ground black pepper
1 hard-cooked egg white, finely chopped

In a jar with a tight-fitting lid, combine all ingredients. Shake well and refrigerate.

NUTRIENT ANALYSIS

Calories	17 kcal
Protein	1 g
Carbohydrate	2 g
Total Fat	1 g
Saturated	0 g
Polyunsaturated	0 g
Monounsaturated	0 g
Cholesterol	0 mg
Sodium	19 mg
Potassium	53 mg
Calcium	14 mg

YOGURT DRESSING

MAKES 1 CUP
SERVES 16;
1 TABLESPOON PER SERVING

1 cup plain nonfat yogurt
2 tablespoons low-fat sour cream
2 tablespoons honey
½ teaspoon paprika
¼ teaspoon cayenne pepper

Place all ingredients in a small bowl. Stir with a wire whisk until mixed thoroughly. Cover and refrigerate.

NUTRIENT ANALYSIS	
Calories	19 kcal
Protein	1 g
Carbohydrate	4 g
Total Fat	0 g
Saturated	0 g
Polyunsaturated	0 g
Monounsaturated	0 g
Cholesterol	1 mg
Sodium	14 mg
Potassium	50 mg
Calcium	38 mg

VINAIGRETTE DRESSING

MAKES 1 CUP
SERVES 16;
1 TABLESPOON PER SERVING

1/3 cup acceptable vegetable oil
2 tablespoons fresh lemon juice
2 tablespoons tarragon vinegar
1 teaspoon chopped fresh parsley or 1/2 teaspoon dry parsley flakes
1/2 teaspoon freshly ground black pepper
1/4 teaspoon dry mustard powder
1/8 teaspoon garlic powder
1 hard-cooked egg white, finely chopped (optional)
1 tablespoon plain low-fat yogurt (optional)

In a jar with a tight-fitting lid, combine all ingredients. Shake well and refrigerate. Serve with cooked or raw chilled vegetables or with fresh tomato slices.

NUTRIENT ANALYSIS

Calories	41 kcal
Protein	0 g
Carbohydrate	0 g
Total Fat	5 g
Saturated	1 g
Polyunsaturated	3 g
Monounsaturated	1 g
Cholesterol	0 mg
Sodium	0 mg
Potassium	5 mg
Calcium	1 mg

REDUCED-CALORIE RANCH DRESSING

MAKES 1½ CUPS
SERVES 24;
1 TABLESPOON PER SERVING

1 cup low-fat buttermilk
½ cup plain low-fat yogurt
1 tablespoon Dijon mustard
2 teaspoons minced onion
1 tablespoon fresh dill
1 tablespoon chopped fresh parsley
½ teaspoon garlic powder
¼ teaspoon freshly ground black pepper

In a jar with a tight-fitting lid, combine all ingredients. Shake well to blend. Refrigerate for at least 2 hours, allowing flavors to blend.

NUTRIENT ANALYSIS

Calories	8 kcal
Protein	1 g
Carbohydrate	1 g
Total Fat	0 g
Saturated	0 g
Polyunsaturated	0 g
Monounsaturated	0 g
Cholesterol	1 mg
Sodium	22 mg
Potassium	31 mg
Calcium	23 mg

ORANGE-YOGURT DRESSING

MAKES 1¼ CUPS
SERVES 20;
1 TABLESPOON PER SERVING

1 cup plain nonfat yogurt
¼ cup orange juice
1 teaspoon honey

In a small bowl, mix all ingredients until well blended. Cover and refrigerate.

NUTRIENT ANALYSIS

Calories	9 kcal
Protein	1 g
Carbohydrate	2 g
Total Fat	0 g
Saturated	0 g
Polyunsaturated	0 g
Monounsaturated	0 g
Cholesterol	0 mg
Sodium	9 mg
Potassium	37 mg
Calcium	25 mg

LEMON–POPPY SEED DRESSING

MAKES 1 CUP
SERVES 16;
1 TABLESPOON PER SERVING

1/2 cup frozen lemonade concentrate, undiluted
1/3 cup honey
2 tablespoons acceptable vegetable oil
1 teaspoon poppy seeds

Combine all ingredients in a small mixing bowl. Beat with rotary beater until smooth. Serve over fruit salad.

NUTRIENT ANALYSIS

Calories	54 kcal
Protein	0 g
Carbohydrate	10 g
Total Fat	2 g
Saturated	0 g
Polyunsaturated	1 g
Monounsaturated	0 g
Cholesterol	0 mg
Sodium	2 mg
Potassium	11 mg
Calcium	4 mg

TOFU MAYONNAISE

MAKES ¾ CUP
SERVES 12;
1 TABLESPOON PER SERVING

½ pound firm tofu
½ teaspoon dry mustard
⅛ teaspoon cayenne pepper
2 tablespoons fresh lemon juice
3 tablespoons acceptable vegetable oil
2 tablespoons water

In a food processor or blender, process tofu, mustard, cayenne pepper and lemon juice until mixed. With machine still running, add oil very slowly and then add water. Blend until smooth. Stop the machine a few times during processing and scrape the sides.

Keeps up to 3 months when refrigerated in an airtight container.

NUTRIENT ANALYSIS

Calories	45 kcal
Protein	2 g
Carbohydrate	1 g
Total Fat	4 g
Saturated	1 g
Polyunsaturated	3 g
Monounsaturated	1 g
Cholesterol	0 mg
Sodium	2 mg
Potassium	26 mg
Calcium	20 mg

FISH

Herbed Fillet of Sole

Fish Fillets Supreme

Rolled Fish Fillets

Oven-Fried Fish

Crispy Baked Fish

Southern Catfish Fillets

Fish Steaks with Thyme

Poached Salmon Steaks

Tuna-Macaroni Casserole

Tuna Oriental

Fresh, fabulous fish!

It's everything you could want in an entrée: low in calories, low in fat, low in salt, but high in taste.

Most fish contains about two-thirds the calories of an equal serving of red meat. For instance, a 3½-ounce broiled hamburger has about 290 calories; an equal serving of swordfish has just 154.

Fish is also higher in protein and lower in fat than red meat. A 3½-ounce serving of flounder gives you 30 grams of protein and 8 grams of fat for a very reasonable 202 calories. A similar-size serving of beef rump supplies somewhat less protein (24 grams) and three times the amount of fat (27 grams) for 347 calories.

It's not only the amount of fat that's different in fish, it's also the *kind* of fat. Beef contains saturated fat and cholesterol, while most of the fat in fish is unsaturated, with only a small amount of cholesterol. Certain kinds of fish contain a special kind of fat called Omega-3 fatty acids, which research suggests may have a protective effect on the heart. Fish rich in Omega-3 fatty acids include salmon, mackerel, trout, haddock and albacore tuna.

And what about salt? More good news: Even saltwater fish is low in salt but packed to the gills with vitamins and minerals. Best of all, fish is one of the easiest foods to prepare—simply broil it in just a little margarine—and one that truly needs "only a little lemon juice" to be delectable.

Just remember when shopping to opt for fresh rather than frozen fish because fish is usually frozen in brine. And anyway, the fresher the fish, the better it tastes.

So dive into this chapter. You'll net exciting and healthful fish dishes like Herbed Fillet of Sole, Southern Catfish Fillets, Tuna Oriental, and Poached Salmon Steaks—don't let them get away.

HERBED FILLET OF SOLE

SERVES 4

1/3 cup fresh lemon juice
1/4 teaspoon dry mustard powder
1/2 teaspoon tarragon
2 tablespoons acceptable margarine, softened
1 pound fillet of sole

Preheat broiler.

Combine lemon juice, mustard and tarragon. Set aside.

Spread margarine in a flat baking dish and add fish. Brush fish with seasoned lemon juice. Broil 2 to 3 inches from the heat 5 to 8 minutes for thin fillets (10 to 12 minutes for thicker fillets). Brush once or twice with lemon juice mixture during broiling.

Fish is done when it is firm and flakes easily with a fork. Do not overcook.

NUTRIENT ANALYSIS

Calories	147 kcal
Protein	19 g
Carbohydrate	1 g
Total Fat	7 g
Saturated	1 g
Polyunsaturated	2 g
Monounsaturated	3 g
Cholesterol	53 mg
Sodium	88 mg
Potassium	293 mg
Calcium	18 mg

FISH FILLETS SUPREME

SERVES 6

1½ cups water
2 tablespoons fresh lemon juice
1½ pounds cod fillets
Vegetable oil spray
⅛ teaspoon freshly ground black pepper
2 large fresh tomatoes, sliced ¼ inch thick
½ medium green bell pepper, finely chopped
2 tablespoons finely chopped onion
¼ cup dry bread crumbs
½ teaspoon basil
1 tablespoon acceptable vegetable oil

NUTRIENT ANALYSIS	
Calories	156 kcal
Protein	23 g
Carbohydrate	7 g
Total fat	4 g
Saturated	1 g
Polyunsaturated	2 g
Monounsaturated	1 g
Cholesterol	60 mg
Sodium	130 mg
Potassium	469 mg
Calcium	29 mg

Combine water and lemon juice. Pour over fish fillets and let stand 30 minutes. Drain fillets.

Preheat oven to 350° F.

Spray an ovenproof pan lightly with vegetable oil spray. Place fish in prepared pan. Season with black pepper. Place tomato slices over fish and sprinkle with green pepper and onion.

Combine bread crumbs, basil and oil. Blend well. Spread seasoned crumb mixture evenly over tomatoes.

Bake uncovered 25 minutes or until fish is firm and flakes easily with a fork. Do not overcook.

ROLLED FISH FILLETS

SERVES 8

2 pounds fish fillets
3 tablespoons fresh lemon juice
1½ cups water or more
1 bay leaf

Dip fish fillets in lemon juice. Drain. Beginning with the narrow end, roll each fillet as for jelly roll and secure with a toothpick.

Place water in large saucepan. (Water should be 2 inches deep.) Add bay leaf and bring to a boil. Carefully place rolled fillets in boiling water, cover and reduce heat. Simmer 5 minutes or until fish is firm and flakes easily with a fork.

Carefully transfer fillets to a heated serving platter. Remove toothpicks.

For an elegant entrée, serve with Yogurt-Dill Sauce (see page 207) or chopped toasted almonds.

NUTRIENT ANALYSIS

Calories	105 kcal
Protein	21 g
Carbohydrate	0 g
Total Fat	1 g
Saturated	0 g
Polyunsaturated	1 g
Monounsaturated	0 g
Cholesterol	60 mg
Sodium	94 mg
Potassium	310 mg
Calcium	17 mg

OVEN-FRIED FISH

SERVES 4

Vegetable oil spray
2 tablespoons acceptable margarine, melted
1 tablespoon fresh lemon juice
1/4 teaspoon freshly ground black pepper
1/4 teaspoon paprika
1/4 teaspoon basil
1/8 teaspoon garlic powder
1 pound fillet of flounder or other fish
1/4 cup dry bread crumbs

NUTRIENT ANALYSIS	
Calories	173 kcal
Protein	21 g
Carbohydrate	5 g
Total Fat	7 g
Saturated	1 g
Polyunsaturated	3 g
Monounsaturated	3 g
Cholesterol	56 mg
Sodium	135 mg
Potassium	306 mg
Calcium	27 mg

Lightly spray a shallow baking dish with vegetable oil spray. Preheat oven to 475° F.

Combine margarine, lemon juice, pepper, paprika, basil and garlic powder. Mix well. Dip fish in margarine-herb mixture and roll in bread crumbs.

Arrange fish in a single layer in a baking dish. Spoon remaining margarine mixture over fish. Bake uncovered 15 minutes or until fish flakes easily with a fork. Do not overcook.

CRISPY BAKED FISH

SERVES 4

Vegetable oil spray
1 cup whole-wheat bread crumbs
½ teaspoon freshly ground black pepper
4 tablespoons fresh minced parsley
2 tablespoons reduced-calorie mayonnaise
1 tablespoon water
2 drops hot pepper sauce
1¼ pounds fish fillets
4 lemon wedges

NUTRIENT ANALYSIS	
Calories	185 kcal
Protein	28 g
Carbohydrate	7 g
Total Fat	4 g
Saturated	1 g
Polyunsaturated	2 g
Monounsaturated	1 g
Cholesterol	77 mg
Sodium	230 mg
Potassium	441 mg
Calcium	39 mg

Preheat oven to 350° F. Lightly spray a baking sheet with vegetable oil spray. Set aside.

Place bread crumbs in the work bowl of a food processor fitted with a metal blade. Process until very fine. Sprinkle crumbs onto an ungreased baking sheet and bake 5 to 7 minutes, or until lightly browned.

Combine prepared bread crumbs, black pepper and parsley in a shallow pan and set aside.

Raise oven temperature to 450° F.

Combine mayonnaise, water and hot pepper sauce in a shallow bowl and mix well.

Dip fish in mayonnaise mixture and then dredge in bread crumbs.

Place fish on prepared baking sheet. Bake 17 to 18 minutes, or until fish flakes easily.

Serve with lemon wedges.

SOUTHERN CATFISH FILLETS

SERVES 4

Vegetable oil spray
4 5-ounce catfish fillets
1/2 teaspoon freshly ground black pepper
1/2 cup low-fat milk
4 drops hot pepper sauce
1/2 cup cornmeal
1/4 cup fresh minced parsley
1/4 teaspoon cayenne pepper
Lemon wedges (optional)

NUTRIENT ANALYSIS	
Calories	254 kcal
Protein	33 g
Carbohydrate	15 g
Total Fat	6 g
Saturated	1 g
Polyunsaturated	2 g
Monounsaturated	2 g
Cholesterol	86 mg
Sodium	56 mg
Potassium	822 mg
Calcium	143 mg

Preheat oven to 450° F. Lightly spray a baking dish with vegetable oil spray.

Sprinkle fillets with black pepper. Set aside.

In a shallow dish, combine milk and hot pepper sauce. In another dish, combine cornmeal, parsley and cayenne pepper. Dip fillets in milk mixture and then roll in cornmeal mixture. Place fillets in prepared baking dish and bake 15 to 17 minutes, or until done.

Serve with lemon wedges if desired.

FISH STEAKS WITH THYME

SERVES 4

Vegetable oil spray
1¼ pounds fish steaks, such as swordfish, tuna or mako shark
2 tablespoons acceptable vegetable oil
1 teaspoon dried thyme leaves
½ teaspoon freshly ground black pepper
1 tablespoon acceptable margarine, melted

NUTRIENT ANALYSIS*	
Calories	241 kcal
Protein	27 g
Carbohydrate	0 g
Total Fat	14 g
Saturated	2 g
Polyunsaturated	6 g
Monounsaturated	4 g
Cholesterol	75 mg
Sodium	36 mg
Potassium	653 mg
Calcium	93 mg

* Using swordfish.

Lightly spray top of grill with vegetable oil spray. Preheat grill.

Rub fish steaks with oil, thyme and pepper. Cover and let sit in refrigerator 30 to 60 minutes.

Remove fish steaks from refrigerator and place on heated grill at least 6 inches from the coals or fire. Cook 2 to 3 minutes on each side.

For an attractive crosshatch pattern, grill fish 1 to 1½ minutes and then rotate fish ¼ of a turn. Grill another 1 to 1½ minutes and flip to other side. Grill 1 to 1½ minutes and then rotate fish ¼ of a turn.

Remove from grill and brush with melted margarine.

POACHED SALMON STEAKS

SERVES 4

1 pound salmon steaks
3/4 cup water
3/4 cup dry white table wine
1 medium onion, chopped
1 bay leaf
1/4 teaspoon freshly ground black pepper
1/8 teaspoon ground cloves
1/8 teaspoon thyme

Place salmon in a large nonstick skillet. Add remaining ingredients. If necessary, add additional water so fish is barely covered with liquid. Simmer over low heat 15 to 20 minutes or until salmon is firm and flakes easily with a fork.

Drain liquid and serve fish with Yogurt-Dill Sauce (see page 207).

NUTRIENT ANALYSIS

Calories	147 kcal
Protein	26 g
Carbohydrate	0 g
Total Fat	4 g
Saturated	1 g
Polyunsaturated	2 g
Monounsaturated	1 g
Cholesterol	71 mg
Sodium	33 mg
Potassium	618 mg
Calcium	84 mg

TUNA-MACARONI CASSEROLE

SERVES 4

1 cup uncooked macaroni
Vegetable oil spray
1 tablespoon acceptable vegetable oil
2 tablespoons chopped onion
1 tablespoon all-purpose flour
1/4 teaspoon curry powder
1/4 teaspoon onion powder
1/8 teaspoon freshly ground black pepper
1 tablespoon finely chopped fresh parsley or 1/2 tablespoon dry parsley flakes
1 cup skim milk
1/2 cup no-salt-added canned tomatoes, drained and chopped
1 6 1/2-ounce can unsalted tuna packed in spring water, drained, rinsed and flaked
2 tablespoons acceptable margarine, melted
1/4 cup dry bread crumbs

Cook macaroni as directed on package, omitting salt. Drain and set aside.

Preheat oven to 350° F. Lightly spray a 1 1/2-quart ovenproof casserole dish with vegetable oil spray.

Heat oil in a saucepan. Add chopped onion and sauté until tender. Add flour, curry and onion powders, pepper and parsley. Mix thoroughly. Gradually stir in milk, blending well. Cook, stirring constantly, until mixture comes to a boil. Remove from heat.

Add macaroni, tomatoes and tuna. Pour into prepared pan.

In a small bowl, combine melted margarine and bread crumbs. Sprinkle evenly over top of tuna-macaroni mixture. Bake 30 to 35 minutes or until sauce is bubbly.

NUTRIENT ANALYSIS

Calories	327 kcal
Protein	20 g
Carbohydrate	38 g
Total Fat	10 g
Saturated	2 g
Polyunsaturated	4 g
Monounsaturated	4 g
Cholesterol	9 mg
Sodium	106 mg
Potassium	397 mg
Calcium	112 mg

TUNA ORIENTAL

SERVES 3

½ green bell pepper, cut in ¼-inch strips
1 small onion, thinly sliced
2 teaspoons acceptable vegetable oil
⅓ cup pineapple juice
1½ teaspoons cornstarch
⅔ cup pineapple chunks, canned in natural juices, drained
1 tablespoon sugar
1 tablespoon cider vinegar
1 6½-ounce can unsalted tuna packed in spring water, drained, rinsed and flaked
⅛ teaspoon freshly ground black pepper
Dash hot pepper sauce

Sauté green pepper and onion in oil, leaving slightly crisp. Mix pineapple juice with cornstarch and add to green pepper and onion mixture. Cook, stirring gently, until thickened. Add remaining ingredients. Cook 5 minutes, stirring occasionally.

This dish is good served over rice.

NUTRIENT ANALYSIS

Calories	178 kcal
Protein	17 g
Carbohydrate	20 g
Total Fat	3 g
Saturated	0 g
Polyunsaturated	2 g
Monounsaturated	1 g
Cholesterol	10 mg
Sodium	30 mg
Potassium	330 mg
Calcium	26 mg

POULTRY

Golden Baked Chicken

Lemon-Baked Chicken

Roast Chicken

Oven-Fried Chicken

Chicken à l'Orange

Chicken Dijon

Chicken with Yogurt-Cilantro Sauce

Chicken Paprikash

Chicken Primavera

Chicken Marengo

Arroz con Pollo (Chicken with Rice)

Chicken Cacciatore

Chicken Enchiladas

Chicken Tuscany

Chicken with Ginger and Snow Peas

Lemon-Barbecued Chicken

Roast Turkey

Turkey Stew

Turkey with Rosemary

Turkey Sausage Patties

In many ways, poultry is a cook's best friend. It's high in protein, low in fat, flavorful, versatile and inexpensive.

Chicken, turkey and other poultry contain protein and B vitamins with fewer calories per serving than red meat. Their gentle flavors lend themselves well to a wide variety of cooking techniques. Virtually every cuisine in the world has a poultry specialty.

From the delicately tart taste of Lemon-Baked Chicken to the ultra-spicy kick of Chicken Cacciatore, you'll find a variety of dishes here to please a variety of palates.

But don't stop there. As long as you're careful of added salt and fat, go ahead and create your own poultry dishes with spices from Africa, Israel and Mexico. With cayenne pepper, curry, turmeric or cumin, and so many other popular spices, you can create almost infinite taste sensations.

If you want to save money preparing these recipes, buy whole chickens and cut them up yourself—you can save as much as 30 percent on the cost. Plus, you'll have the necks, backs and bones for making your own low-sodium broth.

As for turkey, well, at holiday time—or any time—everyone loves a stuffed turkey. To keep it moist, stuff it with moisture-producing materials instead of bread stuffing, which tends to soak up fats and moisture. For example, coarsely chop a bunch of parsley, a couple of leeks, an onion, a few stalks of celery, a couple of apples and an orange with peel, then pack the cavity with this mixture of fruits and vegetables. (Discard them when cooking is finished.) This lends flavor as well as moistness to the meat.

Wrap the bird in foil and baste with a flavorful, low-sodium broth every 45 minutes. You can still have bread stuffing: Just prepare it on the side so you can control the amount of fat and salt it contains.

Poultry dishes are among America's family favorites. Try these recipes and you'll see why.

GOLDEN BAKED CHICKEN

SERVES 4

2½-pound frying chicken, cut in pieces, skinned, all visible fat removed
3 tablespoons acceptable margarine, melted
2 tablespoons fresh lemon juice
½ teaspoon paprika
⅛ teaspoon freshly ground black pepper
⅛ teaspoon garlic powder

Preheat oven to 375° F.

Rinse chicken and pat dry.

Place chicken on a rack in a shallow baking dish. Combine remaining ingredients and brush about half of mixture on chicken. Brush chicken with remaining margarine mixture again once or twice during baking. Bake 1 hour.

NUTRIENT ANALYSIS

Calories	316 kcal
Protein	38 g
Carbohydrate	1 g
Total Fat	17 g
Saturated	4 g
Polyunsaturated	5 g
Monounsaturated	6 g
Cholesterol	109 mg
Sodium	108 mg
Potassium	371 mg
Calcium	31 mg

LEMON-BAKED CHICKEN

SERVES 4

Vegetable oil spray
2½-pound frying chicken, cut in pieces, skinned, all visible fat removed
2 tablespoons acceptable vegetable oil
¼ cup fresh lemon juice
2 teaspoons oregano or tarragon (optional)
⅛ teaspoon garlic powder
2 tablespoons chopped fresh parsley
¼ teaspoon paprika

NUTRIENT ANALYSIS	
Calories	271 kcal
Protein	33 g
Carbohydrate	1 g
Total Fat	14 g
Saturated	3 g
Polyunsaturated	6 g
Monounsaturated	4 g
Cholesterol	95 mg
Sodium	94 mg
Potassium	335 mg
Calcium	28 mg

Preheat oven to 350° F. Lightly spray an ovenproof casserole dish with vegetable oil spray.

Rinse chicken and pat dry. Place chicken pieces in prepared casserole.

In a small bowl, combine oil, lemon juice, oregano or tarragon and garlic powder. Brush about half of mixture on chicken. Cover and bake 35 minutes.

Remove cover. Brush with remainder of oil-lemon mixture. Continue baking, uncovered, 20 minutes longer or until tender.

Sprinkle with parsley and paprika before serving.

ROAST CHICKEN

SERVES 6

1 4- to 4½-pound chicken
½ teaspoon poultry seasoning
¼ teaspoon freshly ground black pepper
¼ teaspoon paprika
1 lemon

NUTRIENT ANALYSIS	
Calories	206 kcal
Protein	33 g
Carbohydrate	0 g
Total Fat	7 g
Saturated	2 g
Polyunsaturated	2 g
Monounsaturated	2 g
Cholesterol	94 mg
Sodium	89 mg
Potassium	304 mg
Calcium	23 mg

Preheat oven to 350° F.

Remove parts from inside cavity of chicken and discard. Rinse chicken and pat dry. Sprinkle seasonings over chicken, and place whole lemon inside cavity.

Place chicken on a roasting rack, breast side up, in a deep roasting pan. Bake 1¼ to 1½ hours.

Chicken is done if clear juices run from the thigh when pierced with a fork or when thermometer inserted in the thigh registers 180° to 185° F.

Serve on a heated platter and remove skin after carving.

For a delicious flavor combination, serve this with Mushroom and Herb Dressing (page 178). The dressing may be stuffed into the chicken before roasting or cooked in a casserole dish alongside the roasting pan.

OVEN-FRIED CHICKEN

SERVES 6

1 chicken (2½ to 3 pounds) cut into serving pieces, skinned, all visible fat removed
½ cup plain nonfat yogurt
2 cloves garlic, minced
2 cups whole-wheat bread crumbs
¼ cup minced fresh parsley sprigs
1 teaspoon basil
1 teaspoon oregano
4 tablespoons grated Parmesan cheese
¼ teaspoon freshly ground black pepper
1 tablespoon acceptable margarine

NUTRIENT ANALYSIS	
Calories	329 kcal
Protein	31 g
Carbohydrate	27 g
Total Fat	10 g
Saturated	3 g
Polyunsaturated	2 g
Monounsaturated	3 g
Cholesterol	74 mg
Sodium	391 mg
Potassium	362 mg
Calcium	159 mg

Preheat oven to 350° F.

Rinse chicken and pat dry. Set aside.

In a medium bowl, combine yogurt and garlic. Set aside. In a medium bowl, toss bread crumbs with parsley, basil, oregano, cheese and pepper. Dip each piece of chicken in the yogurt mixture and then roll it in the crumb mixture.

In a large nonstick skillet, heat margarine over medium-high heat. Add chicken pieces and cook about 5 minutes on each side, or until evenly browned.

Transfer chicken pieces to a 13 × 9-inch baking dish. Bake 30 to 35 minutes.

CHICKEN À L'ORANGE

SERVES 4

$2\frac{1}{2}$-pound frying chicken, cut in pieces, skinned, all visible fat removed
$\frac{1}{2}$ cup all-purpose flour
2 teaspoons freshly grated orange peel
1 teaspoon paprika
$\frac{1}{2}$ teaspoon freshly ground black pepper
1 tablespoon acceptable vegetable oil
$\frac{1}{2}$ cup water
$1\frac{1}{2}$ cups orange juice
2 tablespoons firmly packed brown sugar
$\frac{1}{4}$ teaspoon ground ginger
$\frac{1}{8}$ teaspoon ground cinnamon
$\frac{1}{4}$ cup finely chopped pecans

Rinse chicken and pat dry. Set aside.

Combine flour, orange peel, paprika and pepper. Set aside 2 tablespoons flour mixture and coat chicken with remainder.

Brown chicken in oil in a large, heavy nonstick skillet over medium-high heat. Pour off fat. Add water. Cover and simmer over low heat 30 minutes or until tender.

Remove chicken to a warm serving platter.

Pour drippings from pan, reserving 2 tablespoons and discarding remainder. Return reserved 2 tablespoons of drippings to skillet over medium-high heat. Add reserved seasoned flour mixture. Blend well. Add orange juice, brown sugar, ginger and cinnamon. Cook, stirring constantly, until thickened.

Serve chicken topped with orange sauce and pecans.

NUTRIENT ANALYSIS

Calories	410 kcal
Protein	36 g
Carbohydrate	30 g
Total Fat	16 g
Saturated	3 g
Polyunsaturated	5 g
Monounsaturated	6 g
Cholesterol	95 mg
Sodium	94 mg
Potassium	571 mg
Calcium	46 mg

CHICKEN DIJON

SERVES 6

1½ pounds boneless chicken breasts, skinned, all visible fat removed
2 tablespoons acceptable margarine
2 tablespoons flour
1 cup skim milk
¼ teaspoon freshly ground black pepper
1 to 2 teaspoons Dijon mustard
¼ cup low-sodium chicken broth
1 clove garlic, cut in half
¼ teaspoon freshly ground black pepper
1 medium zucchini, sliced
2 medium carrots, sliced
½ medium red bell pepper, cut into strips
1 tablespoon chopped fresh parsley

Rinse chicken and pat dry. Set aside.

In a small saucepan, melt margarine over medium heat. Add flour, stirring constantly. Cook 1 to 2 minutes. Add milk, stirring constantly. Raise heat and bring mixture to a boil, then reduce heat immediately so liquid simmers. Stir in 1/4 teaspoon pepper, and mustard. Add enough chicken broth to thin sauce to desired consistency.

Rub chicken with garlic clove and sprinkle with 1/4 teaspoon pepper. Poach or steam breasts 12 to 15 minutes, or until meat is white throughout.

Steam vegetables until tender-crisp. Place around chicken pieces. Pour sauce over chicken and sprinkle chopped parsley on top.

NUTRIENT ANALYSIS

Calories	215 kcal
Protein	27 g
Carbohydrate	9 g
Total Fat	7 g
Saturated	2 g
Polyunsaturated	2 g
Monounsaturated	3 g
Cholesterol	63 mg
Sodium	113 mg
Potassium	476 mg
Calcium	92 mg

CHICKEN WITH YOGURT-CILANTRO SAUCE

SERVES 4

4 boneless chicken breasts, skinned, all visible fat removed
2 tablespoons olive oil
2 tablespoons lime juice
1/4 teaspoon freshly ground black pepper
4 ounces plain nonfat yogurt
1 tablespoon minced cilantro
1 tablespoon minced mint
1/2 teaspoon cumin
4 wedges fresh lime

NUTRIENT ANALYSIS

Calories	221 kcal
Protein	28 g
Carbohydrate	3 g
Total Fat	10 g
Saturated	2 g
Polyunsaturated	1 g
Monounsaturated	6 g
Cholesterol	67 mg
Sodium	85 mg
Potassium	329 mg
Calcium	76 mg

Rinse chicken and pat dry. Set aside.

In a shallow dish, combine oil, lime juice and black pepper. Place chicken breasts in dish and turn until well coated. Cover and refrigerate at least 2 hours.

To make the sauce, combine yogurt, cilantro, mint and cumin in a small bowl. Set aside.

Preheat broiler or grill.

Remove chicken breasts from refrigerator 20 to 30 minutes before cooking. Cook by broiling or grilling 4 to 5 minutes on each side.

Serve sauce over chicken breasts and garnish with lime wedges.

CHICKEN PAPRIKASH

SERVES 6

Vegetable oil spray
1 3- to 3½-pound chicken
2 tablespoons acceptable margarine
1 medium red onion, sliced
2 tablespoons sweet Hungarian paprika
1 fresh tomato, peeled and chopped
½ cup low-sodium chicken broth
2 tablespoons flour
½ cup plain nonfat yogurt
2 tablespoons low-fat sour cream

NUTRIENT ANALYSIS	
Calories	257 kcal
Protein	31 g
Carbohydrate	7 g
Total Fat	11 g
Saturated	3 g
Polyunsaturated	3 g
Monounsaturated	4 g
Cholesterol	84 mg
Sodium	108 mg
Potassium	474 mg
Calcium	91 mg

Preheat oven to 350° F. Lightly spray baking dish with vegetable oil spray.

Rinse chicken and cut into serving pieces. Remove skin and visible fat. Melt margarine in a large nonstick skillet over medium heat. Brown chicken lightly on all sides. Remove chicken and set aside.

Add onion and paprika to skillet and cook 1 minute. Add tomato and chicken broth and cook for another 2 to 3 minutes. Return chicken to pan. Reduce heat, cover and simmer 30 to 40 minutes. Remove chicken.

Sprinkle flour into skillet and cook 2 to 3 minutes. In a small bowl, whisk yogurt and sour cream together. Add to skillet and then remove skillet from heat. Pour sauce over chicken pieces and serve hot.

CHICKEN PRIMAVERA

SERVES 6

1 16-ounce can no-salt-added tomatoes, chopped
1 medium red onion, chopped
1 medium zucchini, chopped
1 medium yellow squash, chopped
½ cup sliced fresh mushrooms
½ cup low-sodium chicken broth
1 pound fettucine noodles
2 cups diced cooked chicken
1 cup frozen peas
¼ teaspoon freshly ground black pepper
¼ teaspoon red pepper flakes

NUTRIENT ANALYSIS	
Calories	467 kcal
Protein	28 g
Carbohydrate	78 g
Total Fat	5 g
Saturated	1 g
Polyunsaturated	1 g
Monounsaturated	1 g
Cholesterol	39 mg
Sodium	79 mg
Potassium	778 mg
Calcium	96 mg

In a large saucepan over medium-high heat, combine tomatoes, onion, zucchini, squash, mushrooms and chicken broth. Bring to a boil and reduce heat. Simmer 30 minutes.

Cook fettucine noodles according to package directions, omitting salt. Drain and set aside. Keep warm.

Add chicken, peas and black and red pepper to tomato mixture. Cook another 5 to 10 minutes. Spoon sauce over warm fettucine noodles.

CHICKEN MARENGO

SERVES 6

Vegetable oil spray
1 4- to 4½-pound chicken
½ teaspoon freshly ground black pepper
2 tablespoons acceptable vegetable oil
1 medium red onion, chopped
2 cloves garlic, minced
1 large fresh tomato, peeled and chopped or 1 cup no-salt-added canned tomatoes
½ pound fresh mushrooms, sliced
½ cup low-sodium chicken broth

NUTRIENT ANALYSIS	
Calories	296 kcal
Protein	39 g
Carbohydrate	4 g
Total Fat	13 g
Saturated	3 g
Polyunsaturated	5 g
Monounsaturated	4 g
Cholesterol	107 mg
Sodium	111 mg
Potassium	551 mg
Calcium	38 mg

Preheat oven to 350° F. Lightly spray a 9 × 13-inch baking dish with vegetable oil spray.

Rinse chicken and cut into serving pieces. Remove skin and visible fat. Sprinkle with pepper. Place oil in a large nonstick skillet over medium-high heat. Add chicken and brown lightly on all sides. Remove chicken to prepared baking dish.

Place onion and garlic in skillet and sauté until soft. Add tomatoes, mushrooms and chicken broth and cook about 5 minutes. Pour mixture over chicken.

Place in oven and bake 30 to 40 minutes, or until chicken is done.

ARROZ CON POLLO (Chicken with Rice)

SERVES 6

1½ pounds boneless chicken breasts, skinned, all visible fat removed
1 tablespoon acceptable margarine
2 cloves garlic, minced
¼ teaspoon freshly ground black pepper
¼ teaspoon paprika
¼ cup chopped onion
¼ cup chopped green bell pepper
1 tablespoon acceptable vegetable oil
1 cup uncooked rice
2 cups low-sodium chicken broth
½ cup chopped fresh tomatoes
⅛ teaspoon saffron or turmeric
½ cup cooked green peas

Preheat oven to 350° F.

Rinse chicken and pat dry. Set aside.

In a small saucepan over medium heat, melt margarine. Add garlic, black pepper and paprika. Mix well. Remove from heat and brush on chicken breasts.

Place chicken in an ovenproof dish and bake, uncovered, 20 to 25 minutes, or until meat has turned white throughout.

Meanwhile, in a large nonstick skillet over medium heat, sauté the onion and green pepper in oil 5 to 6 minutes or until soft. Add rice and cook another 2 to 3 minutes, stirring frequently. Add chicken broth, tomatoes and saffron or turmeric and stir to mix thoroughly. Cover and simmer over low heat 20 to 25 minutes. Add green peas and cooked chicken and cook an additional 10 minutes. Serve immediately.

NUTRIENT ANALYSIS

Calories	299 kcal
Protein	28 g
Carbohydrate	27 g
Total Fat	8 g
Saturated	2 g
Polyunsaturated	3 g
Monounsaturated	2 g
Cholesterol	62 mg
Sodium	90 mg
Potassium	369 mg
Calcium	35 mg

CHICKEN CACCIATORE

SERVES 6

6 split chicken breasts, skinned, all visible fat removed
2 tablespoons acceptable vegetable oil
1 clove garlic, minced
1 medium onion, chopped
2 tablespoons chopped green bell pepper
4 fresh tomatoes, peeled and chopped
1/4 cup dry white table wine
1/4 teaspoon rosemary
1 bay leaf
1/4 teaspoon basil
1/8 teaspoon freshly ground black pepper

NUTRIENT ANALYSIS

Calories	204 kcal
Protein	27 g
Carbohydrate	5 g
Total Fat	8 g
Saturated	2 g
Polyunsaturated	4 g
Monounsaturated	2 g
Cholesterol	66 mg
Sodium	72 mg
Potassium	440 mg
Calcium	41 mg

Rinse chicken and pat dry. Set aside.

Heat oil and garlic in a large nonstick skillet over medium-high heat. Add chicken and brown. Remove chicken and set aside. Add onion and green pepper to skillet, and sauté until tender. Pour off fat.

Return chicken to skillet. Add remaining ingredients. Cover and simmer over low heat 30 minutes, or until chicken is tender.

Remove bay leaf before serving.

May be served over rice.

CHICKEN ENCHILADAS

SERVES 4;
2 ENCHILADAS PER SERVING

3/4 pound boneless chicken breasts, skinned, all visible fat removed
1/4 cup chopped onion
1 clove garlic, minced
1/4 teaspoon chili powder
1/2 teaspoon cumin
2 tablespoons acceptable margarine
2 tablespoons flour
1 1/2 cups skim milk
1/4 teaspoon freshly ground black pepper
1 teaspoon fresh lemon juice
1 cup grated low-fat Monterey Jack cheese
8 corn tortillas
3 tablespoons chopped, canned hot chili peppers

Preheat oven to 350° F. Rinse chicken and pat dry.

Poach or steam chicken breasts 5 to 6 minutes, or until white throughout. Cool under running water and dice into ¼-inch cubes. Place in a small bowl and mix with onion, garlic, chili powder and cumin.

In a small saucepan over medium heat, melt margarine and add flour. Cook 1 to 2 minutes, stirring frequently. Whisk in skim milk, stirring constantly. Bring mixture to a boil and reduce heat. Stir in pepper, lemon juice and half of cheese. Reserve remainder of cheese.

In a nonstick pan over medium heat or in a microwave oven, briefly heat each tortilla on each side until soft.

Place tortillas on flat surface and add 1 to 2 tablespoons of chicken and 1 tablespoon of reserved cheese. Roll and place seam side down in a 9 × 13 × 2-inch baking dish. Repeat for each tortilla. Pour sauce over enchiladas and top with chili peppers. Bake 20 to 25 minutes.

NUTRIENT ANALYSIS

Calories	339 kcal
Protein	32 g
Carbohydrate	30 g
Total Fat	10 g
Saturated	2 g
Polyunsaturated	3 g
Monounsaturated	4 g
Cholesterol	50 mg
Sodium	684 mg
Potassium	517 mg
Calcium	371 mg

CHICKEN TUSCANY

SERVES 4

$2\frac{1}{2}$-pound frying chicken, cut in pieces, skinned, all visible fat removed
2 tablespoons acceptable margarine, melted
1 teaspoon oregano
¼ teaspoon garlic powder
1 teaspoon paprika
¾ cup dry bread crumbs

Preheat oven to 350° F. Rinse chicken and pat dry. Set aside.

Place melted margarine in a shallow baking dish. In separate flat dish, mix together oregano, garlic powder, paprika and bread crumbs.

Dip chicken pieces in melted margarine, then roll each piece in seasoned crumbs, coating evenly.

Place in a shallow baking dish. Bake uncovered 1 hour, or until chicken is tender.

NUTRIENT ANALYSIS

Calories	334 kcal
Protein	35 g
Carbohydrate	14 g
Total Fat	14 g
Saturated	3 g
Polyunsaturated	4 g
Monounsaturated	5 g
Cholesterol	96 mg
Sodium	230 mg
Potassium	357 mg
Calcium	55 mg

CHICKEN WITH GINGER AND SNOW PEAS

SERVES 6

1¼ pounds boneless chicken breasts, skinned, all visible fat removed
6 ounces snow peas
1 tablespoon cornstarch
½ cup low-sodium chicken broth
1 teaspoon freshly ground black pepper
1 tablespoon low-sodium soy sauce
2 tablespoons acceptable vegetable oil
2 cloves garlic, minced
½ teaspoon minced fresh ginger

NUTRIENT ANALYSIS	
Calories	174 kcal
Protein	22 g
Carbohydrate	4 g
Total Fat	7 g
Saturated	1 g
Polyunsaturated	3 g
Monounsaturated	2 g
Cholesterol	52 mg
Sodium	153 mg
Potassium	271 mg
Calcium	27 mg

Rinse chicken and pat dry. Slice into thin strips. Set aside. Remove ends from snow peas and discard. Set snow peas aside.

In a small nonplastic bowl, mix cornstarch, chicken broth, pepper and soy sauce. Set aside.

Heat oil in a wok or large, heavy nonstick skillet over high heat. Add chicken and cook 4 to 5 minutes, turning frequently. Add garlic, ginger and snow peas and cook another 2 to 3 minutes. Add soy sauce mixture and cook another 2 to 3 minutes, or until sauce thickens. If mixture begins to burn, remove wok or skillet from heat momentarily, or add a small amount of low-sodium chicken broth.

This dish is excellent served over rice.

LEMON-BARBECUED CHICKEN

SERVES 4

2½-pound frying chicken, quartered, skinned, all visible fat removed
Dash paprika
Dash cayenne pepper
¼ cup fresh lemon juice
¼ cup honey
1 tablespoon sesame seeds, toasted

NUTRIENT ANALYSIS	
Calories	287 kcal
Protein	34 g
Carbohydrate	18 g
Total Fat	9 g
Saturated	2 g
Polyunsaturated	2 g
Monounsaturated	3 g
Cholesterol	95 mg
Sodium	95 mg
Potassium	341 mg
Calcium	29 mg

Preheat broiler. Rinse chicken and pat dry.

Season chicken lightly with paprika and pepper. Combine lemon juice and honey in a small saucepan, mixing thoroughly. Heat over medium heat until warm and set aside 2 tablespoons. Coat chicken pieces with about half of the rest of the lemon-honey mixture.

Place chicken on broiler rack. Broil 4 to 5 inches from the heat for 15 minutes. Baste occasionally with remaining lemon-honey mixture. Turn pieces over, baste and broil 15 minutes longer or until tender. Combine sesame seeds and the reserved 2 tablespoons lemon-honey mixture. Spoon over chicken just before serving.

This also may be cooked on a charcoal grill.

ROAST TURKEY

SERVES 12

1 turkey (about 12 pounds)
½ teaspoon freshly ground black pepper
½ teaspoon poultry seasoning
3 stalks celery, chopped
1 medium onion, chopped
2 carrots, chopped
⅓ cup chopped fresh parsley
¼ cup acceptable margarine, melted

NUTRIENT ANALYSIS	
Calories	499 kcal
Protein	75 g
Carbohydrate	0 g
Total Fat	20 g
Saturated	5 g
Polyunsaturated	5 g
Monounsaturated	6 g
Cholesterol	214 mg
Sodium	203 mg
Potassium	700 mg
Calcium	53 mg

Thaw turkey completely, rinse and pat dry. Remove parts from cavity of turkey. Preheat oven to 425° F.

Sprinkle pepper and poultry seasoning inside cavity of turkey. Add vegetables and parsley. Truss. Place bird on a rack in a roasting pan. Brush with melted margarine. Bake 15 minutes and reduce heat to 325° F. Cook turkey, basting often, until internal temperature reaches 185° F. when tested at the thigh. Let turkey rest 15 to 20 minutes before cutting. Discard vegetables and parsley. Carve, remove skin and serve.

TURKEY STEW

SERVES 6

1¼ pounds uncooked turkey breast, skinned, all visible fat removed
¼ cup flour
3 tablespoons acceptable margarine
2 cloves garlic, minced
2 cups low-sodium chicken broth
1½ cups sliced carrots
1½ cups sliced celery
1 cup green peas
1 teaspoon fresh lemon juice
Freshly ground black pepper to taste

NUTRIENT ANALYSIS	
Calories	234 kcal
Protein	25 g
Carbohydrate	12 g
Total Fat	9 g
Saturated	2 g
Polyunsaturated	3 g
Monounsaturated	3 g
Cholesterol	56 mg
Sodium	130 mg
Potassium	453 mg
Calcium	44 mg

Rinse turkey breast and pat dry. Cut into ½-inch cubes and dredge in flour.

Melt margarine in a large pot over medium heat. Add turkey and sauté until lightly browned, about 4 to 5 minutes. Add garlic and cook 1 to 2 minutes. Add chicken broth, carrots and celery. Bring to a boil. Reduce heat and simmer 45 to 60 minutes. Add peas and cook 5 additional minutes. Add lemon juice and black pepper and serve.

TURKEY WITH ROSEMARY

SERVES 4

1 pound turkey tenderloins
1 tablespoon olive oil
1 clove garlic, minced
1 tablespoon chopped fresh rosemary
1/4 teaspoon freshly ground black pepper
1 teaspoon fresh lemon juice
1/4 cup low-sodium chicken broth
1 tablespoon white table wine

NUTRIENT ANALYSIS	
Calories	178 kcal
Protein	27 g
Carbohydrate	1 g
Total Fat	7 g
Saturated	1 g
Polyunsaturated	1 g
Monounsaturated	3 g
Cholesterol	67 mg
Sodium	66 mg
Potassium	258 mg
Calcium	18 mg

Preheat oven to 350° F. Rinse turkey and pat dry. Set aside.

Place olive oil, garlic, rosemary, pepper and lemon juice in a shallow pan and stir until well mixed. Dip tenderloins in mixture until well coated. Place on a baking pan and bake 10 minutes. Turn and bake another 5 to 10 minutes, or until done.

Remove and slice tenderloins across grain. Place turkey slices on a warm serving platter.

Place broth and wine in a skillet over medium-high heat. Cook 2 to 3 minutes. Remove from heat and pour over turkey slices. Serve immediately.

TURKEY SAUSAGE PATTIES

SERVES 4

¾ pound ground turkey
¼ teaspoon freshly ground black pepper
¼ teaspoon basil
¼ teaspoon sage
¼ teaspoon oregano
⅛ teaspoon allspice
⅛ teaspoon nutmeg
⅛ teaspoon dill weed
⅛ teaspoon chili powder (optional)
⅛ teaspoon hot pepper sauce (optional)
⅛ teaspoon garlic powder
1 egg white
2 tablespoons water

NUTRIENT ANALYSIS	
Calories	121 kcal
Protein	20 g
Carbohydrate	0 g
Total Fat	4 g
Saturated	1 g
Polyunsaturated	1 g
Monounsaturated	1 g
Cholesterol	53 mg
Sodium	64 mg
Potassium	194 mg
Calcium	19 mg

Preheat broiler.

Combine all ingredients in a medium bowl and mix thoroughly. Shape into 4 patties and place on a rack in a shallow pan. Broil 2 to 4 inches from heat for 10 to 15 minutes. Turn patties and broil 5 to 10 minutes, or until done.

Serve these as breakfast patties with French Toast, Pancakes or Apple-Filled Crepes (see recipes, pages 163, 227 and 245).

MEATS

Beef Bourguignon

Peppered Roast Beef

Beef Stroganoff

Lime-Marinated Steak

Chili

Meat Loaf

Beef Goulash

Soft Tacos

Spaghetti with Meat Sauce

Lemon Veal with Spinach

Lamb Curry

Mediterranean Pork Chops

Hungarian Pork Chops

Can lean red meat be part of a low-sodium, low-modified-fat eating plan? You bet. It just plays a smaller role in your overall diet than perhaps you've been used to in the past.

Instead of being the centerpiece of a meal, meats are now taking a supporting role. They are often supplemented by high-fiber grains and legumes, and surrounded by salads and leafy vegetables.

Meats add potassium, B vitamins, zinc and iron to your diet. They also add saturated fat. You can limit the fat you get by looking for the leanest cuts of fresh meat and trimming all visible fat before cooking. And sodium won't be a problem if you follow the recipes here.

Meat is versatile, too. You can prepare Peppered Roast Beef as an evening meal for the family, then slice it for sandwiches for the next day's lunchbox. Mexican food need not be high in fat or salt to be delicious, as our Soft Tacos will show you.

Having a dinner party? Impress your guests and help your heart at the same time by serving our Lemon Veal with Spinach, a tangy gourmet dish. Or turn to the exotic tastes of India with our Lamb Curry.

BEEF BOURGUIGNON

SERVES 9

2 pounds lean beef chuck roast, visible fat removed, cut into cubes
1/4 cup all-purpose flour
1/8 teaspoon freshly ground black pepper
2 tablespoons acceptable vegetable oil
1/2 cup chopped onion
1 clove garlic, minced
1/4 teaspoon thyme
1/4 teaspoon basil
1/4 teaspoon oregano
1/8 teaspoon rosemary
1/8 teaspoon marjoram
1 tablespoon chopped fresh parsley
1/2 cup dry red table wine
1 cup water
2 cups finely chopped fresh tomatoes
2 cups diced raw carrots
3 cups diced raw potatoes

NUTRIENT ANALYSIS	
Calories	252 kcal
Protein	22 g
Carbohydrate	18 g
Total Fat	10 g
Saturated	3 g
Polyunsaturated	2 g
Monounsaturated	4 g
Cholesterol	54 mg
Sodium	70 mg
Potassium	611 mg
Calcium	26 mg

Coat beef with flour and pepper. Brown meat in oil. Add onion and garlic, and cook until tender. Pour off fat. Add thyme, basil, oregano, rosemary, marjoram, parsley, wine and water.

Cover and simmer 1 hour, stirring occasionally, adding more water if necessary to keep the bottom of the pan covered.

Add tomatoes and simmer 1 additional hour. Add carrots and potatoes. Simmer 30 minutes.

PEPPERED ROAST BEEF

SERVES 18

5 pounds beef round roast, all visible fat removed
2 tablespoons acceptable vegetable oil
1 teaspoon fresh, coarsely ground black pepper
1 medium onion, sliced
1 medium carrot, sliced
1 large stalk celery, sliced
½ cup dry red table wine

NUTRIENT ANALYSIS	
Calories	202 kcal
Protein	25 g
Carbohydrate	1 g
Total Fat	10 g
Saturated	4 g
Polyunsaturated	1 g
Monounsaturated	4 g
Cholesterol	67 mg
Sodium	65 mg
Potassium	384 mg
Calcium	12 mg

Preheat oven to 350° F.

Rub meat with oil and pepper, and place in an open roasting pan. Insert meat thermometer so tip reaches center of thickest part. Arrange onion, carrot and celery slices around meat. Pour wine over meat and vegetables. Place in oven and cook uncovered 1½ hours, or until meat thermometer registers desired degree of doneness.

If more liquid is needed, baste with additional wine during the roasting period. Do not use drippings from the roast for basting.

Skim fat from pan juices or remove juices with bulb baster and discard fat. Remove meat from pan and slice thin. Spoon pan juices over meat and serve immediately.

BEEF STROGANOFF

SERVES 5

1/3 cup plain low-fat yogurt
1 pound beef tenderloin or sirloin steak, 1/2 inch thick, all visible fat removed
1/8 teaspoon freshly ground black pepper
1/2 pound fresh mushrooms, sliced
1 medium onion, sliced
3 tablespoons acceptable vegetable oil
3 tablespoons all-purpose flour
2 cups low-sodium beef broth, heated
2 tablespoons no-salt-added tomato paste
1 teaspoon dry mustard powder
1/8 teaspoon oregano
1/8 teaspoon dill weed
2 tablespoons dry table sherry

NUTRIENT ANALYSIS*

Calories	276 kcal
Protein	23 g
Carbohydrate	10 g
Total Fat	16 g
Saturated	4 g
Polyunsaturated	5 g
Monounsaturated	5 g
Cholesterol	53 mg
Sodium	88 mg
Potassium	576 mg
Calcium	52 mg

* Using beef tenderloin.

Place a double-thick layer of fine-mesh cotton cheesecloth or paper coffee filters inside a colander that does not rust. Place the colander in a bowl, leaving enough space for some of the yogurt whey to drain out of the colander. Pour the yogurt into the prepared colander and refrigerate for 30 minutes.

Cut meat into thin strips about 2 inches long. Sprinkle with pepper and set aside.

In a large nonstick skillet, sauté mushrooms and onion in oil. Remove mushrooms and onion and set aside. Place meat strips in same skillet and lightly brown on all sides. Remove meat and set aside. Mix flour into oil in skillet. Add beef broth. Bring to a boil. Reduce heat and simmer, stirring constantly, until thickened. Add tomato paste, mustard powder, oregano, dill weed and sherry. Stir. Add beef, mushrooms and onions. Cover tightly and simmer 1 to 1½ hours, or until beef has reached desired degree of doneness. Stir in yogurt; heat for 5 minutes, but do not boil.

This dish may be served over rice or noodles.

LIME-MARINATED STEAK

SERVES 4

2 tablespoons acceptable vegetable oil
½ cup fresh lime juice
½ teaspoon hot pepper sauce
½ teaspoon garlic powder
1 18-ounce boneless top round steak, visible fat removed
2 teaspoons freshly ground black pepper
Lime wedges to garnish

In a large nonplastic dish, combine oil, lime juice, hot pepper sauce and garlic powder, stirring to mix well. Add steak to marinade and turn to coat well. Cover and place in refrigerator for 6 to 8 hours, turning a few times.

Preheat grill or broiler.

Remove steak from marinade and sprinkle with black pepper. Cook 3 to 4 minutes on each side. Transfer to a cutting board and slice thinly across grain of meat. Garnish with lime wedges.

NUTRIENT ANALYSIS

Calories	255 kcal
Protein	31 g
Carbohydrate	1 g
Total Fat	13 g
Saturated	3 g
Polyunsaturated	4 g
Monounsaturated	4 g
Cholesterol	83 mg
Sodium	60 mg
Potassium	451 mg
Calcium	11 mg

CHILI

SERVES 6

¾ cup dried kidney beans
3 cups water
1 pound lean ground beef
½ cup chopped onion
½ green bell pepper, chopped
1 16-ounce can no-salt-added tomatoes, chopped
1 6-ounce can no-salt-added tomato paste
¾ cup water
1 tablespoon Chili Powder *(see recipe, page 40)*
½ teaspoon oregano
¼ teaspoon garlic powder
⅛ teaspoon freshly ground black pepper
1 bay leaf

NUTRIENT ANALYSIS	
Calories	255 kcal
Protein	20 g
Carbohydrate	20 g
Total Fat	11 g
Saturated	4 g
Polyunsaturated	1 g
Monounsaturated	5 g
Cholesterol	42 mg
Sodium	78 mg
Potassium	843 mg
Calcium	58 mg

Place beans and water in a saucepan. Bring to a boil and cook 2 minutes. Set aside for 1 hour without draining.

Return beans to heat and simmer for 1 hour or until beans are tender. Drain, rinse and set aside.

Brown ground beef, onion and green pepper together. Pour off fat. Add kidney beans and remaining ingredients. Simmer over low heat 1½ hours, stirring occasionally.

Remove bay leaf and serve hot.

MEAT LOAF

SERVES 6

½ cup skim milk
2 slices bread, broken into pieces
1 pound lean ground beef
2 egg whites, slightly beaten
½ cup chopped onion
2 teaspoons chopped celery
1 medium fresh tomato, peeled and chopped
2 tablespoons low-sodium ketchup
1 tablespoon fresh lemon juice
⅛ teaspoon freshly ground black pepper
⅛ teaspoon dry mustard powder
⅛ teaspoon sage
⅛ teaspoon garlic powder

NUTRIENT ANALYSIS	
Calories	204 kcal
Protein	17 g
Carbohydrate	9 g
Total Fat	11 g
Saturated	4 g
Polyunsaturated	1 g
Monounsaturated	5 g
Cholesterol	43 mg
Sodium	110 mg
Potassium	339 mg
Calcium	45 mg

Preheat oven to 375° F.

Pour milk over bread and allow to stand 5 minutes. Add remaining ingredients and mix well.

Form into a loaf and place on a rack in a shallow roasting pan. Bake 1½ hours.

BEEF GOULASH

SERVES 6

1 cup uncooked macaroni
1 pound lean ground beef
½ pound fresh mushrooms, sliced
1 cup chopped onion
1 clove garlic, minced
1 6-ounce can no-salt-added tomato paste
¾ cup water
1 cup Ketchup (see recipe, page 197) or low-sodium ketchup
1 small bay leaf
1 teaspoon sugar
½ teaspoon freshly ground black pepper
¼ teaspoon oregano
¼ teaspoon basil

NUTRIENT ANALYSIS	
Calories	329 kcal
Protein	19 g
Carbohydrate	36 g
Total Fat	12 g
Saturated	5 g
Polyunsaturated	1 g
Monounsaturated	5 g
Cholesterol	42 mg
Sodium	72 mg
Potassium	855 mg
Calcium	46 mg

Cook macaroni according to package directions, omitting salt. Drain and set aside.

Brown ground beef with mushrooms, onion and garlic. Pour off fat. Add remaining ingredients. Simmer gently about 15 minutes. Add cooked, drained macaroni. Simmer 5 minutes. Remove bay leaf and serve.

SOFT TACOS

SERVES 6; 2 TACOS PER SERVING

1 pound lean ground beef
1 16-ounce can tomato puree
½ teaspoon Chili Powder (see recipe, page 40)
¼ teaspoon garlic powder
¼ teaspoon onion powder
¼ teaspoon sugar
¼ teaspoon freshly ground black pepper
12 flour tortillas
½ cup chopped green bell pepper
½ cup chopped onion
2 fresh tomatoes, chopped
½ head lettuce, shredded

NUTRIENT ANALYSIS	
Calories	507 kcal
Protein	23 g
Carbohydrate	67 g
Total Fat	19 g
Saturated	8 g
Polyunsaturated	1 g
Monounsaturated	8 g
Cholesterol	50 mg
Sodium	458 mg
Potassium	771 mg
Calcium	95 mg

Brown meat in a large nonstick skillet. Pour off fat. Add tomato puree, Chili Powder, garlic and onion powders, sugar and black pepper. Mix well. Cook uncovered over low heat 20 minutes or until thick, stirring occasionally.

Heat tortillas in a nonstick skillet over medium-high heat or in a microwave oven.

Spoon meat mixture onto hot tortillas and top with green pepper, onion, tomatoes and lettuce. Fold tortilla over filling and serve.

SPAGHETTI WITH MEAT SAUCE

SERVES 6

1 pound lean ground beef
1 medium onion, chopped
1 clove garlic, minced
5 medium fresh tomatoes, peeled and chopped, or 1 28-ounce can no-salt-added tomatoes, chopped
1 6-ounce can no-salt-added tomato paste
½ cup dry red table wine
½ teaspoon oregano
½ teaspoon basil
½ teaspoon fennel seeds
⅛ teaspoon freshly ground black pepper
1 8-ounce package spaghetti

NUTRIENT ANALYSIS	
Calories	370 kcal
Protein	21 g
Carbohydrate	45 g
Total Fat	12 g
Saturated	5 g
Polyunsaturated	1 g
Monounsaturated	5 g
Cholesterol	42 mg
Sodium	66 mg
Potassium	826 mg
Calcium	45 mg

Brown ground beef in a large nonstick skillet. Pour off fat. Add remaining ingredients except spaghetti. Cover and simmer over low heat 1½ hours, stirring occasionally. If sauce appears too thick, add water.

Cook spaghetti according to package directions, omitting salt. Drain.

Pour sauce over spaghetti and serve.

LEMON VEAL WITH SPINACH

SERVES 6

1½ pounds lean veal, cut into cubes
3 tablespoons acceptable vegetable oil
1 large onion, chopped
¼ cup water
1 tablespoon fresh lemon juice
¼ teaspoon freshly ground black pepper
½ teaspoon crushed fennel seeds
3 green onions with tops, chopped
2 10-ounce packages frozen spinach
1 lemon, cut into 6 wedges

NUTRIENT ANALYSIS	
Calories	194 kcal
Protein	20 g
Carbohydrate	5 g
Total Fat	11 g
Saturated	2 g
Polyunsaturated	4 g
Monounsaturated	3 g
Cholesterol	72 mg
Sodium	117 mg
Potassium	477 mg
Calcium	121 mg

Brown veal in oil in a large, heavy nonstick skillet. Add chopped onion, cooking until onion is tender. Pour off fat. Add water, lemon juice, pepper and crushed fennel seeds. Cover and simmer over low heat 1 hour, or until veal is tender, stirring occasionally. (More water may be added if needed.)

Add green onions and spinach. Cover and return to simmer. Cook over low heat until spinach is tender, about 5 to 10 minutes.

Place on warm serving platter and garnish with lemon wedges.

LAMB CURRY

SERVES 8

3 tablespoons all-purpose flour
1/8 teaspoon freshly ground black pepper
2 pounds lean lamb, all visible fat removed, cut into cubes
2 tablespoons acceptable vegetable oil
1/2 cup finely chopped onion
2 teaspoons curry powder
3 cups water
2 teaspoons fresh lemon juice

Combine flour and pepper. Roll lamb in seasoned flour. Place oil in a large nonstick skillet over medium-high heat. Add lamb and brown on all sides. Pour off fat. Add onion, curry powder and water. Cover and simmer over low heat, stirring occasionally, for 1 hour or until meat is tender. Stir in lemon juice.

This dish is very good served over rice.

NUTRIENT ANALYSIS

Calories	206 kcal
Protein	23 g
Carbohydrate	3 g
Total Fat	11 g
Saturated	3 g
Polyunsaturated	2 g
Monounsaturated	4 g
Cholesterol	73 mg
Sodium	58 mg
Potassium	289 mg
Calcium	13 mg

MEDITERRANEAN PORK CHOPS

SERVES 4

1 teaspoon acceptable vegetable oil
4 loin pork chops, very lean, ½ inch thick, all visible fat removed
½ teaspoon marjoram
⅛ teaspoon garlic powder
⅛ teaspoon onion powder
⅛ teaspoon freshly ground black pepper
½ cup water

Place oil in a large nonstick skillet over medium-high heat. Add pork chops and brown evenly. Pour off fat.

In a small bowl, mix seasonings together. Sprinkle over chops. Add water and cover tightly. Reduce heat and simmer over low heat 1 hour or until tender.

NUTRIENT ANALYSIS

Calories	172 kcal
Protein	18 g
Carbohydrate	0 g
Total Fat	10 g
Saturated	3 g
Polyunsaturated	2 g
Monounsaturated	4 g
Cholesterol	60 mg
Sodium	46 mg
Potassium	248 mg
Calcium	7 mg

HUNGARIAN PORK CHOPS

SERVES 4

⅔ cup plain low-fat yogurt
Vegetable oil spray
4 loin pork chops, very lean, ½ inch thick, all visible fat removed
1 teaspoon acceptable vegetable oil
1 teaspoon paprika
½ teaspoon caraway seeds
½ teaspoon dill weed
½ teaspoon onion powder
½ teaspoon garlic powder
½ cup water

NUTRIENT ANALYSIS

Calories	201 kcal
Protein	20 g
Carbohydrate	4 g
Total Fat	11 g
Saturated	4 g
Polyunsaturated	2 g
Monounsaturated	5 g
Cholesterol	63 mg
Sodium	76 mg
Potassium	364 mg
Calcium	86 mg

Place a double-thick layer of fine-mesh cotton cheesecloth or paper coffee filters inside a colander that does not rust. Place the colander in a bowl, leaving enough space for some of the yogurt whey to drain out of the colander. Pour the yogurt into the prepared colander and refrigerate for 30 minutes.

Lightly spray a heavy nonstick skillet with vegetable oil spray. Place over medium-high heat. Add chops and oil and brown evenly. Pour off fat. In a small bowl, mix seasonings together. Sprinkle over chops. Add water to skillet. Reduce heat, cover tightly and simmer 1 hour or until tender. Add more water if necessary.

Remove chops and keep warm. Add yogurt to liquid in pan and stir to mix well. Heat for 5 minutes, but do not boil. Pour sauce over chops and serve.

VEGETARIAN ENTRÉES

Spaghetti with Mushroom Sauce

Spaghetti Squash

Spinach Lasagna

Pizza Hero

Zucchini Frittata

Fettucine Alfredo

Vegetarian Chili

Cheese Blintzes

French Toast

No-Cholesterol Egg Substitute

Almost everyone likes an occasional meatless meal. Hearty vegetarian fare is great for weight watchers, too—and for those keeping an eye on their cholesterol levels.

You can get all the daily protein you need by combining grains, legumes and vegetables in interesting ways in casseroles, vegetable pizzas and stir-fries.

Try Spaghetti with Mushroom Sauce or Spinach Lasagna for a taste of the old country, or Fettucine Alfredo, which, despite no salt and little fat in the recipe here, is wonderful and rich-tasting.

For an out-West flavor, try Vegetarian Chili. Made with beans and bulgur wheat, it offers the hearty taste of that old Texas favorite, and you can make it as spicy as your tastebuds can stand!

Breakfast used to mean bacon and eggs, but no more. For healthful alternatives, try these new versions of two old favorites: Cheese Blintzes and French Toast. With a few slight alterations, they can be made without salt and little fat for a nutritious breakfast.

Here, too, is a recipe that's a must for every low-fat kitchen: No-Cholesterol Egg Substitute. Use it anywhere you need an egg. That includes omelettes, baking, casseroles . . . anything.

SPAGHETTI WITH MUSHROOM SAUCE

SERVES 6

3 tablespoons acceptable margarine
1 cup sliced fresh mushrooms
1/3 cup chopped onion
1 clove garlic, minced
1 16-ounce can no-salt-added tomatoes, chopped
1 6-ounce can no-salt-added tomato paste
1/2 cup water
1 tablespoon sugar
1 bay leaf
1/4 teaspoon basil
1/4 teaspoon oregano
1/8 teaspoon freshly ground black pepper
1 8-ounce package spaghetti

NUTRIENT ANALYSIS	
Calories	260 kcal
Protein	7 g
Carbohydrate	44 g
Total Fat	7 g
Saturated	1 g
Polyunsaturated	2 g
Monounsaturated	3 g
Cholesterol	0 mg
Sodium	32 mg
Potassium	564 mg
Calcium	49 mg

Melt margarine in a large nonstick skillet over medium-high heat. Add mushrooms, onion and garlic. Sauté until onion is tender. Stir in remaining ingredients except spaghetti. Cover and simmer over low heat 2 hours, stirring occasionally. If sauce appears too thick, add additional water. Remove bay leaf.

Cook spaghetti according to package directions, omitting salt. Drain. Pour sauce over spaghetti and serve.

SPAGHETTI SQUASH

SERVES 4

1 spaghetti squash, approximately 4 pounds
1 tablespoon olive oil
1 medium onion, chopped
1/2 pound fresh mushrooms, sliced
1/3 cup white table wine
1 16-ounce can no-salt-added tomato sauce
1 16-ounce can no-salt-added tomatoes
2 cloves garlic, minced
1/4 teaspoon freshly ground black pepper
1 cup sliced fresh carrots
2 cups cooked fresh broccoli florets
1 small zucchini, sliced
1/4 cup Parmesan cheese
2 tablespoons chopped fresh parsley

Preheat oven to 350° F. Place whole squash in a baking dish with a little water. Pierce squash with a fork a few times. Place in oven and bake 1 hour, or until squash can easily be pierced with a fork.

Meanwhile, place oil in a large saucepan over medium heat. Add onion and cook until soft. Add mushrooms and wine and cook another 2 to 3 minutes. Add tomato sauce, tomatoes, garlic and pepper. Simmer 3 to 4 minutes. Add carrots, broccoli and zucchini and allow to simmer 5 minutes.

Halve squash lengthwise and remove seeds. Scrape the squash lengthwise with a fork so the strands resemble spaghetti. Place on serving platter and pour spaghetti sauce over the squash. Sprinkle with Parmesan cheese and parsley. Toss and serve.

NUTRIENT ANALYSIS	
Calories	320 kcal
Protein	12 g
Carbohydrate	59 g
Total Fat	8 g
Saturated	2 g
Polyunsaturated	2 g
Monounsaturated	3 g
Cholesterol	4 mg
Sodium	180 mg
Potassium	1759 mg
Calcium	229 mg

SPINACH LASAGNA

SERVES 8

Vegetable oil spray
1 pound lasagna noodles, white or spinach
¼ cup shredded part-skim mozzarella cheese
2 tablespoons Parmesan cheese
1¼ cups shredded part-skim mozzarella cheese
6 tablespoons Parmesan cheese
3 cups low-fat cottage cheese (drained)
3 cups chopped raw spinach
4 cups Tomato Sauce (see recipe, page 201)

Preheat oven to 350° F. Lightly spray a 9 × 13 × 2½-inch baking dish with vegetable oil spray. Set aside.

Place noodles in a large pan of unsalted boiling water. Cook until soft but not completely cooked. (It is best to slightly undercook noodles because they will be easier to handle during assembly, and they will continue to cook while in the oven.) Drain noodles and rinse under cold running water.

In a small bowl, combine ¼ cup mozzarella and 2 tablespoons Parmesan cheese. Stir to mix well and set aside. In a medium bowl, combine 1¼ cups mozzarella with 6 tablespoons Parmesan cheese and all of the cottage cheese and spinach. Stir to mix well and set aside.

Spread a thin layer of Tomato Sauce in the bottom of the baking dish. Add about one-third of the noodles in a single layer. Spread one-half of cottage cheese mixture on top. Add a thin coating of sauce. Add another layer of noodles and top with cottage cheese mixture and a thin coating of sauce. Top with the remaining noodles and cover with remaining sauce and reserved mozzarella-and-Parmesan mixture.

Bake 30 to 40 minutes. Let stand 10 to 15 minutes. Cut into 8 equal portions and serve.

NUTRIENT ANALYSIS

Calories	432 kcal
Protein	30 g
Carbohydrate	60 g
Total Fat	8 g
Saturated	5 g
Polyunsaturated	1 g
Monounsaturated	2 g
Cholesterol	23 mg
Sodium	594 mg
Potassium	688 mg
Calcium	343 mg

PIZZA HERO

SERVES 2; ½ ROLL PER SERVING

1 6-inch submarine roll
¼ cup no-salt-added spaghetti sauce
1 ounce part-skim mozzarella cheese, shredded
¼ cup sliced fresh mushrooms
4 thin slices of onion
3 green bell pepper rings

Preheat oven to 400° F.

Split roll in half lengthwise and place on baking sheet, cut sides up. Pour spaghetti sauce over roll halves and top with cheese, mushrooms, onion slices and bell pepper.

Place in oven and heat about 5 minutes, or until cheese is melted. Serve warm.

NUTRIENT ANALYSIS

Calories	175 kcal
Protein	8 g
Carbohydrate	25 g
Total Fat	5 g
Saturated	2 g
Polyunsaturated	1 g
Monounsaturated	2 g
Cholesterol	8 mg
Sodium	288 mg
Potassium	290 mg
Calcium	136 mg

ZUCCHINI FRITTATA

SERVES 4

1 large egg
3 large egg whites
1 tablespoon olive oil
1 medium zucchini, diced
3 medium green onions, with tops, sliced
2 cloves garlic, minced
1 16-ounce can no-salt-added tomatoes
½ teaspoon commercial Italian seasoning
¼ teaspoon freshly ground black pepper
1 cup grated part-skim mozzarella cheese

NUTRIENT ANALYSIS	
Calories	186 kcal
Protein	14 g
Carbohydrate	11 g
Total Fat	10 g
Saturated	4 g
Polyunsaturated	1 g
Monounsaturated	4 g
Cholesterol	84 mg
Sodium	220 mg
Potassium	530 mg
Calcium	281 mg

Preheat oven to 350° F.

In a small bowl, whisk together egg and egg whites. Set aside.

Heat oil in a 10-inch nonstick skillet with ovenproof handle, over medium heat. Add zucchini and cook until soft, about 5 minutes. Add green onions and cook another minute. Add garlic, tomatoes, Italian seasoning and pepper and cook another 3 to 4 minutes.

Add egg mixture to vegetables and stir to mix well. Sprinkle cheese on top and place skillet in oven. Bake 5 to 6 minutes, or until mixture is firm.

Change oven setting to Broil and cook an additional 2 to 3 minutes, or until golden brown. Serve immediately.

This dish works well for dinner and for breakfast or brunch.

FETTUCINE ALFREDO

SERVES 4

1 pound fettucine noodles
2 tablespoons acceptable margarine
2 tablespoons flour
1½ cups skim milk
⅓ cup Parmesan cheese
1 teaspoon fresh lemon juice
⅛ teaspoon ground white pepper
2 tablespoons chopped fresh parsley
2 tablespoons Parmesan cheese

NUTRIENT ANALYSIS	
Calories	612 kcal
Protein	23 g
Carbohydrate	104 g
Total Fat	10 g
Saturated	3 g
Polyunsaturated	3 g
Monounsaturated	4 g
Cholesterol	9 mg
Sodium	224 mg
Potassium	433 mg
Calcium	280 mg

Cook fettucine noodles according to package directions, omitting salt. Set aside and keep warm.

Melt margarine in a medium saucepan over medium heat. Add flour. Cook 1 to 2 minutes, stirring constantly. Whisk in milk and bring to a boil. Reduce heat to low and add more milk if thinner consistency is desired. Add ⅓ cup Parmesan cheese, lemon juice and pepper.

Pour sauce over warm fettucine noodles and garnish with parsley and remaining 2 tablespoons Parmesan cheese.

VEGETARIAN CHILI

SERVES 6

1 cup dry kidney beans
6 cups water
3 tablespoons acceptable vegetable oil
2 cups chopped onions
2 cups chopped green bell peppers
2 cloves garlic, minced
1 cup no-salt-added canned tomatoes, chopped
2 cups water
1 cup bulgur
1½ tablespoons chili powder (or to taste)
¼ teaspoon cayenne pepper
½ teaspoon freshly ground black pepper
2 tablespoons ground cumin
1 tablespoon fresh lemon juice

NUTRIENT ANALYSIS	
Calories	362 kcal
Protein	12 g
Carbohydrate	62 g
Total Fat	9 g
Saturated	1 g
Polyunsaturated	5 g
Monounsaturated	2 g
Cholesterol	0 mg
Sodium	34 mg
Potassium	599 mg
Calcium	67 mg

Soak beans overnight in 3 cups of water.

Drain beans and place them in a large saucepan. Add 3 cups of fresh water and cook, uncovered, 1½ hours, or until tender. Drain, rinse and set aside.

In a large saucepan or Dutch oven, place oil, onions, green peppers and garlic. Sauté 8 to 10 minutes, or until vegetables are soft. Add tomatoes, 2 cups of water and bulgur. Simmer 45 to 60 minutes. Add cooked kidney beans and remaining ingredients and cook an additional 10 minutes. Serve hot.

CHEESE BLINTZES

SERVES 11;
2 BLINTZES PER SERVING

2 cups (1 pound) unsalted dry-curd cottage cheese
1 egg white
¼ cup sugar
½ teaspoon grated fresh lemon peel
2 tablespoons fresh lemon juice
1 recipe Crepes (page 229)
1 tablespoon acceptable margarine

NUTRIENT ANALYSIS	
Calories	170 kcal
Protein	8 g
Carbohydrate	19 g
Total Fat	7 g
Saturated	1 g
Polyunsaturated	2 g
Monounsaturated	3 g
Cholesterol	2 mg
Sodium	30 mg
Potassium	70 mg
Calcium	35 mg

To make filling, combine cottage cheese, egg white, sugar, lemon peel and lemon juice in a medium bowl and beat well.

Place 1 tablespoon of filling in center of each crepe and fold in an envelope shape.

Melt margarine in large nonstick skillet over medium heat. Add blintzes and heat for approximately 10 minutes, or until heated thoroughly.

Blintzes may be refrigerated for up to 5 hours before heating.

To serve blintzes as a breakfast entrée, top with a sprinkle of ground cinnamon and sugar or with warm applesauce and cinnamon.

FRENCH TOAST

SERVES 5

1 recipe No-Cholesterol Egg Substitute (see recipe, page 164)
1/4 cup skim milk
1/4 teaspoon vanilla
1/8 teaspoon ground cinnamon
5 slices day-old bread
2 tablespoons acceptable margarine

In a medium shallow bowl, mix Egg Substitute, skim milk, vanilla and cinnamon. Dip bread slices in egg mixture.

Melt margarine in a large nonstick skillet over medium-high heat. Add bread slices and lightly brown.

May be served with margarine and syrup or jelly.

NUTRIENT ANALYSIS

Calories	153 kcal
Protein	6 g
Carbohydrate	14 g
Total Fat	8 g
Saturated	1 g
Polyunsaturated	3 g
Monounsaturated	3 g
Cholesterol	1 mg
Sodium	183 mg
Potassium	102 mg
Calcium	50 mg

NO-CHOLESTEROL EGG SUBSTITUTE

SERVES 1

4 large egg whites
1 tablespoon acceptable vegetable oil
1 tablespoon nonfat dry milk powder
3 drops yellow food coloring

NUTRIENT ANALYSIS

Calories	202 kcal
Protein	16 g
Carbohydrate	4 g
Total Fat	14 g
Saturated	2 g
Polyunsaturated	8 g
Monounsaturated	3 g
Cholesterol	1 mg
Sodium	242 mg
Potassium	264 mg
Calcium	60 mg

Place all ingredients in a medium bowl. Mix until thoroughly blended.

Use in place of 2 whole eggs in recipes. (This substitution may require some experimenting in baking since it will not work effectively in every cake and cookie recipe.)

No-Cholesterol Scrambled Eggs
Add a dash of thyme and a dash of freshly ground black pepper to mixture. Spray a small nonstick skillet with vegetable oil spray. Place skillet over medium heat and add egg mixture. Stir occasionally until eggs are fully cooked. Serve immediately.

No-Cholesterol Omelet
Spray a small omelet pan or nonstick skillet with vegetable oil spray. Place over medium heat and add egg mixture. Cook until lightly browned. Turn omelet and brown other side. Place chopped fresh tomatoes or sautéed sliced mushrooms, onions, green bell pepper or chives in center of omelet and fold in half. Serve immediately.

VEGETABLES

Gingered Carrots

Dilled Summer Squash

Vegetable Medley

Baked Tomatoes

Sautéed Cauliflower

Stir-Fried Cabbage with Noodles

Baked Beans

Sweet and Sour Green Beans

Green Beans and Corn

Eggplant Mexicana

Mushroom and Herb Dressing

Scalloped Potatoes

Potatoes O'Brien

Hash-Brown Potatoes

Potato Pancakes

Oven-Fried Potatoes with Oregano

Scalloped Sweet Potatoes

Sweet Potato Casserole

Seasoned Rice

Brown Rice Pilaf

Rice and Vegetable Pilaf

The 1941 edition of the *Fannie Farmer Cookbook* instructed cooks to boil green beans for at least 20 minutes. Today we laugh at the idea.

Gone are the days when vegetables were cooked until limp. Now we want vegetables tender-crisp, and often, even raw. Since overcooking can leach vegetables of vitamins and minerals, braising, steaming and stir-frying have become the cook's preferred cooking methods. And with great results!

Steaming is a wonderful way to cook vegetables because it doesn't use fats or oils and leaves most of the vitamins and minerals right where you want them—in your food.

If you're skeptical that vegetables can be tasty without added fat and salt, these recipes should convince you. From crunchy, tangy Gingered Carrots to spicy Eggplant Mexicana, you'll find that flavorful vegetable dishes are easier to make than you think.

And with the hundreds of kinds of vegetables grown throughout the world, it's a cinch to come up with a different combination of veggies every day of the year. There's simply no excuse for having broccoli 365 days in a row!

Even the simplest vegetables have a lot to recommend them. For instance, buy summer squash when the skin is soft enough not to need peeling, then try the Dilled Summer Squash or Vegetable Medley recipes here. Unforgettable!

The humble potato is high in carbohydrates and low in fat. Each potato has a good amount of iron and potassium, some calcium, phosphorous and vitamins B_1, C and niacin. All for about 100 calories a potato. Try Hash-Brown Potatoes for breakfast, Potato Pancakes for lunch and Scalloped Potatoes for dinner.

The trick with vegetables is adding flavor without inflating the fat, sodium or calorie count. These recipes are a start. After that, use your imagination, fresh herbs and spices. You'll surprise yourself.

GINGERED CARROTS

SERVES 5

1 pound raw carrots, peeled and cut into ¼-inch slices
¼ teaspoon ground ginger
1 teaspoon sugar
1 tablespoon acceptable margarine, melted
2 tablespoons finely chopped fresh parsley or 1 tablespoon dry parsley flakes

Place carrots in a saucepan. Add just enough water to cover. Boil 10 to 12 minutes or until barely tender. Drain.

Add ginger and sugar to melted margarine and pour over carrots. Stir gently.

Sprinkle with parsley and serve immediately.

NUTRIENT ANALYSIS	
Calories	62 kcal
Protein	1 g
Carbohydrate	10 g
Total Fat	2 g
Saturated	0 g
Polyunsaturated	1 g
Monounsaturated	1 g
Cholesterol	0 mg
Sodium	56 mg
Potassium	200 mg
Calcium	29 mg

DILLED SUMMER SQUASH

SERVES 4

1/4 cup water
2 medium summer squash, sliced
1 1/2 teaspoons finely chopped onion
1/2 teaspoon dill seed, crushed
1/8 teaspoon freshly ground black pepper
1 tablespoon acceptable margarine

Bring water to a boil in a medium saucepan over high heat. Add squash, onion, dill seed and pepper. Reduce heat to medium and cook 10 minutes or until squash is tender. Drain and dot with margarine. Serve immediately.

NUTRIENT ANALYSIS

Calories	60 kcal
Protein	2 g
Carbohydrate	8 g
Total Fat	3 g
Saturated	1 g
Polyunsaturated	1 g
Monounsaturated	1 g
Cholesterol	0 mg
Sodium	3 mg
Potassium	332 mg
Calcium	48 mg

VEGETABLE MEDLEY

SERVES 4

1 tablespoon acceptable margarine
2 medium yellow summer squash, sliced
1 medium zucchini, sliced
1 medium yellow onion, diced
3 medium fresh tomatoes, diced
½ cup frozen corn
1 clove garlic, minced
½ teaspoon oregano
½ teaspoon basil
¼ teaspoon freshly ground black pepper

In a large pan over medium heat melt margarine. Add squash, zucchini and onion. Sauté 3 to 4 minutes. Add tomatoes, corn, garlic and seasonings and cook another 2 to 3 minutes. Serve immediately.

NUTRIENT ANALYSIS

Calories	123 kcal
Protein	4 g
Carbohydrate	22 g
Total Fat	4 g
Saturated	1 g
Polyunsaturated	1 g
Monounsaturated	1 g
Cholesterol	0 mg
Sodium	16 mg
Potassium	788 mg
Calcium	92 mg

BAKED TOMATOES

SERVES 4

Vegetable oil spray
2 fresh tomatoes, cut in halves
1 tablespoon olive oil
1/2 teaspoon chopped fresh parsley or
1/4 teaspoon dried parsley flakes
1/4 teaspoon oregano
1/4 teaspoon basil

Preheat oven to 350° F. Lightly spray a 9 × 9-inch baking dish with vegetable oil spray.

Place tomato halves in baking dish, cut side up. Drizzle oil over tomatoes. Sprinkle remaining ingredients on top and bake 20 to 30 minutes. Serve hot.

NUTRIENT ANALYSIS	
Calories	44 kcal
Protein	1 g
Carbohydrate	3 g
Total Fat	4 g
Saturated	0 g
Polyunsaturated	0 g
Monounsaturated	3 g
Cholesterol	0 mg
Sodium	6 mg
Potassium	150 mg
Calcium	8 mg

SAUTÉED CAULIFLOWER

SERVES 4

1 head (1 pound) fresh or 1 10-ounce package frozen cauliflower
2 teaspoons acceptable vegetable oil
¼ teaspoon thyme
¾ teaspoon cider vinegar
½ clove garlic, minced
Dash freshly ground black pepper
2 teaspoons minced fresh parsley or 1 teaspoon dried parsley flakes

NUTRIENT ANALYSIS	
Calories	48 kcal
Protein	2 g
Carbohydrate	6 g
Total Fat	3 g
Saturated	0 g
Polyunsaturated	1 g
Monounsaturated	1 g
Cholesterol	0 mg
Sodium	26 mg
Potassium	203 mg
Calcium	27 mg

Break fresh cauliflower into small florets and cook or steam in unsalted water until just tender, 10 to 12 minutes. If using frozen cauliflower, cook according to directions on package, omitting salt. Drain.

Combine oil, thyme, vinegar and garlic in a large pan or skillet. Cook over moderate heat 5 minutes. Add drained cauliflower, sprinkle with pepper and stir gently. Simmer until hot. Sprinkle with parsley and serve immediately.

STIR-FRIED CABBAGE WITH NOODLES

SERVES 6

1 cup dry no-cholesterol noodles
3 cups finely chopped cabbage
1 tablespoon acceptable margarine
3/4 teaspoon caraway seeds
1/2 teaspoon onion powder

Cook noodles according to package directions, omitting salt.

Stir-fry chopped cabbage in margarine over medium heat until cabbage is tender but still crisp, about 5 to 8 minutes. Add drained noodles, caraway seeds and onion powder. Stir together gently. Serve immediately.

NUTRIENT ANALYSIS

Calories	48 kcal
Protein	1 g
Carbohydrate	7 g
Total Fat	2 g
Saturated	0 g
Polyunsaturated	1 g
Monounsaturated	1 g
Cholesterol	0 mg
Sodium	7 mg
Potassium	48 mg
Calcium	14 mg

BAKED BEANS

SERVES 6

½ pound (1 cup) dried navy beans
4 cups water
Vegetable oil spray
1 loin-end pork chop, very lean
1 cup Chili Sauce *(see recipe, page 200)*
¾ cup chopped onion
2 tablespoons light molasses
1 tablespoon firmly packed brown sugar
1½ teaspoons dry mustard powder
¼ teaspoon garlic powder
1 cup water

NUTRIENT ANALYSIS	
Calories	233 kcal
Protein	12 g
Carbohydrate	41 g
Total Fat	4 g
Saturated	1 g
Polyunsaturated	1 g
Monounsaturated	1 g
Cholesterol	10 mg
Sodium	32 mg
Potassium	688 mg
Calcium	102 mg

Place beans and water in a large saucepan over high heat. Bring to a boil and cook 2 minutes. Remove from heat and let stand 1 hour.

Return beans to heat and simmer 1 hour, or until beans are tender. Drain, rinse and set aside.

Preheat oven to 350° F. Lightly spray a 1½-quart casserole dish with vegetable oil spray.

Place beans in prepared casserole and set aside.

Brown pork chop in a small nonstick skillet over medium-high heat. Cut into small cubes and add to beans.

Add remaining ingredients and mix well. Cover and bake 4 hours. If needed, add additional water during cooking.

SWEET AND SOUR GREEN BEANS

SERVES 4

1 10-ounce package frozen or 1 pound fresh green beans, cut in 1-inch pieces
1 teaspoon acceptable margarine
½ teaspoon all-purpose flour
1 tablespoon water
1 tablespoon fresh lemon juice
1 tablespoon sugar
¼ teaspoon dill seeds (optional)
Dash paprika

NUTRIENT ANALYSIS	
Calories	38 kcal
Protein	1 g
Carbohydrate	7 g
Total Fat	1 g
Saturated	0 g
Polyunsaturated	0 g
Monounsaturated	0 g
Cholesterol	0 mg
Sodium	9 mg
Potassium	76 mg
Calcium	30 mg

Cook frozen green beans according to directions on package, omitting salt. If using fresh green beans, cook in ½ cup unsalted water until tender. Drain and set aside.

In a separate pan, melt margarine, stir in flour and brown lightly. Stir in remaining ingredients and cook over low heat until thickened.

Pour over drained green beans and heat 5 minutes. Serve immediately.

GREEN BEANS AND CORN

SERVES 4

1 cup fresh or frozen French-style green beans
1 cup frozen whole kernel corn or fresh, cut from cob
½ cup water
3 tablespoons chopped onion
1 tablespoon acceptable margarine
½ teaspoon basil
½ teaspoon fresh lemon juice
Dash freshly ground black pepper

Cook beans and corn together in water until beans are just tender. Drain and set aside in saucepan.

In a separate pan, sauté onion in margarine until tender. Pour over beans and corn and add basil, lemon juice and pepper. Place saucepan over low heat and simmer until hot.

Succotash
Use fresh lima beans in place of green beans.

GREEN BEANS AND CORN NUTRIENT ANALYSIS	
Calories	69 kcal
Protein	2 g
Carbohydrate	11 g
Total Fat	3 g
Saturated	0 g
Polyunsaturated	1 g
Monounsaturated	1 g
Cholesterol	0 mg
Sodium	8 mg
Potassium	110 mg
Calcium	21 mg

SUCCOTASH NUTRIENT ANALYSIS	
Calories	103 kcal
Protein	4 g
Carbohydrate	17 g
Total Fat	3 g
Saturated	1 g
Polyunsaturated	1 g
Monounsaturated	1 g
Cholesterol	0 mg
Sodium	26 mg
Potassium	248 mg
Calcium	17 mg

EGGPLANT MEXICANA

SERVES 6

1 medium (1 pound) eggplant, peeled and cut into cubes
4 medium fresh tomatoes, peeled and chopped, or 1 16-ounce can no-salt-added tomatoes
1 clove garlic, minced
2 tablespoons chopped onion
1/4 teaspoon Chili Powder (see recipe, page 40)
1/4 teaspoon freshly ground black pepper

Combine all ingredients in a large nonstick skillet and simmer gently 15 to 20 minutes or until eggplant is tender. Serve immediately.

NUTRIENT ANALYSIS

Calories	33 kcal
Protein	1 g
Carbohydrate	7 g
Total Fat	0 g
Saturated	0 g
Polyunsaturated	0 g
Monounsaturated	0 g
Cholesterol	0 mg
Sodium	13 mg
Potassium	314 mg
Calcium	25 mg

MUSHROOM AND HERB DRESSING

SERVES 4

Vegetable oil spray
1 tablespoon acceptable margarine
1/4 cup chopped onions
1 cup chopped fresh mushrooms
2 cups bread crumbs
1/2 teaspoon thyme
1/2 teaspoon basil
1/4 teaspoon freshly ground black pepper
1/4 cup low-sodium chicken broth

NUTRIENT ANALYSIS	
Calories	230 kcal
Protein	7 g
Carbohydrate	38 g
Total Fat	5 g
Saturated	1 g
Polyunsaturated	2 g
Monounsaturated	2 g
Cholesterol	3 mg
Sodium	374 mg
Potassium	150 mg
Calcium	73 mg

Preheat oven to 350° F. Lightly spray a 1½-quart casserole with vegetable oil spray.

Melt margarine in a nonstick skillet over medium heat. Add onions and mushrooms and sauté about 5 minutes, or until soft.

In a medium bowl, combine onion-mushroom mixture, bread crumbs, thyme, basil and black pepper. Add chicken broth and mix well.

Place in prepared casserole and bake uncovered 30 minutes. Or, stuff loosely into a 4- to 4½-pound chicken, such as Roast Chicken (page 112), before roasting.

SCALLOPED POTATOES

SERVES 5

3 tablespoons acceptable margarine
2 tablespoons all-purpose flour
2 cups skim milk
¼ teaspoon freshly ground black pepper
⅛ teaspoon onion powder
⅛ teaspoon garlic powder
Vegetable oil spray
5 medium potatoes, peeled and thinly sliced
½ cup chopped onion

NUTRIENT ANALYSIS	
Calories	190 kcal
Protein	5 g
Carbohydrate	27 g
Total Fat	7 g
Saturated	1 g
Polyunsaturated	2 g
Monounsaturated	3 g
Cholesterol	2 mg
Sodium	59 mg
Potassium	497 mg
Calcium	135 mg

Preheat oven to 350° F.

Melt margarine in a small saucepan. Add flour and mix well. Gradually add milk while stirring constantly. Cook over medium heat, stirring until thickened. Add pepper, onion powder and garlic powder. Stir and remove from heat.

Lightly spray a 1½-quart casserole dish with vegetable oil spray.

Place potatoes and chopped onion in bottom of casserole. Add sauce and stir lightly.

Cover and bake 30 minutes.

Stir gently and bake uncovered an additional 30 to 40 minutes, or until potatoes are tender and lightly browned. Serve hot.

POTATOES O'BRIEN

SERVES 5

5 medium potatoes, unpeeled
2 medium onions, chopped
1 small green bell pepper, chopped
2 tablespoons acceptable vegetable oil
1/8 teaspoon freshly ground black pepper
1/8 teaspoon paprika

Boil potatoes in water 20 to 25 minutes, or until tender. Remove from heat and add cold water until potatoes are cooled slightly. Peel and cut into 1-inch cubes.

In a large nonstick skillet, sauté onions and green pepper in oil until tender. Add potatoes and sprinkle with black pepper and paprika. Cook over medium heat 10 minutes or until potatoes are browned, stirring frequently. Serve hot.

NUTRIENT ANALYSIS

Calories	141 kcal
Protein	2 g
Carbohydrate	21 g
Total Fat	6 g
Saturated	1 g
Polyunsaturated	3 g
Monounsaturated	1 g
Cholesterol	0 mg
Sodium	8 mg
Potassium	376 mg
Calcium	18 mg

HASH-BROWN POTATOES

SERVES 6

1/4 cup acceptable vegetable oil
1/4 teaspoon freshly ground black pepper
1/8 teaspoon onion powder
1/8 teaspoon garlic powder
6 cups chopped or grated peeled potatoes
1/4 teaspoon paprika

Heat oil, pepper and onion and garlic powders in a large nonstick skillet over medium-high heat. Add potatoes and paprika. Cook until potatoes are crisp and browned, stirring frequently.

Drain on paper towels and serve immediately.

NUTRIENT ANALYSIS

Calories	209 kcal
Protein	3 g
Carbohydrate	30 g
Total Fat	9 g
Saturated	1 g
Polyunsaturated	5 g
Monounsaturated	2 g
Cholesterol	0 mg
Sodium	8 mg
Potassium	490 mg
Calcium	13 mg

POTATO PANCAKES

SERVES 8; 1 PANCAKE PER SERVING

1¾ cups grated raw peeled potatoes
2 tablespoons finely chopped onion
2 egg whites
¼ cup all-purpose flour
¾ teaspoon baking powder
¼ teaspoon onion powder
¼ teaspoon garlic powder
⅛ teaspoon freshly ground black pepper
¼ cup (approximately) acceptable vegetable oil

In a large bowl, mix together potatoes and onion.

In a separate mixing bowl, beat egg whites until soft peaks form. Fold into the potato mixture.

Add remaining dry ingredients. Mix well.

Heat a small amount of oil in a large nonstick skillet over medium-high heat. Spoon ⅛ of batter into skillet and spread to ½-inch thickness. Cook until browned, turn and cook second side. Drain on paper towels. Repeat with remainder of batter, using a small amount of oil each time ⅛ of batter is added.

Potato Pancakes with Applesauce and Cinnamon
Add 1 tablespoon warm applesauce and dash of ground cinnamon to top of each pancake.

POTATO PANCAKES NUTRIENT ANALYSIS

Calories	107 kcal
Protein	2 g
Carbohydrate	10 g
Total Fat	7 g
Saturated	1 g
Polyunsaturated	4 g
Monounsaturated	2 g
Cholesterol	0 mg
Sodium	43 mg
Potassium	127 mg
Calcium	22 mg

POTATO PANCAKES WITH APPLESAUCE AND CINNAMON NUTRIENT ANALYSIS

Calories	119 kcal
Protein	2 g
Carbohydrate	13 g
Total Fat	7 g
Saturated	1 g
Polyunsaturated	4 g
Monounsaturated	2 g
Cholesterol	0 mg
Sodium	43 mg
Potassium	137 mg
Calcium	23 mg

OVEN-FRIED POTATOES WITH OREGANO

SERVES 6

3 medium baking potatoes
1 tablespoon olive oil
1/2 teaspoon freshly ground black pepper
1 teaspoon dried oregano
2 tablespoons malt vinegar

NUTRIENT ANALYSIS	
Calories	88 kcal
Protein	1 g
Carbohydrate	16 g
Total Fat	2 g
Saturated	0 g
Polyunsaturated	0 g
Monounsaturated	2 g
Cholesterol	0 mg
Sodium	5 mg
Potassium	266 mg
Calcium	11 mg

Preheat oven to 400° F.

Scrub potatoes thoroughly. Cut each potato lengthwise into 6 wedges. Place wedges in a medium bowl and cover with cold water. Let stand 30 minutes. Drain and pat dry with paper towels.

Place potatoes and oil in a medium bowl and toss to coat evenly.

Place potatoes on baking sheet. Sprinkle with pepper and oregano. Bake 45 to 50 minutes, or until potatoes are tender. Remove from oven and sprinkle with malt vinegar.

SCALLOPED SWEET POTATOES

SERVES 6

Vegetable oil spray
1/4 cup sugar
1/2 teaspoon ground cinnamon
3 raw medium sweet potatoes, peeled, sliced 1/4 inch thick
2 medium apples, sliced
3 tablespoons acceptable margarine

NUTRIENT ANALYSIS	
Calories	165 kcal
Protein	1 g
Carbohydrate	28 g
Total Fat	6 g
Saturated	1 g
Polyunsaturated	2 g
Monounsaturated	3 g
Cholesterol	0 mg
Sodium	8 mg
Potassium	321 mg
Calcium	23 mg

Preheat oven to 350° F. Lightly spray a 1½-quart casserole dish with vegetable oil spray.

Combine sugar and cinnamon in a small bowl and stir to mix thoroughly. Set aside. Place a layer of sweet potatoes in the casserole dish. Add a layer of apples, sprinkle with cinnamon-sugar mixture and dot with margarine. Repeat layers.

Cover and bake 1 hour. Serve hot.

SWEET POTATO CASSEROLE

SERVES 6

4 medium sweet potatoes
Vegetable oil spray
1 tablespoon acceptable margarine
1/4 cup orange juice
2 tablespoons chopped walnuts
1/4 teaspoon nutmeg

Cook whole sweet potatoes in boiling water 25 to 30 minutes or until tender. Meanwhile, preheat oven to 375° F. Lightly spray a 1-quart casserole dish with vegetable oil spray.

Remove potatoes from heat and add cold water until potatoes are cooled slightly. Peel and mash. Add remaining ingredients and mix thoroughly. Place in casserole dish and bake uncovered 25 minutes. Serve hot.

NUTRIENT ANALYSIS

Calories	116 kcal
Protein	2 g
Carbohydrate	20 g
Total Fat	4 g
Saturated	0 g
Polyunsaturated	2 g
Monounsaturated	1 g
Cholesterol	0 mg
Sodium	9 mg
Potassium	393 mg
Calcium	25 mg

SEASONED RICE

SERVES 4

2 tablespoons acceptable margarine
1 medium onion, finely chopped
3/4 cup uncooked long-grain rice
1 1/2 cups low-sodium chicken broth
1/4 teaspoon celery flakes
1/4 teaspoon onion powder
1/4 teaspoon dill weed
1/8 teaspoon freshly ground black pepper

Melt margarine in a nonstick skillet over medium-high heat. Add onion and rice. Brown lightly.

Add remaining ingredients and bring to a boil. Cover, reduce heat and simmer 15 to 25 minutes or until rice is tender, stirring occasionally. Serve immediately.

NUTRIENT ANALYSIS

Calories	184 kcal
Protein	3 g
Carbohydrate	28 g
Total Fat	6 g
Saturated	1 g
Polyunsaturated	2 g
Monounsaturated	3 g
Cholesterol	0 mg
Sodium	25 mg
Potassium	121 mg
Calcium	27 mg

BROWN RICE PILAF

SERVES 4

1 tablespoon acceptable margarine
1 cup uncooked brown rice
2 cups low-sodium chicken broth
¼ teaspoon freshly ground black pepper
2 tablespoons minced fresh parsley sprigs

Melt margarine in a 3-quart saucepan over medium heat. Add rice. Cook 3 to 4 minutes, stirring constantly. Do not brown. Add remaining ingredients and bring to a boil. Cover, reduce heat and simmer 40 to 45 minutes, or until liquid is absorbed.

NUTRIENT ANALYSIS	
Calories	223 kcal
Protein	5 g
Carbohydrate	40 g
Total Fat	4 g
Saturated	1 g
Polyunsaturated	1 g
Monounsaturated	2 g
Cholesterol	0 mg
Sodium	30 mg
Potassium	184 mg
Calcium	27 mg

RICE AND VEGETABLE PILAF

SERVES 6

1 cup low-sodium chicken broth
½ cup long-grain rice
1 cup chopped fresh mushrooms
1 cup shredded carrots
½ cup chopped fresh parsley sprigs
¼ cup sliced green onions, with tops
¼ teaspoon freshly ground black pepper

In a medium saucepan over high heat, bring chicken broth to a boil. Add rice and cover. Reduce heat and simmer 20 minutes. Remove from heat and let stand 5 minutes. Stir in remaining ingredients. Return to low heat and cook another 5 minutes. Fluff with a fork and serve immediately.

NUTRIENT ANALYSIS

Calories	69 kcal
Protein	2 g
Carbohydrate	15 g
Total Fat	0 g
Saturated	0 g
Polyunsaturated	0 g
Monounsaturated	0 g
Cholesterol	0 mg
Sodium	23 mg
Potassium	144 mg
Calcium	23 mg

SAUCES

MOCK SOUR CREAM

MOCK WHIPPED CREAM

MUSHROOM SAUCE

KETCHUP

HOT PREPARED MUSTARD

HORSERADISH SAUCE

CHILI SAUCE

TOMATO SAUCE

CHUNKY TOMATO SAUCE

BARBECUE SAUCE

MEXICAN SALSA

WHITE SAUCE

YOGURT-DILL SAUCE

STRAWBERRY SAUCE

CHOCOLATE SAUCE

Whether you're glazing a dessert, bringing fresh pasta to life or taking a lean cut of meat from the ordinary to the extraordinary, the hallmark of really fine cooking is a creatively prepared sauce.

Unfortunately, most of the commercial sauces we take for granted, such as ketchup, barbecue sauce, chili sauce and tomato sauce, are loaded with salt. Instead, try recipes here for these and other popular condiments. The aroma of homemade tomato sauce with fresh onion, garlic, basil, freshly squeezed lemon juice and just-ground black pepper prepares you for a taste sensation you'll love. Store-bought sauce will taste pretty tame after you try this!

For a different flavor altogether, try Yogurt-Dill Sauce. It's fabulous over fish and great as a dip for cold sliced cucumbers. And to top off a great meal, Strawberry Sauce is certain to dazzle friends and relatives. It's irresistible over Crepes, Angel Food Cake, ice milk or low-fat yogurt.

A sauce is one part of a great cuisine that is easy to experiment with: Substitute wines, spices, homemade low-sodium chicken broth, vinegar, shallots, cornstarch or plenty of fresh herbs for other ingredients wherever you see fit. Just be sure to use acceptable margarines or acceptable vegetable oils in place of butter or other animal fats, and leave out the salt. You'll find that with the creative use of herbs, spices and spirits, you'll enjoy these homemade sauces.

MOCK SOUR CREAM

MAKES 2 CUPS
SERVES 16;
2 TABLESPOONS PER SERVING

1½ cups (12 ounces) unsalted dry-curd cottage cheese
½ cup skim milk
1 tablespoon fresh lemon juice
¼ teaspoon onion powder (optional)

Place all ingredients in a blender and combine on medium-high speed until smooth and creamy. Cover and chill.

NUTRIENT ANALYSIS	
Calories	14 kcal
Protein	3 g
Carbohydrate	1 g
Total Fat	0 g
Saturated	0 g
Polyunsaturated	0 g
Monounsaturated	0 g
Cholesterol	1 mg
Sodium	6 mg
Potassium	18 mg
Calcium	14 mg

MOCK WHIPPED CREAM

MAKES 2 CUPS
SERVES 32;
1 TABLESPOON PER SERVING

1 teaspoon unflavored gelatin
2 teaspoons cold water
3 tablespoons boiling water
½ cup ice water
½ cup nonfat dry milk
3 tablespoons sugar
3 tablespoons acceptable vegetable oil

NUTRIENT ANALYSIS	
Calories	20 kcal
Protein	0 g
Carbohydrate	2 g
Total Fat	1 g
Saturated	0 g
Polyunsaturated	1 g
Monounsaturated	0 g
Cholesterol	0 mg
Sodium	6 mg
Potassium	18 mg
Calcium	13 mg

Chill a small mixing bowl.

In another small bowl, soften gelatin with cold water. Add boiling water, stirring constantly until gelatin is completely dissolved. Cool until tepid.

Place ice water and nonfat dry milk in chilled mixing bowl. Beat at high speed of electric mixer until stiff peaks form. Continue beating and add sugar, oil and gelatin.

Place in freezer for approximately 15 minutes, then transfer to refrigerator until ready to use. Stir before using to retain creamy texture.

MUSHROOM SAUCE

MAKES 2 CUPS
SERVES 8; ¼ CUP PER SERVING

¼ cup chopped onion
½ pound fresh mushrooms, sliced
¼ cup acceptable margarine
1 tablespoon all-purpose flour
⅛ teaspoon freshly ground black pepper
⅛ teaspoon garlic powder
2 cups skim milk
1 tablespoon dry white table wine

NUTRIENT ANALYSIS

Calories	91 kcal
Protein	3 g
Carbohydrate	7 g
Total Fat	6 g
Saturated	1 g
Polyunsaturated	2 g
Monounsaturated	3 g
Cholesterol	1 mg
Sodium	37 mg
Potassium	229 mg
Calcium	88 mg

In a medium nonstick skillet over medium-high heat, sauté onion and mushrooms in margarine until tender. Add flour, pepper and garlic powder and mix well. Gradually add milk, stirring constantly. Cook over medium heat, stirring until thickened. Stir in wine.

Serve hot.

KETCHUP

MAKES 1 QUART
SERVES 64;
1 TABLESPOON PER SERVING

3 6-ounce cans no-salt-added tomato paste
4 cups water
½ cup chopped onion
½ cup chopped celery
½ cup cider vinegar
½ cup sugar
1 tablespoon firmly packed brown sugar
2 tablespoons acceptable margarine
1 teaspoon light molasses
⅛ teaspoon ground cloves
⅛ teaspoon ground cinnamon
⅛ teaspoon basil
⅛ teaspoon tarragon
⅛ teaspoon freshly ground black pepper
⅛ teaspoon onion powder
⅛ teaspoon garlic powder

NUTRIENT ANALYSIS	
Calories	17 kcal
Protein	0 g
Carbohydrate	3 g
Total Fat	0 g
Saturated	0 g
Polyunsaturated	0 g
Monounsaturated	0 g
Cholesterol	0 mg
Sodium	6 mg
Potassium	83 mg
Calcium	5 mg

Place tomato paste, water, onion, celery, vinegar and sugar in a blender or the work bowl of a food processor fitted with a metal blade. Process on medium-high speed until mixture is smooth.

Place tomato mixture and remaining ingredients in a saucepan and simmer uncovered 1½ hours or until ketchup is thickened and reduced to one-half original volume. Stir occasionally.

May be stored in a covered container in refrigerator for 1 month. For longer storage, freeze in small quantities for use as needed.

HOT PREPARED MUSTARD

MAKES ½ CUP
SERVES 8;
1 TABLESPOON PER SERVING

2 tablespoons dry mustard powder
2 tablespoons sugar
¼ cup all-purpose flour
¼ teaspoon onion powder
¼ teaspoon turmeric
2 tablespoons fresh lemon juice
2 tablespoons water

NUTRIENT ANALYSIS

Calories	32 kcal
Protein	1 g
Carbohydrate	6 g
Total Fat	1 g
Saturated	0 g
Polyunsaturated	0 g
Monounsaturated	0 g
Cholesterol	0 mg
Sodium	1 mg
Potassium	18 mg
Calcium	5 mg

Sift dry ingredients together or stir until evenly blended. Add lemon juice and water. Mix well.

Place in covered container and refrigerate.

HORSERADISH SAUCE

MAKES 1½ CUPS
SERVES 24;
1 TABLESPOON PER SERVING

½ medium (6 ounces) horseradish root, peeled
½ cup white vinegar

Cut horseradish into cubes and place in blender. Add vinegar and process until desired consistency. Or finely grate horseradish into a medium bowl and mix with vinegar. Keep refrigerated up to a week in a covered container.

NUTRIENT ANALYSIS	
Calories	3 kcal
Protein	0 g
Carbohydrate	1 g
Total Fat	0 g
Saturated	0 g
Polyunsaturated	0 g
Monounsaturated	0 g
Cholesterol	0 mg
Sodium	7 mg
Potassium	26 mg
Calcium	5 mg

CHILI SAUCE

MAKES 3 CUPS
SERVES 48;
1 TABLESPOON PER SERVING

2 16-ounce cans no-salt-added tomato sauce
½ cup chopped onion
½ cup cider vinegar
½ cup sugar
½ cup chopped celery
½ medium green bell pepper, chopped
2 tablespoons acceptable margarine
1 tablespoon fresh lemon juice
1 teaspoon firmly packed brown sugar
1 teaspoon light molasses
¼ teaspoon hot pepper sauce
⅛ teaspoon ground cloves
⅛ teaspoon ground cinnamon
⅛ teaspoon freshly ground black pepper
⅛ teaspoon basil
⅛ teaspoon tarragon

NUTRIENT ANALYSIS	
Calories	19 kcal
Protein	0 g
Carbohydrate	4 g
Total Fat	1 g
Saturated	0 g
Polyunsaturated	0 g
Monounsaturated	0 g
Cholesterol	0 mg
Sodium	7 mg
Potassium	83 mg
Calcium	5 mg

Place all ingredients in a 3-quart saucepan. Mix thoroughly. Bring to a boil, reduce heat and simmer uncovered 1½ hours or until sauce is thickened and reduced to one-half original volume. Stir occasionally.

May be stored in a covered container in refrigerator for 1 month. For longer storage, freeze in small quantities for use as needed.

TOMATO SAUCE

MAKES 1 QUART
SERVES 8; ½ CUP PER SERVING

2 6-ounce cans no-salt-added tomato paste
3 cups water
¼ cup finely chopped onion
1 clove garlic, minced
2 tablespoons fresh lemon juice
Dash hot pepper sauce
¼ teaspoon basil
⅛ teaspoon freshly ground black pepper

In a medium saucepan, combine all ingredients and mix well. Place over medium-high heat and bring to a boil. Reduce heat, cover and simmer 30 minutes, stirring occasionally. Use in any recipe requiring tomato sauce.

May be stored in a covered container in refrigerator for 1 week. For longer storage, freeze in small quantities for use as needed.

NUTRIENT ANALYSIS

Calories	38 kcal
Protein	2 g
Carbohydrate	9 g
Total Fat	0 g
Saturated	0 g
Polyunsaturated	0 g
Monounsaturated	0 g
Cholesterol	0 mg
Sodium	29 mg
Potassium	410 mg
Calcium	20 mg

CHUNKY TOMATO SAUCE

MAKES 1 CUP
SERVES 4; ¼ CUP PER SERVING

1 tablespoon chopped onion
1 tablespoon chopped green bell pepper
2 tablespoons acceptable margarine
1 tablespoon all-purpose flour
1¼ cups chopped, peeled fresh tomatoes or 1 cup canned no-salt-added tomatoes
Dash freshly ground black pepper

In a large skillet over medium-high heat, sauté onion and green pepper in margarine until tender. Stir in flour until well blended. Add chopped tomatoes and cook, stirring constantly, until tomatoes are tender and sauce is thickened. Add black pepper.

May be stored in a covered container in refrigerator for 1 week. For longer storage, freeze in small quantities for use as needed.

NUTRIENT ANALYSIS

Calories	70 kcal
Protein	1 g
Carbohydrate	4 g
Total Fat	6 g
Saturated	1 g
Polyunsaturated	2 g
Monounsaturated	3 g
Cholesterol	0 mg
Sodium	8 mg
Potassium	136 mg
Calcium	7 mg

BARBECUE SAUCE

SERVES 64;
1 TABLESPOON PER SERVING

2 6-ounce cans no-salt-added tomato paste
2 cups water
½ cup Ketchup (see recipe, page 197) or low-sodium ketchup
¼ cup firmly packed brown sugar
2 tablespoons fresh lemon juice
¼ cup chopped onion
1 clove garlic, minced
2 tablespoons Chili Powder (see recipe, page 40)
2 tablespoons cider vinegar
2 tablespoons acceptable vegetable oil
1 tablespoon chopped fresh parsley
1 teaspoon dry mustard powder
1 teaspoon paprika
⅛ teaspoon freshly ground black pepper
Dash hot pepper sauce (optional)

NUTRIENT ANALYSIS	
Calories	15 kcal
Protein	0 g
Carbohydrate	3 g
Total Fat	1 g
Saturated	0 g
Polyunsaturated	0 g
Monounsaturated	0 g
Cholesterol	0 mg
Sodium	7 mg
Potassium	71 mg
Calcium	5 mg

Combine all ingredients in a saucepan and mix well. Simmer uncovered over low heat 20 minutes.

May be stored in a covered container in refrigerator for 1 month. For longer storage, freeze in small quantities for use as needed.

MEXICAN SALSA

MAKES ¾ CUP
SERVES 12;
1 TABLESPOON PER SERVING

1 large ripe tomato, cored, peeled, seeded and diced
1 teaspoon minced fresh jalapeño or serrano pepper, or to taste
2 tablespoons finely chopped onion
1 to 2 teaspoons fresh lime juice
1 teaspoon finely chopped cilantro

Combine all ingredients in a medium bowl. Mix well. Cover and refrigerate.

NUTRIENT ANALYSIS

Calories	4 kcal
Protein	0 g
Carbohydrate	1 g
Total Fat	0 g
Saturated	0 g
Polyunsaturated	0 g
Monounsaturated	0 g
Cholesterol	0 mg
Sodium	4 mg
Potassium	35 mg
Calcium	2 mg

WHITE SAUCE

MAKES 1¼ CUPS
SERVES 10;
2 TABLESPOONS PER SERVING

2 tablespoons acceptable margarine
3 tablespoons flour
2 cups skim milk
1 teaspoon fresh lemon juice
¼ teaspoon freshly ground black pepper, or to taste

In a 1-quart saucepan heat margarine over medium heat. Add flour and cook 1 to 2 minutes, stirring frequently. Gradually add milk, stirring constantly. Add seasonings and stir until mixture thickens.

White Sauce with Parmesan Cheese

Add ½ cup Parmesan cheese for a great sauce to serve over pasta.

WHITE SAUCE NUTRIENT ANALYSIS

Calories	45 kcal
Protein	2 g
Carbohydrate	4 g
Total Fat	2 g
Saturated	0 g
Polyunsaturated	1 g
Monounsaturated	1 g
Cholesterol	1 mg
Sodium	26 mg
Potassium	85 mg
Calcium	62 mg

WHITE SAUCE WITH PARMESAN CHEESE NUTRIENT ANALYSIS

Calories	64 kcal
Protein	4 g
Carbohydrate	4 g
Total Fat	4 g
Saturated	1 g
Polyunsaturated	1 g
Monounsaturated	1 g
Cholesterol	4 mg
Sodium	101 mg
Potassium	90 mg
Calcium	117 mg

White Sauce with Dijon Mustard
Add 2 tablespoons Dijon mustard, or to taste.

WHITE SAUCE WITH DIJON MUSTARD NUTRIENT ANALYSIS	
Calories	48 kcal
Protein	2 g
Carbohydrate	4 g
Total Fat	3 g
Saturated	0 g
Polyunsaturated	1 g
Monounsaturated	1 g
Cholesterol	1 mg
Sodium	64 mg
Potassium	89 mg
Calcium	64 mg

YOGURT-DILL SAUCE

MAKES 1⅛ CUPS
SERVES 18;
1 TABLESPOON PER SERVING

1 cup plain nonfat yogurt
2 tablespoons low-fat sour cream
2 teaspoons dried dill weed
1 teaspoon prepared mustard
½ teaspoon sugar
¼ teaspoon freshly ground black pepper
½ teaspoon fresh lemon juice

Place all ingredients in a small bowl. Stir to mix thoroughly. Cover and refrigerate.

Serve cold as an accompaniment for hot or chilled fish. May also be used as a dip for raw vegetables or as a dressing for sliced cucumbers.

NUTRIENT ANALYSIS	
Calories	11 kcal
Protein	1 g
Carbohydrate	1 g
Total Fat	0 g
Saturated	0 g
Polyunsaturated	0 g
Monounsaturated	0 g
Cholesterol	1 mg
Sodium	16 mg
Potassium	46 mg
Calcium	36 mg

STRAWBERRY SAUCE

MAKES APPROXIMATELY 1 CUP
SERVES 4; APPROXIMATELY ¼ CUP PER SERVING

1 pound fresh strawberries
1 tablespoon acceptable margarine
1 tablespoon orange juice
1 tablespoon sugar

Wash berries, remove stems and slice berries lengthwise so that slices are heart shaped.

In a nonstick pan, heat margarine and orange juice over medium setting. Add strawberries and cook for 2 to 3 minutes, stirring frequently. Add sugar and cook for 2 minutes longer. Mixture should be slightly thickened. Serve immediately.

This topping is great over plain low-fat yogurt, ice milk or angel food cake.

NUTRIENT ANALYSIS

Calories	61 kcal
Protein	1 g
Carbohydrate	9 g
Total Fat	3 g
Saturated	0 g
Polyunsaturated	1 g
Monounsaturated	1 g
Cholesterol	0 mg
Sodium	2 mg
Potassium	135 mg
Calcium	13 mg

CHOCOLATE SAUCE

MAKES 1 CUP
SERVES 16;
1 TABLESPOON PER SERVING

3 tablespoons cocoa
½ cup sugar
⅓ cup skim milk
1 tablespoon acceptable margarine, melted
1 teaspoon vanilla

Combine cocoa and sugar in a small bowl. Set aside.

In a medium saucepan, heat milk and margarine over medium-high heat. Slowly add cocoa-sugar mixture, stirring constantly. Bring to a boil, remove from heat and add vanilla. Mixture will thicken as it cools.

This sauce is delicious over angel food cake or ice milk.

NUTRIENT ANALYSIS

Calories	35 kcal
Protein	0 g
Carbohydrate	7 g
Total Fat	1 g
Saturated	0 g
Polyunsaturated	0 g
Monounsaturated	0 g
Cholesterol	0 mg
Sodium	3 mg
Potassium	29 mg
Calcium	8 mg

BREADS

On the following pages are recipes for delicious breads, biscuits, muffins, pancakes and more—all made from scratch. Kids will love the Gingerbread and the Blueberry Muffins. Try Oat Bran and Yogurt Muffins and Banana Bread for delicious lunchbox desserts or snacks.

Soups and salads will taste especially homemade with our Seasoned Croutons scattered on top. And for special desserts or main dishes, impress your guests with our delicate Crepes.

Fresh-baked bread is a wonderful gift for friends, family, even just for yourself. If you're baking breads without salt, however, there are a few tips you should know.

First, yeast bread made without salt will rise more quickly than normal bread dough. If you allow the dough to rise too much, your bread will be coarse and have a strong yeasty taste. You can help prevent this from happening by punching the dough lightly with two fingers periodically when it is rising in the bowl. When the indentation remains and the dough no longer springs back, it is ready to be shaped. Allow the loaves and rolls to rise only until slightly less than double in size before placing them in the oven.

Baking bread is an easy way to get children involved in healthful cooking. Let them help by measuring ingredients, shaping the loaves and forming buns with the extra dough. With luck, this early initiation will be the start of a lifelong habit.

BASIC WHITE BREAD

MAKES 2 LARGE LOAVES;
18 SLICES PER LOAF
SERVES 36; 1 SLICE PER SERVING

Vegetable oil spray
1 package dry yeast
1/4 cup lukewarm water
3 tablespoons sugar
2 tablespoons acceptable vegetable oil
1 3/4 cups skim milk, scalded and cooled to lukewarm
5 to 5 1/2 cups all-purpose flour

Preheat oven to 425° F. Lightly spray a large bowl and 2 9 × 5 × 3-inch loaf pans lightly with vegetable oil spray. Set aside.

Soak yeast in water for 5 minutes without stirring. In a large bowl, combine sugar, oil and milk. Add dissolved yeast. Stir in 3 cups of flour and beat until smooth. Gradually add more flour until mixture becomes stiff enough to handle. With some of remaining flour, lightly dust a clean, dry board or tabletop. Knead dough until smooth and elastic, using small amounts of remaining flour. Place kneaded dough in prepared bowl, turning dough to coat entire surface with oil. Cover loosely and let rise in a warm place until almost double in size, or when, if pressed with two fingers, an indentation remains in dough. Punch dough down, divide into 2 equal parts and let rest for 3 to 5 minutes.

Roll each piece into a 9 × 12-inch rectangle. Starting with the narrow side, roll up dough tightly. Seal ends by pinching them together, and place loaf seam side down in prepared pans. Cover loosely and let rise in warm place until sides of dough reach top of pan, 30 to 45 minutes.

Bake 25 to 30 minutes. Remove loaves from pans immediately and cool on a rack.

Dinner Rolls
Preheat oven to 425° F. Lightly spray a baking sheet with vegetable oil spray.

Make dough as for white bread. Divide it into 2 equal parts. Roll out 1 part and divide into 12 equal sections. Shape each into a ball and place on baking sheets with sides touching for soft rolls or 1½ inches apart for crusty rolls. Let rise until almost doubled in size. Bake 15 to 20 minutes, or until brown. Remove from baking sheet and cool on a rack.

NUTRIENT ANALYSIS*

Calories	76 kcal
Protein	2 g
Carbohydrate	14 g
Total Fat	1 g
Saturated	0 g
Polyunsaturated	1 g
Monounsaturated	0 g
Cholesterol	0 mg
Sodium	7 mg
Potassium	40 mg
Calcium	17 mg

* One slice of loaf.

WHITE BREAD VARIATIONS

The Basic White Bread recipe (page 214) can be used as a basis for several different kinds of breads. A few variations are outlined below. Be creative and try a few of your own ideas for tasty breads.

Whole-Wheat Bread

Use 4 cups whole-wheat or graham flour and 1 to 1½ cups all-purpose flour in place of the all-purpose flour called for in the recipe. Light molasses may be used in place of sugar.

NUTRIENT ANALYSIS	
Calories	74 kcal
Protein	3 g
Carbohydrate	14 g
Total Fat	1 g
Saturated	0 g
Polyunsaturated	1 g
Monounsaturated	0 g
Cholesterol	0 mg
Sodium	7 mg
Potassium	77 mg
Calcium	21 mg

Rye Bread

Use 2½ cups rye flour and 2½ to 3 cups all-purpose flour in place of the all-purpose flour called for in the recipe. Use ¼ cup dark molasses in place of sugar. If desired, 1 tablespoon caraway seeds may be added. Dough will not rise as much as white bread dough. Round loaves may be formed and baked on prepared baking sheets.

NUTRIENT ANALYSIS

Calories	70 kcal
Protein	2 g
Carbohydrate	13 g
Total Fat	1 g
Saturated	0 g
Polyunsaturated	1 g
Monounsaturated	0 g
Cholesterol	0 mg
Sodium	7 mg
Potassium	68 mg
Calcium	24 mg

Herb Bread

Many different seeds, herbs or herb combinations may be used with white bread recipes. Add any of the following to dough mixture with the first addition of flour: 1 teaspoon sage and 1 tablespoon caraway seeds; 1 tablespoon oregano and 1 teaspoon basil; 1 tablespoon dill seed and 2 tablespoons grated onion; or 1/4 cup each finely chopped fresh chives and parsley.

NUTRIENT ANALYSIS*

Calories	76 kcal
Protein	2 g
Carbohydrate	14 g
Total Fat	1 g
Saturated	0 g
Polyunsaturated	1 g
Monounsaturated	0 g
Cholesterol	0 mg
Sodium	7 mg
Potassium	40 mg
Calcium	17 mg

* With chives and parsley.

Raisin Bread

Add 1 cup seedless raisins to white dough mixture during first addition of flour.

NUTRIENT ANALYSIS

Calories	89 kcal
Protein	2 g
Carbohydrate	18 g
Total Fat	1 g
Saturated	0 g
Polyunsaturated	1 g
Monounsaturated	0 g
Cholesterol	0 mg
Sodium	8 mg
Potassium	75 mg
Calcium	19 mg

Cinnamon Bread

Prepare Basic White Bread recipe. Divide dough into 2 equal parts and roll each piece into a 9 × 12-inch rectangle. For each loaf, brush dough with 2 teaspoons acceptable vegetable oil and sprinkle with a mixture of ¼ cup sugar and 1 teaspoon ground cinnamon. Roll and seal as directed for Basic White Bread.

NUTRIENT ANALYSIS

Calories	91 kcal
Protein	2 g
Carbohydrate	17 g
Total fat	1 g
Saturated	0 g
Polyunsaturated	1 g
Monounsaturated	0 g
Cholesterol	0 mg
Sodium	7 mg
Potassium	40 mg
Calcium	19 mg

Swedish Bread

Increase sugar in Basic White Bread recipe to 1/3 cup. Add 4 shelled, pulverized cardamom seeds, 1/2 cup finely chopped dried apricots and 3/4 cup seedless raisins to white dough mixture during first addition of flour.

NUTRIENT ANALYSIS	
Calories	92 kcal
Protein	2 g
Carbohydrate	18 g
Total Fat	1 g
Saturated	0 g
Polyunsaturated	1 g
Monounsaturated	0 g
Cholesterol	0 mg
Sodium	8 mg
Potassium	83 mg
Calcium	19 mg

Cinnamon Rolls

Prepare Basic White Bread Recipe. Divide dough into 2 equal parts and roll into rectangles about 1/4 inch thick. Mix 1 cup firmly packed brown sugar, 1 tablespoon ground cinnamon and 1 cup chopped walnuts. Brush dough with 1/4 cup melted acceptable margarine and sprinkle with brown sugar mixture. Roll the dough tightly into cylinders and cut in 1-inch slices. Place cut side up with sides touching on prepared baking sheet. Allow to rise until almost doubled in size, about 35 minutes. Bake in preheated 400° F. oven 30 to 35 minutes or until golden brown. Invert on rack to cool. While warm, drizzle with a glaze made by mixing 1 cup powdered sugar, 1 teaspoon vanilla and 1 to 2 tablespoons water.

NUTRIENT ANALYSIS

Calories	146 kcal
Protein	3 g
Carbohydrate	25 g
Total Fat	4 g
Saturated	1 g
Polyunsaturated	2 g
Monounsaturated	1 g
Cholesterol	0 mg
Sodium	9 mg
Potassium	79 mg
Calcium	29 mg

BISCUITS

SERVES 12; 1 BISCUIT PER SERVING

2 cups all-purpose flour
1 tablespoon baking powder
¼ cup acceptable vegetable oil
⅔ cup skim milk

Preheat oven to 450° F.

In a medium bowl, combine flour and baking powder. Set aside.

In a small bowl, combine oil and milk. Pour all at once into dry ingredients. Stir until mixture clings together and forms a ball. Knead on waxed paper 18 to 20 times without using additional flour. Gently pat or roll out until dough is ½ inch thick. Cut with 2-inch round cutter and place close together with edges touching on ungreased baking sheet. Bake 12 to 15 minutes.

Herb-Seasoned Biscuits

Add one or more of the following to the flour mixture: 1 teaspoon garlic powder; 1 teaspoon onion powder; 2 teaspoons dried parsley flakes; 2 teaspoons dill weed; ½ teaspoon sage.

Drop Biscuits

Add 2 additional tablespoons skim milk and stir dough until well mixed. Drop by spoonfuls onto ungreased baking sheet.

BISCUITS NUTRIENT ANALYSIS	
Calories	115 kcal
Protein	2 g
Carbohydrate	15 g
Total Fat	5 g
Saturated	1 g
Polyunsaturated	3 g
Monounsaturated	1 g
Cholesterol	0 mg
Sodium	80 mg
Potassium	42 mg
Calcium	66 mg

DROP BISCUITS NUTRIENT ANALYSIS	
Calories	116 kcal
Protein	3 g
Carbohydrate	16 g
Total Fat	5 g
Saturated	1 g
Polyunsaturated	3 g
Monounsaturated	1 g
Cholesterol	0 mg
Sodium	81 mg
Potassium	46 mg
Calcium	69 mg

CORN MUFFINS

SERVES 8;
1 LARGE MUFFIN PER SERVING

Vegetable oil spray
1 cup all-purpose flour
1 tablespoon sugar (optional)
¾ cup yellow or white cornmeal
2 teaspoons baking powder
2 egg whites, lightly beaten
1 cup skim milk
2 tablespoons acceptable vegetable oil

NUTRIENT ANALYSIS	
Calories	145 kcal
Protein	4 g
Carbohydrate	23 g
Total Fat	4 g
Saturated	1 g
Polyunsaturated	2 g
Monounsaturated	1 g
Cholesterol	1 mg
Sodium	102 mg
Potassium	93 mg
Calcium	87 mg

Preheat oven to 425° F. Lightly spray muffin tin with vegetable oil spray.

In a large bowl, sift together flour, sugar, cornmeal and baking powder. In a medium bowl, combine egg whites, milk and oil. Pour all at once into dry ingredients. Stir just enough to blend. Pour batter into prepared muffin cups until each is ⅔ full. Bake 15 to 20 minutes, or until golden brown. Allow muffins to cool 2 minutes before removing from pan.

Corn Bread

Pour batter into an 8-inch square baking pan that has been sprayed lightly with vegetable oil spray. Bake 20 to 25 minutes, or until golden brown. Allow to cool 2 minutes before removing from pan.

BLUEBERRY MUFFINS

SERVES 12; 1 MUFFIN PER SERVING

Vegetable oil spray
1 cup unsweetened blueberries, fresh or frozen
1¾ cups all-purpose flour
2½ teaspoons baking powder
⅓ cup sugar
2 egg whites, slightly beaten
¼ cup acceptable vegetable oil
½ cup skim milk
1 teaspoon sugar

NUTRIENT ANALYSIS	
Calories	137 kcal
Protein	3 g
Carbohydrate	21 g
Total Fat	5 g
Saturated	1 g
Polyunsaturated	3 g
Monounsaturated	1 g
Cholesterol	0 mg
Sodium	76 mg
Potassium	53 mg
Calcium	55 mg

Preheat oven to 400° F. Lightly spray a muffin tin with vegetable oil spray.

Wash and drain fresh or frozen berries. Set aside.

In a large bowl, sift flour, baking powder and ⅓ cup sugar together.

In a small bowl, combine egg whites, oil and milk. Pour all at once into dry ingredients. Stir just enough to blend. Gently stir in blueberries. Pour batter into prepared muffin tin, filling each cup ⅔ full. Sprinkle lightly with 1 teaspoon sugar and bake 20 to 25 minutes, or until browned. Allow muffins to cool 2 minutes before removing from pan.

OAT BRAN AND YOGURT MUFFINS

SERVES 24; 1 MUFFIN PER SERVING

Vegetable oil spray
2 cups whole-wheat flour
½ cup oat bran
1 cup all-purpose flour
1 teaspoon baking soda
1 tablespoon sugar
1 egg white
2 cups plain nonfat yogurt
¼ cup honey
2 tablespoons acceptable vegetable oil
1 cup raisins

NUTRIENT ANALYSIS	
Calories	111 kcal
Protein	4 g
Carbohydrate	22 g
Total Fat	2 g
Saturated	0 g
Polyunsaturated	1 g
Monounsaturated	0 g
Cholesterol	0 mg
Sodium	55 mg
Potassium	161 mg
Calcium	49 mg

Preheat oven to 425° F. Lightly spray muffin pans with vegetable oil spray.

Combine whole-wheat flour, oat bran, all-purpose flour, baking soda and sugar in a large mixing bowl. Set aside. In a medium bowl, beat together egg white, yogurt, honey and oil. Add yogurt mixture to dry ingredients and mix well. Fold in raisins.

Place mixture in muffin pans, filling each cup ⅔ full. Bake 15 to 20 minutes.

BANANA BREAD

SERVES 16; 1 SLICE PER SERVING

Vegetable oil spray
1/3 cup acceptable vegetable oil
1/3 cup sugar
1 cup mashed ripe banana (2 to 3 medium bananas)
1 3/4 cups sifted all-purpose flour
1/4 teaspoon cinnamon
1/8 teaspoon nutmeg
2 teaspoons baking powder
3 egg whites
1/3 cup sugar

NUTRIENT ANALYSIS

Calories	135 kcal
Protein	2 g
Carbohydrate	21 g
Total Fat	5 g
Saturated	1 g
Polyunsaturated	3 g
Monounsaturated	1 g
Cholesterol	0 mg
Sodium	47 mg
Potassium	85 mg
Calcium	27 mg

Preheat oven to 350° F. Lightly spray a 5 × 9-inch loaf pan with vegetable oil spray.

In a large mixing bowl, beat oil and 1/3 cup sugar together. Add banana and mix well.

In a medium bowl, sift flour, spices and baking powder together. Add to batter and beat.

In a separate bowl, beat egg whites until foamy. Gradually add 1/3 cup sugar and beat until egg whites form soft peaks. Fold egg whites into the batter.

Pour into loaf pan and bake 55 minutes.

Remove from oven and allow to stand 10 minutes. Invert bread on a wire rack to cool.

GINGERBREAD

SERVES 8

½ cup low-fat milk
2 teaspoons cider vinegar
Vegetable oil spray
¾ cup light molasses
½ cup acceptable vegetable oil
1 egg white
1 cup all-purpose flour
1 cup whole-wheat flour
1 teaspoon ground ginger
½ teaspoon baking soda
½ teaspoon ground cinnamon
¼ cup raisins

NUTRIENT ANALYSIS	
Calories	327 kcal
Protein	5 g
Carbohydrate	47 g
Total Fat	14 g
Saturated	2 g
Polyunsaturated	8 g
Monounsaturated	3 g
Cholesterol	1 mg
Sodium	80 mg
Potassium	488 mg
Calcium	119 mg

Combine milk and vinegar and allow to stand 10 minutes.

Preheat oven to 350° F. Lightly spray a 9-inch square baking pan with vegetable oil spray.

Place prepared milk, molasses, oil and egg white in a mixing bowl. Beat until blended. In a medium bowl, combine flours, ginger, baking soda and cinnamon. Add flour mixture to liquid mixture. Mix until evenly distributed. Fold in raisins.

Pour into prepared pan. Bake 30 to 35 minutes. Remove from oven and allow to cool in pan.

PANCAKES

SERVES 5;
3 4-INCH PANCAKES PER SERVING

1½ cups all-purpose flour
2 tablespoons sugar
1 tablespoon baking powder
¼ teaspoon ground cinnamon
1 egg white
¼ cup acceptable vegetable oil
1½ cups skim milk
½ teaspoon vanilla
Vegetable oil spray

PANCAKES NUTRIENT ANALYSIS

Calories	272 kcal
Protein	7 g
Carbohydrate	35 g
Total Fat	11 g
Saturated	2 g
Polyunsaturated	7 g
Monounsaturated	3 g
Cholesterol	1 mg
Sodium	224 mg
Potassium	168 mg
Calcium	208 mg

In a large bowl, sift dry ingredients together.

In a medium bowl, beat egg white until foamy. Add oil, milk and vanilla. Mix well. Add to dry ingredients. Beat only until batter is smooth.

Lightly spray a griddle or nonstick skillet with vegetable oil spray. Preheat griddle or skillet and spoon batter in ¼-cup portions onto cooking surface. When bubbles form and begin to break, turn and brown on other side. Serve immediately, or layer between waxed paper, freeze and reheat in toaster when needed.

Blueberry Pancakes
Add ½ cup blueberries to batter.

Pancakes with Walnuts

Add ¼ cup chopped walnuts to batter.

BLUEBERRY PANCAKES NUTRIENT ANALYSIS	
Calories	280 kcal
Protein	7 g
Carbohydrate	37 g
Total Fat	11 g
Saturated	2 g
Polyunsaturated	7 g
Monounsaturated	3 g
Cholesterol	1 mg
Sodium	224 mg
Potassium	181 mg
Calcium	209 mg

PANCAKES WITH WALNUTS NUTRIENT ANALYSIS	
Calories	311 kcal
Protein	8 g
Carbohydrate	36 g
Total Fat	15 g
Saturated	2 g
Polyunsaturated	9 g
Monounsaturated	4 g
Cholesterol	1 mg
Sodium	224 mg
Potassium	198 mg
Calcium	214 mg

Wheat-Germ Pancakes

Add ½ cup toasted wheat germ to batter.

WHEAT-GERM PANCAKES NUTRIENT ANALYSIS	
Calories	315 kcal
Protein	10 g
Carbohydrate	41 g
Total Fat	13 g
Saturated	2 g
Polyunsaturated	7 g
Monounsaturated	3 g
Cholesterol	1 mg
Sodium	224 mg
Potassium	275 mg
Calcium	213 mg

CREPES

SERVES 22;
1 6-INCH CREPE PER SERVING

3/4 cup skim milk
3/4 cup cold water
2 egg whites
1 1/2 cups sifted all-purpose flour
1/3 cup acceptable margarine, melted
2 tablespoons rum or orange liqueur (optional)
1 tablespoon sugar
4 drops yellow food coloring
Vegetable oil spray

NUTRIENT ANALYSIS	
Calories	60 kcal
Protein	1 g
Carbohydrate	7 g
Total Fat	3 g
Saturated	0 g
Polyunsaturated	1 g
Monounsaturated	1 g
Cholesterol	0 mg
Sodium	10 mg
Potassium	27 mg
Calcium	13 mg

Place all ingredients in a large mixing bowl. Beat well. Cover and refrigerate for 2 hours or overnight. Batter will be thin.

Spray a small nonstick skillet lightly with vegetable oil spray. Place over moderate heat. Pour 2 tablespoons batter in center of skillet. Tilt pan in all directions until batter covers bottom of pan. Return to heat for about 1 minute. Shake pan sharply to loosen crepe. Lift edges with a spatula and turn the crepe over when lightly browned. Brown lightly, approximately 1/2 minute, on the other side.

If first crepe appears too thick, beat in 2 to 3 tablespoons additional water.

Spray skillet lightly again with vegetable oil spray. Pour 2 tablespoons batter into skillet and proceed as before. Repeat process with remaining batter.

Crepes may be stacked with waxed paper between each

and refrigerated overnight or frozen. Crepes should be at room temperature when used, for ease in rolling.

For a deliciously simple dessert, brush rolled crepes with margarine, warm in oven and serve topped with maple syrup, powdered sugar or cinnamon-sugar. (See recipes for Apple-Filled Crepes, Banana Crepes, and Strawberry Crepes on pages 245, 246 and 247.)

SEASONED CROUTONS

MAKES 2 CUPS
SERVES 8; 1/4 CUP PER SERVING

1/2 teaspoon onion powder
1/4 teaspoon garlic powder
1/4 teaspoon dill weed
1/8 teaspoon freshly ground black pepper
1/4 cup acceptable margarine, softened
4 slices bread

NUTRIENT ANALYSIS	
Calories	85 kcal
Protein	1 g
Carbohydrate	7 g
Total Fat	6 g
Saturated	1 g
Polyunsaturated	2 g
Monounsaturated	3 g
Cholesterol	0 mg
Sodium	66 mg
Potassium	19 mg
Calcium	14 mg

Preheat oven to 300° F.

In a small bowl, add seasonings to margarine and mix well. Spread margarine mixture on one side of each slice of bread. Cut bread into 1/2-inch cubes. Place on a cookie sheet and bake 15 to 20 minutes, or until crisp and dry.

Cool and store in a tightly covered container. Use as a garnish for soups or salads.

DESSERTS

Applesauce Cake
Angel Food Cake
Chocolate Cake
Quick Frosting
Denver Chocolate Pudding Cake
Carrot Cake
Oatmeal Cookies
Peanut Butter Cookies
Walnut Delights
Date Rounds
Pralines
Apple-Filled Crepes
Banana Crepes
Matzo Crumb Piecrust
Piecrust
Cherry Pie
Apple Pie
Pumpkin Pie
Citrus Chiffon
Apple Crisp
Baked Pears
Orange Pudding
Raspberry Sorbet
Fresh Fruit Cobbler
Baked Custard
Vanilla Pudding
Fruit-Rice Pudding
Spiced Fruit
Brownies
Fudge

On these pages you'll find a selection of delectable goodies guaranteed to please, from Raspberry Sorbet, southern Pralines, and Fresh Fruit Cobbler, to Baked Custard and Peanut Butter Cookies. How can we do this on a low-sodium, low-fat diet? Easy. The trick is omitting most of the salt and using the right kind of fat.

Dessert is as American as . . . well, Apple Pie, which is here along with Cherry and Pumpkin, and two wonderful piecrust recipes: regular Piecrust and Matzo Crumb Piecrust.

Fruit still makes a great dessert, especially if you innovate a bit. For example, serve strawberries, pineapple chunks, grapes and melon balls on small skewers or layered in a parfait dish and chilled, with a tablespoon of liqueur on top. Need other ideas? Look for the recipes in this section for Baked Pears, Apple Crisp, Fruit-Rice Pudding and Spiced Fruit.

If ice cream is your favorite dessert, skip the saturated fat and cholesterol by substituting low-fat frozen yogurt, ice milk or sherbet. Top it off with Chocolate Sauce (page 209) for a winning finale to any meal.

Need an impressive dessert for company? Denver Chocolate Pudding Cake looks and tastes like a rich confection, but its ingredients make it a healthful treat.

Every family has a few favorite desserts that are hard to give up. Happily, maybe you don't have to. Just look closely at the ingredients list and, if possible, substitute low-sodium, low-fat ingredients for those high in sodium and fat. It can be that easy.

The very best desserts, the ones that taste great and are good for you, are the ones you make yourself. Try these and be convinced.

APPLESAUCE CAKE

SERVES 9

Vegetable oil spray
1/2 cup acceptable margarine
1 cup sugar
2 egg whites
1 1/2 cups applesauce
2 cups all-purpose flour
1 1/2 teaspoons baking powder
1 teaspoon ground cloves
1 teaspoon nutmeg
2 teaspoons ground cinnamon
1/2 cup raisins

NUTRIENT ANALYSIS

Calories	330 kcal
Protein	4 g
Carbohydrate	57 g
Total Fat	11 g
Saturated	2 g
Polyunsaturated	3 g
Monounsaturated	5 g
Cholesterol	0 mg
Sodium	69 mg
Potassium	144 mg
Calcium	51 mg

Preheat oven to 350° F. Lightly spray a 9-inch square cake pan with vegetable oil spray.

In a large mixing bowl, cream margarine with sugar until fluffy. Add egg whites and beat well. Add applesauce and beat.

In a medium bowl, sift dry ingredients together. Add to margarine mixture and mix well. Stir in raisins. Pour into prepared pan and bake 45 minutes. Serve warm.

ANGEL FOOD CAKE

SERVES 12

1 cup sifted cake flour
½ cup sugar
1¼ cups (10 to 12) egg whites, room temperature
1 teaspoon cream of tartar
½ teaspoon vanilla
½ teaspoon almond extract
¾ cup sugar

NUTRIENT ANALYSIS

Calories	122 kcal
Protein	4 g
Carbohydrate	27 g
Total Fat	0 g
Saturated	0 g
Polyunsaturated	0 g
Monounsaturated	0 g
Cholesterol	0 mg
Sodium	68 mg
Potassium	61 mg
Calcium	3 mg

Preheat oven to 350° F.

In 2 medium bowls, sift together flour and ½ cup sugar 3 times.

In a large mixing bowl, beat egg whites until foamy. Add cream of tartar, vanilla and almond extract. Continue beating until soft, moist, glossy peaks form. Gradually add ¾ cup sugar and continue beating at high speed until volume increases and stiff peaks form. By hand, gently fold in sifted flour-sugar mixture only until all flour is moistened.

Pour into a 9-inch tube pan. Cut through batter carefully with a thin spatula to break up large air pockets. Bake 40 to 45 minutes.

Remove from oven and invert pan for 1½ hours, or until cold. Remove cake from pan before storing.

Strawberry Sauce (see recipe, page 208) makes a delicious topping for this cake.

CHOCOLATE CAKE

SERVES 16

Vegetable oil spray
2½ cups all-purpose flour
⅓ cup cocoa
3½ teaspoons baking powder
⅔ cup acceptable vegetable oil
¾ cup water
½ cup skim milk
1 teaspoon vanilla
4 egg whites
¼ teaspoon cream of tartar
1¾ cups sugar

NUTRIENT ANALYSIS*	
Calories	241 kcal
Protein	3 g
Carbohydrate	36 g
Total Fat	10 g
Saturated	2 g
Polyunsaturated	5 g
Monounsaturated	2 g
Cholesterol	0 mg
Sodium	85 mg
Potassium	81 mg
Calcium	56 mg

* Unfrosted.

Preheat oven to 375° F. Lightly spray a 9 × 13-inch cake pan or 2 layer-cake pans with vegetable oil spray. Line pan with waxed paper cut to fit the bottom.

In a large mixing bowl, sift flour, cocoa and baking powder together.

In a small bowl, mix oil, water, milk and vanilla together. Add to flour mixture and beat until well combined. Batter will resemble a thick paste.

In a medium mixing bowl, beat egg whites until foamy. Add cream of tartar and gradually add sugar, beating until egg whites form soft peaks. Fold egg whites into batter.

Pour into prepared pan and bake 35 to 40 minutes, or until toothpick inserted in center of pan comes out clean.

Remove from oven and let cool on wire rack for 5 minutes. Remove cake from pan and serve warm or cold.

Serve this cake plain or frost with Quick Frosting (see recipe, page 237). Remember to allow cake to cool completely before frosting.

QUICK FROSTING

FROSTS 1 9×13-INCH OR 1 2-LAYER CAKE; SERVES 16

2 large egg whites
1½ cups powdered sugar
¼ teaspoon cream of tartar
⅓ cup water
1 teaspoon vanilla
1 tablespoon fresh lemon juice
¼ teaspoon grated lemon peel

NUTRIENT ANALYSIS	
Calories	49 kcal
Protein	0 g
Carbohydrate	12 g
Total Fat	0 g
Saturated	0 g
Polyunsaturated	0 g
Monounsaturated	0 g
Cholesterol	0 mg
Sodium	10 mg
Potassium	9 mg
Calcium	0 mg

In a medium mixing bowl, combine egg whites, sugar, cream of tartar and water. Beat with electric mixer 1 minute.

Place in double boiler over boiling water and beat about 5 minutes with electric mixer. Remove from heat and stir in vanilla, lemon juice and lemon peel. Beat 1 additional minute.

This frosting is delicious on Chocolate Cake (see recipe, page 236).

DENVER CHOCOLATE PUDDING CAKE

SERVES 9

Vegetable oil spray
1 cup all-purpose flour
¾ cup sugar
2 teaspoons baking powder
3 tablespoons acceptable margarine, melted
3 tablespoons cocoa
½ cup skim milk
½ teaspoon vanilla
½ cup firmly packed brown sugar
½ cup sugar
¼ cup cocoa
1½ cups cold water or cold coffee

NUTRIENT ANALYSIS

Calories	250 kcal
Protein	3 g
Carbohydrate	52 g
Total Fat	5 g
Saturated	2 g
Polyunsaturated	1 g
Monounsaturated	2 g
Cholesterol	0 mg
Sodium	78 mg
Potassium	163 mg
Calcium	79 mg

Preheat oven to 350° F. Lightly spray a 9-inch square baking pan with vegetable oil spray.

In a large bowl, sift flour, ¾ cup sugar and baking powder together.

In a small bowl, combine margarine and 3 tablespoons cocoa. Add to dry ingredients.

Beat in milk and vanilla.

Pour into prepared pan. Sprinkle the brown sugar, ½ cup sugar, and ¼ cup cocoa over the top of the batter one at a time but do not mix. Pour water (or coffee) over the top. Bake 40 minutes. To serve, cut cake into 9 equal pieces. Invert each piece onto a dessert plate.

Serve plain or with Mock Whipped Cream (see recipe, page 195).

CARROT CAKE

SERVES 16

Vegetable oil spray
1/4 cup acceptable vegetable oil
1 cup honey
2 egg whites
1/2 teaspoon vanilla
2 cups shredded carrots
1 cup all-purpose flour
1 cup whole-wheat flour
1/4 cup nonfat dry milk powder
1 teaspoon ground cinnamon
1/8 teaspoon nutmeg
1 tablespoon baking powder

NUTRIENT ANALYSIS	
Calories	158 kcal
Protein	3 g
Carbohydrate	30 g
Total Fat	4 g
Saturated	0 g
Polyunsaturated	2 g
Monounsaturated	1 g
Cholesterol	0 mg
Sodium	77 mg
Potassium	100 mg
Calcium	59 mg

Preheat oven to 350° F. Lightly spray a 9 × 13-inch baking dish with vegetable oil spray.

In a medium mixing bowl, combine oil and honey and beat until smooth. Beat in egg whites and vanilla. Stir in carrots. Set aside.

In a large mixing bowl, combine remaining ingredients. Add liquid mixture and mix thoroughly. Pour into prepared baking pan. Bake 25 to 30 minutes. Remove from oven and allow to cool in pan.

OATMEAL COOKIES

SERVES 30; 1 COOKIE PER SERVING

Vegetable oil spray
1/2 cup acceptable margarine
1/2 cup firmly packed brown sugar
1 tablespoon water
1/4 teaspoon vanilla
1 1/2 cups all-purpose flour
1 cup quick-cooking oatmeal, uncooked

NUTRIENT ANALYSIS	
Calories	72 kcal
Protein	1 g
Carbohydrate	10 g
Total Fat	3 g
Saturated	1 g
Polyunsaturated	1 g
Monounsaturated	1 g
Cholesterol	0 mg
Sodium	2 mg
Potassium	29 mg
Calcium	6 mg

Preheat oven to 350° F. Lightly spray a cookie sheet with vegetable oil spray.

In a large mixing bowl, cream margarine with brown sugar. Stir in water and vanilla. Add flour, mixing well. Stir in oatmeal. Form dough into 1-inch balls and place 2 inches apart on prepared cookie sheet. Flatten with a fork that has been dipped in flour.

Bake 15 minutes, or until lightly browned. Transfer to cooling rack immediately.

PEANUT BUTTER COOKIES

SERVES 48; 1 COOKIE PER SERVING

Vegetable oil spray
½ cup acceptable margarine
½ cup sugar
½ cup firmly packed brown sugar
1 egg
1 cup unsalted peanut butter
½ teaspoon vanilla
1½ cups all-purpose flour
1¼ teaspoons baking powder

NUTRIENT ANALYSIS	
Calories	79 kcal
Protein	2 g
Carbohydrate	8 g
Total Fat	5 g
Saturated	1 g
Polyunsaturated	1 g
Monounsaturated	2 g
Cholesterol	4 mg
Sodium	11 mg
Potassium	52 mg
Calcium	10 mg

Preheat oven to 350° F. Lightly spray a cookie sheet with vegetable oil spray.

In a large mixing bowl, cream margarine and sugars. Stir in egg. Add peanut butter and vanilla and beat.

In a medium bowl, sift flour and baking powder together. Add to margarine mixture and mix well.

Form dough into 1½-inch balls and place 3 inches apart on prepared cookie sheet. Flatten with a fork. Bake 15 minutes or until done. Allow cookies to cool 2 to 3 minutes on cookie sheet before transferring to cooling rack.

WALNUT DELIGHTS

SERVES 24; 1 COOKIE PER SERVING

Vegetable oil spray
1½ cups all-purpose flour
2 tablespoons powdered sugar
½ cup acceptable margarine
1 cup finely chopped walnuts
1 teaspoon vanilla
3 tablespoons (approximately) cold water
⅓ cup powdered sugar

NUTRIENT ANALYSIS	
Calories	102 kcal
Protein	2 g
Carbohydrate	9 g
Total Fat	7 g
Saturated	1 g
Polyunsaturated	3 g
Monounsaturated	2 g
Cholesterol	0 mg
Sodium	2 mg
Potassium	34 mg
Calcium	7 mg

Preheat oven to 350° F. Lightly spray a cookie sheet with vegetable oil spray.

In a large bowl, sift flour and sugar together. Cut in margarine with a fork or pastry blender. Mix in walnuts, vanilla and enough cold water to make a soft dough.

Form into small rolls 1 inch long and ½ inch thick. Place 2 inches apart on prepared cookie sheet. Bake 25 to 30 minutes, or until firm. While cookies are still warm, roll them in powdered sugar.

DATE ROUNDS

SERVES 30; 1 COOKIE PER SERVING

½ cup acceptable margarine
⅓ cup powdered sugar
1 tablespoon skim milk
1 teaspoon vanilla
1¼ cups sifted all-purpose flour
⅔ cup chopped dates
½ cup chopped walnuts
⅓ cup powdered sugar

Preheat oven to 300° F.

In a large bowl, cream margarine with ⅓ cup powdered sugar. Add milk and vanilla and mix. Add flour and stir well. Mix in dates and nuts.

Form dough in 1-inch balls and place 2 inches apart on ungreased cookie sheet. Bake 20 to 25 minutes, or until lightly browned. While cookies are still warm, roll them in the remaining powdered sugar.

NUTRIENT ANALYSIS

Calories	79 kcal
Protein	1 g
Carbohydrate	10 g
Total Fat	4 g
Saturated	1 g
Polyunsaturated	2 g
Monounsaturated	2 g
Cholesterol	0 mg
Sodium	2 mg
Potassium	43 mg
Calcium	6 mg

PRALINES

SERVES 72; 1 COOKIE PER SERVING

Vegetable oil spray
1 cup acceptable margarine
1 cup firmly packed brown sugar
1 egg
1 tablespoon vanilla
1½ cups sifted all-purpose flour
1 cup chopped, toasted pecans

Preheat oven to 350° F. Lightly spray a cookie sheet with vegetable oil spray.

In a large mixing bowl, cream margarine with sugar. Add egg and vanilla and beat. Add flour and mix well. Mix in nuts.

Drop by teaspoonfuls on prepared cookie sheet. Bake 12 minutes, or until lightly browned. Remove from oven and allow to cool on rack.

NUTRIENT ANALYSIS

Calories	55 kcal
Protein	0 g
Carbohydrate	5 g
Total Fat	4 g
Saturated	1 g
Polyunsaturated	1 g
Monounsaturated	2 g
Cholesterol	3 mg
Sodium	3 mg
Potassium	21 mg
Calcium	5 mg

APPLE-FILLED CREPES

SERVES 10; 1 CREPE PER SERVING

Vegetable oil spray
2 tablespoons acceptable margarine
5 apples, peeled and sliced (Golden Delicious apples preferred)
1/4 cup sugar
1 tablespoon fresh lemon juice
1 teaspoon grated lemon peel
1/8 teaspoon nutmeg
10 crepes (1/2 of recipe for Crepes, page 229)

NUTRIENT ANALYSIS

Calories	136 kcal
Protein	2 g
Carbohydrate	21 g
Total Fat	5 g
Saturated	1 g
Polyunsaturated	2 g
Monounsaturated	2 g
Cholesterol	0 mg
Sodium	14 mg
Potassium	88 mg
Calcium	17 mg

Preheat oven to 325° F. Lightly spray a 9-inch square covered casserole dish with vegetable oil spray.

To make filling, melt margarine in a large nonstick skillet. Add remaining ingredients and cook until apples are tender, stirring occasionally. Remove from heat. Spoon 2/3 of apple mixture into center of crepes. Roll. Place seam side down in prepared baking dish. Spoon remaining apple mixture over top of crepes. Cover and bake 25 minutes or until hot.

To serve as a dessert, sprinkle with powdered sugar before serving. Serve for brunch with Turkey Sausage Patties (see recipe, page 131).

BANANA CREPES

SERVES 10; 1 CREPE PER SERVING

1/3 cup acceptable margarine
1/2 cup orange marmalade
2 tablespoons sugar
1 tablespoon cornstarch
3 large bananas, sliced
10 crepes (1/2 of recipe for Crepes, page 229)

BANANA CREPES NUTRIENT ANALYSIS *

Calories	212 kcal
Protein	2 g
Carbohydrate	31 g
Total Fat	9 g
Saturated	2 g
Polyunsaturated	3 g
Monounsaturated	4 g
Cholesterol	0 mg
Sodium	17 mg
Potassium	199 mg
Calcium	22 mg

* Without added powdered sugar, yogurt or nutmeg.

To make filling, place margarine and marmalade in a medium saucepan over medium heat. Stir constantly until margarine melts.

In a small bowl, mix sugar and cornstarch together. Slowly stir into margarine mixture. Cook over medium heat, stirring constantly, until mixture is smooth and bubbly. Remove from heat. Fold in bananas.

Spoon filling into center of 10 warm crepes. Roll.

Banana Crepes with Powdered Sugar
Top each warm crepe with approximately 1 teaspoon powdered sugar.

Banana Crepes with Yogurt and Nutmeg
Top each warm crepe with 2 tablespoons plain low-fat yogurt and 1/8 teaspoon nutmeg.

BANANA CREPES WITH POWDERED SUGAR NUTRIENT ANALYSIS

Calories	222 kcal
Protein	2 g
Carbohydrate	34 g
Total Fat	9 g
Saturated	2 g
Polyunsaturated	3 g
Monounsaturated	4 g
Cholesterol	0 mg
Sodium	17 mg
Potassium	199 mg
Calcium	22 mg

BANANA CREPES WITH YOGURT AND NUTMEG NUTRIENT ANALYSIS

Calories	233 kcal
Protein	4 g
Carbohydrate	34 g
Total Fat	10 g
Saturated	2 g
Polyunsaturated	3 g
Monounsaturated	4 g
Cholesterol	2 mg
Sodium	38 mg
Potassium	272 mg
Calcium	78 mg

Strawberry Crepes

(Omit banana filling.) Refrigerate unfilled crepes. Remove from refrigerator just before using. Place 2 tablespoons vanilla ice milk in center of each crepe and roll up. Top each crepe with 1/4 cup Strawberry Sauce (see recipe, page 208).

STRAWBERRY CREPES NUTRIENT ANALYSIS

Calories	150 kcal
Protein	3 g
Carbohydrate	20 g
Total Fat	7 g
Saturated	1 g
Polyunsaturated	2 g
Monounsaturated	3 g
Cholesterol	2 mg
Sodium	27 mg
Potassium	198 mg
Calcium	49 mg

MATZO CRUMB PIECRUST

MAKES 1 9-INCH PIE SHELL; SERVES 8

1 cup unsalted matzo meal
1/4 cup sugar
1/4 teaspoon ground cinnamon (optional)
1/4 cup acceptable margarine, melted

Preheat oven to 350° F.

In a small bowl, mix matzo meal and sugar together. Add cinnamon and margarine and mix thoroughly. Press firmly into a 9-inch pie plate. Bake 20 minutes, or until lightly browned.

This crust is particularly suited to a pudding or cream pie filling prepared without egg yolk, and with skim milk or nonfat dry milk, such as Citrus Chiffon (recipe, page 254).

NUTRIENT ANALYSIS *

Calories	140 kcal
Protein	2 g
Carbohydrate	20 g
Total Fat	6 g
Saturated	1 g
Polyunsaturated	2 g
Monounsaturated	3 g
Cholesterol	0 mg
Sodium	2 mg
Potassium	22 mg
Calcium	4 mg

* For 1/8 of pie shell.

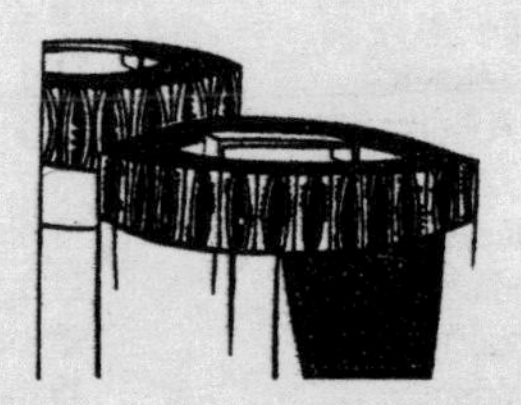

PIECRUST

MAKES PASTRY FOR 1 2-CRUST PIE OR 2 9-INCH PIE SHELLS

2¼ cups all-purpose flour
½ teaspoon sugar
⅓ cup cold skim milk
½ cup plus 1 tablespoon acceptable vegetable oil
1 teaspoon sugar (optional)

NUTRIENT ANALYSIS *

Calories	258 kcal
Protein	4 g
Carbohydrate	25 g
Total Fat	16 g
Saturated	2 g
Polyunsaturated	9 g
Monounsaturated	4 g
Cholesterol	0 mg
Sodium	6 mg
Potassium	48 mg
Calcium	18 mg

* For ⅛ of a double-crust pie shell.

In a medium bowl, combine flour and sugar. Stir to mix. Pour milk and oil into a measuring cup. Do not stir. Add all at once to flour. Stir with fork until well mixed. Form into a smooth ball with hands.

Roll out between 2 12-inch squares of waxed paper using short, brisk strokes until pastry reaches edge of paper. Peel off top paper. Invert crust and place on a pie plate. Carefully peel off paper and gently fit crust into pie plate.

For 2-crust pie, place fruit filling in piecrust and top with second crust; flute edges and make slits in top crust. Sprinkle crust with 1 teaspoon sugar, if desired, and bake according to filling directions.

To prebake single-crust pie shells, flute the edges and prick pastry with a fork. Preheat oven to 450° F.

Place several large raw dried beans on top of crust. Or place a sheet of waxed paper and another pie plate of the same size on top before baking. These methods will help prevent the crust from shrinking.

Bake piecrust 12 to 14 minutes, or until lightly browned.

CHERRY PIE

MAKES 1 9-INCH PIE; SERVES 8

1⅓ cups sugar
⅓ cup all-purpose flour
½ teaspoon ground cinnamon
2 16-ounce cans sour cherries, drained
⅛ teaspoon almond extract
Piecrust (see recipe, page 249)
1 tablespoon acceptable margarine

CHERRY PIE NUTRIENT ANALYSIS

Calories	506 kcal
Protein	5 g
Carbohydrate	85 g
Total Fat	17 g
Saturated	2 g
Polyunsaturated	10 g
Monounsaturated	4 g
Cholesterol	0 mg
Sodium	10 mg
Potassium	219 mg
Calcium	31 mg

Preheat oven to 425° F.

In a medium bowl, combine sugar, flour and cinnamon. In a small bowl, combine cherries and almond extract. Add to flour mixture.

Line pan with piecrust and fill with cherry mixture. Dot with margarine and top with second crust. Seal edges and make slits in top crust. Bake 35 to 45 minutes.

Blueberry Pie
Use 4 cups fresh or frozen unsweetened blueberries in place of cherries and reduce sugar to 1 cup.

Peach Pie
Use 2½ to 3 pounds (10 medium) peaches, peeled and sliced, in place of cherries and reduce sugar to ⅔ cup.

BLUEBERRY PIE NUTRIENT ANALYSIS

Calories	421 kcal
Protein	5 g
Carbohydrate	63 g
Total Fat	17 g
Saturated	2 g
Polyunsaturated	10 g
Monounsaturated	4 g
Cholesterol	0 mg
Sodium	11 mg
Potassium	119 mg
Calcium	25 mg

PEACH PIE NUTRIENT ANALYSIS

Calories	413 kcal
Protein	5 g
Carbohydrate	61 g
Total Fat	17 g
Saturated	2 g
Polyunsaturated	10 g
Monounsaturated	4 g
Cholesterol	0 mg
Sodium	7 mg
Potassium	344 mg
Calcium	28 mg

APPLE PIE

MAKES 1 9-INCH PIE; SERVES 8

1 cup sugar
1 teaspoon ground cinnamon
2½ pounds (8 medium) tart, firm apples, peeled, cored and sliced
Piecrust (see recipe, page 249)
1 tablespoon acceptable margarine

Preheat oven to 425° F.

In a medium bowl, combine sugar and cinnamon. Add sliced apples. Mix thoroughly.

Line pan with piecrust and fill with mixture. Dot with margarine and top with second crust. Seal edges and make slits in top crust. Bake 35 to 45 minutes.

NUTRIENT ANALYSIS	
Calories	426 kcal
Protein	4 g
Carbohydrate	66 g
Total Fat	17 g
Saturated	2 g
Polyunsaturated	10 g
Monounsaturated	4 g
Cholesterol	0 mg
Sodium	10 mg
Potassium	160 mg
Calcium	26 mg

PUMPKIN PIE

MAKES 1 9-INCH PIE; SERVES 8

2/3 cup firmly packed brown sugar
1 teaspoon ground cinnamon
1/2 teaspoon ground ginger
1/4 teaspoon ground cloves
1 1/2 cups (1 16-ounce can) pumpkin
1 13-ounce can evaporated skim milk
3 egg whites, beaten until foamy
1/2 recipe Piecrust (see recipe, page 249), unbaked

Preheat oven to 400° F.

In a medium bowl, mix together brown sugar, spices and pumpkin. Add milk and egg whites and beat until thoroughly mixed.

Line pan with piecrust and fill with mixture. Bake 45 to 50 minutes, or until knife inserted near center of pie comes out clean.

NUTRIENT ANALYSIS	
Calories	265 kcal
Protein	8 g
Carbohydrate	41 g
Total Fat	8 g
Saturated	1 g
Polyunsaturated	5 g
Monounsaturated	2 g
Cholesterol	2 mg
Sodium	92 mg
Potassium	398 mg
Calcium	195 mg

CITRUS CHIFFON

SERVES 8

1/4 cup cold water
2 teaspoons unflavored gelatin
1/2 cup hot water
1/2 cup sugar
2 teaspoons grated lemon peel
3/4 cup orange juice
2 tablespoons fresh lemon juice
1/3 cup nonfat dry milk powder

NUTRIENT ANALYSIS	
Calories	70 kcal
Protein	2 g
Carbohydrate	16 g
Total Fat	0 g
Saturated	0 g
Polyunsaturated	0 g
Monounsaturated	0 g
Cholesterol	1 mg
Sodium	18 mg
Potassium	98 mg
Calcium	38 mg

Place cold water in a medium saucepan and sprinkle gelatin over water. Allow to stand 5 minutes. Add hot water and sugar.

Place saucepan over medium-high heat and stir constantly until gelatin is dissolved.

Remove from heat. Stir in lemon peel and orange and lemon juices. Chill until thickened to the consistency of unbeaten egg white.

Sprinkle milk powder over gelatin mixture. Using an electric mixer, beat until light and fluffy. Pour into a serving bowl or a 1-quart mold and chill 8 hours or overnight. Unmold or spoon into serving dishes.

If desired, serve with fresh strawberries or orange slices.

APPLE CRISP

SERVES 8

Vegetable oil spray
1½ pounds (5 medium) apples, cored and sliced, unpeeled
2 tablespoons fresh lemon juice
¼ teaspoon ground cinnamon
⅔ cup all-purpose flour
½ cup firmly packed brown sugar
½ cup uncooked oatmeal
⅓ cup acceptable margarine

Preheat oven to 375° F. Lightly spray a 2-quart casserole dish with vegetable oil spray. Arrange apples in prepared dish. Sprinkle with lemon juice and cinnamon.

In a medium bowl, combine flour, brown sugar and oatmeal. Cut in margarine with a fork or pastry blender until mixture is crumbly. Spread over fruit. Bake 40 minutes or until apples are tender.

APPLE CRISP
NUTRIENT ANALYSIS

Calories	213 kcal
Protein	2 g
Carbohydrate	35 g
Total Fat	8 g
Saturated	1 g
Polyunsaturated	3 g
Monounsaturated	4 g
Cholesterol	0 mg
Sodium	10 mg
Potassium	150 mg
Calcium	22 mg

Peach Crisp
Use $1\frac{1}{2}$ pounds (6 medium) fresh peaches (pitted, peeled and sliced) in place of apples.

Blueberry Crisp
Use 3 cups fresh or frozen unsweetened blueberries in place of apples.

PEACH CRISP NUTRIENT ANALYSIS	
Calories	212 kcal
Protein	3 g
Carbohydrate	34 g
Total Fat	8 g
Saturated	1 g
Polyunsaturated	3 g
Monounsaturated	4 g
Cholesterol	0 mg
Sodium	8 mg
Potassium	256 mg
Calcium	24 mg

BLUEBERRY CRISP NUTRIENT ANALYSIS	
Calories	204 kcal
Protein	2 g
Carbohydrate	32 g
Total Fat	8 g
Saturated	1 g
Polyunsaturated	3 g
Monounsaturated	4 g
Cholesterol	0 mg
Sodium	11 mg
Potassium	130 mg
Calcium	23 mg

BAKED PEARS

SERVES 4

4 fresh pears, cut in half, peeled and cored
1/4 cup water
1/4 cup sugar
4 lemon slices
1/4 teaspoon ground ginger

Preheat oven to 350° F.

Place pears in a baking dish. Set aside.

Place water and sugar in a small saucepan over medium-high heat. Bring to a boil. Add lemon and ginger. Pour syrup mixture over pears.

Cover and bake 30 to 45 minutes or until tender. Turn once during baking period. Serve warm to accompany meat or chilled for dessert.

NUTRIENT ANALYSIS

Calories	91 kcal
Protein	0 g
Carbohydrate	24 g
Total Fat	0 g
Saturated	0 g
Polyunsaturated	0 g
Monounsaturated	0 g
Cholesterol	0 mg
Sodium	0 mg
Potassium	97 mg
Calcium	9 mg

ORANGE PUDDING

SERVES 4

1/4 cup cold water
1 tablespoon unflavored gelatin
3/4 cup hot water
1/3 cup sugar
1 cup orange juice
1 tablespoon fresh lemon juice
1 teaspoon grated orange rind (optional)

Place cold water in a medium saucepan and sprinkle gelatin over water. Allow to stand 5 minutes. Add hot water and sugar.

Place saucepan over medium-high heat and stir constantly until gelatin is dissolved.

Remove from heat. Stir in remaining ingredients. Pour into 4 half-cup custard cups or a 2-cup mold and chill until firm.

Orange Whip

Chill gelatin until thickened to the consistency of unbeaten egg white. Beat with rotary beater or electric mixer until light and foamy. Chill until firm.

If desired, serve with orange sections or fresh berries.

Fruit Pudding

Chill gelatin until thickened to the consistency of unbeaten egg white. Stir in 1 1/2 cups fresh or canned, drained, cut-up fruit. Chill until firm.

ORANGE PUDDING OR ORANGE WHIP NUTRIENT ANALYSIS

Calories	96 kcal
Protein	2 g
Carbohydrate	23 g
Total Fat	0 g
Saturated	0 g
Polyunsaturated	0 g
Monounsaturated	0 g
Cholesterol	0 mg
Sodium	4 mg
Potassium	123 mg
Calcium	7 mg

FRUIT PUDDING NUTRIENT ANALYSIS

Calories	133 kcal
Protein	2 g
Carbohydrate	32 g
Total Fat	0 g
Saturated	0 g
Polyunsaturated	0 g
Monounsaturated	0 g
Cholesterol	0 mg
Sodium	4 mg
Potassium	276 mg
Calcium	15 mg

RASPBERRY SORBET

SERVES 4

1 cup sugar
1¾ cups water
3 cups fresh raspberries
2 tablespoons fresh lemon juice

In a medium saucepan over medium-high heat, combine sugar and water and bring to a boil. Boil until sugar is dissolved. Remove from heat and allow to cool.

In a blender or the work bowl of a food processor fitted with a metal blade, combine sugar-water mixture, raspberries and lemon juice. Process until pureed.

Pour mixture into a 9-inch square pan and freeze until firm.

If a smoother consistency is desired, press pureed mixture through a sieve before freezing.

NUTRIENT ANALYSIS

Calories	232 kcal
Protein	1 g
Carbohydrate	59 g
Total Fat	1 g
Saturated	0 g
Polyunsaturated	0 g
Monounsaturated	0 g
Cholesterol	0 mg
Sodium	3 mg
Potassium	149 mg
Calcium	23 mg

FRESH FRUIT COBBLER

SERVES 6

Vegetable oil spray
3 cups fresh fruit (cherries, blueberries, blackberries, peaches or apricots)
¾ cup sugar
1 tablespoon cornstarch
1 cup boiling water
½ teaspoon ground cinnamon
1 tablespoon acceptable margarine
½ recipe Biscuits, uncooked (see recipe, page 220)

Preheat oven to 400° F. Lightly spray a shallow 1½-quart baking dish with vegetable oil spray.

Rinse fruit and drain. Peel and slice peaches or apricots. Remove pits from cherries. Set aside.

In a medium saucepan, combine sugar and cornstarch and mix well. Pour boiling water gradually into sugar mixture, stirring constantly. Place over medium-high heat. Bring to a boil and add fruit. Stir to mix well and remove from heat.

Pour into prepared baking dish. Sprinkle cinnamon over top and dot with margarine. Drop spoonfuls of biscuit dough on top of fruit. Bake 25 to 30 minutes or until biscuits are done.

Canned Fruit Cobbler

Use 3 cups canned fruit packed in juices, drained, in place of fresh fruit. (Canned cherries or blueberries are recommended.) Reserve juice in which fruit was packed; add cold water to make 1 cup. Stir cornstarch into cold juice until dissolved. Cook until thickened, stirring constantly, and combine with fruit. Proceed as directed above.

FRESH FRUIT COBBLER NUTRIENT ANALYSIS*

Calories	287 kcal
Protein	3 g
Carbohydrate	54 g
Total Fat	7 g
Saturated	1 g
Polyunsaturated	4 g
Monounsaturated	2 g
Cholesterol	0 mg
Sodium	81 mg
Potassium	219 mg
Calcium	81 mg

* Using fresh cherries.

CANNED FRUIT COBBLER NUTRIENT ANALYSIS*

Calories	314 kcal
Protein	3 g
Carbohydrate	62 g
Total Fat	7 g
Saturated	1 g
Polyunsaturated	3 g
Monounsaturated	2 g
Cholesterol	0 mg
Sodium	84 mg
Potassium	189 mg
Calcium	78 mg

* Using canned cherries.

BAKED CUSTARD

SERVES 6

Vegetable oil spray
2½ cups skim milk
¼ cup sugar
4 egg whites
1 teaspoon vanilla
1 tablespoon table sherry
Few drops yellow food coloring
Dash nutmeg

Preheat oven to 325° F. Lightly spray 6 custard cups with vegetable oil spray.

In a large mixing bowl, combine milk, sugar, egg whites, vanilla, sherry and food coloring. Mix thoroughly. Pour into prepared custard cups. Sprinkle with nutmeg.

Place custard cups in a pan of hot water and bake 50 minutes or until knife inserted near center of custard comes out clean.

NUTRIENT ANALYSIS

Calories	80 kcal
Protein	6 g
Carbohydrate	14 g
Total Fat	0 g
Saturated	0 g
Polyunsaturated	0 g
Monounsaturated	0 g
Cholesterol	2 mg
Sodium	89 mg
Potassium	204 mg
Calcium	128 mg

VANILLA PUDDING

SERVES 5

1/3 cup sugar
1/4 cup cornstarch
2 3/4 cups skim milk
2 tablespoons acceptable margarine
1 teaspoon vanilla
3 drops yellow food coloring (optional)

Combine sugar and cornstarch in a medium saucepan and mix well. Add 1 cup of milk and stir until sugar is dissolved and cornstarch is evenly dispersed. Stir in remaining milk.

Place saucepan over medium heat. Bring to a boil, stirring constantly. Boil 1 minute. Remove from heat. Stir in margarine, vanilla and food coloring. Chill.

Vanilla pudding may be served in parfait glasses layered with fresh strawberries or other fruit or used as a filling for Matzo Crumb Piecrust (see recipe, page 248).

VANILLA PUDDING NUTRIENT ANALYSIS

Calories	167 kcal
Protein	5 g
Carbohydrate	27 g
Total Fat	5 g
Saturated	1 g
Polyunsaturated	2 g
Monounsaturated	2 g
Cholesterol	2 mg
Sodium	71 mg
Potassium	226 mg
Calcium	168 mg

Chocolate Pudding
Increase sugar to ⅔ cup and add 3 tablespoons cocoa to sugar and cornstarch mixture. Omit yellow food coloring.

Butterscotch Pudding
Substitute brown sugar for white sugar. Increase margarine to 3 tablespoons. Omit yellow food coloring.

CHOCOLATE PUDDING NUTRIENT ANALYSIS	
Calories	229 kcal
Protein	5 g
Carbohydrate	41 g
Total Fat	6 g
Saturated	2 g
Polyunsaturated	2 g
Monounsaturated	2 g
Cholesterol	2 mg
Sodium	71 mg
Potassium	291 mg
Calcium	173 mg

BUTTERSCOTCH PUDDING NUTRIENT ANALYSIS	
Calories	192 kcal
Protein	5 g
Carbohydrate	28 g
Total Fat	7 g
Saturated	1 g
Polyunsaturated	2 g
Monounsaturated	3 g
Cholesterol	2 mg
Sodium	76 mg
Potassium	277 mg
Calcium	181 mg

FRUIT-RICE PUDDING

SERVES 6

1¼ cups unsalted cooked rice
1 cup canned fruit cocktail, drained
¼ cup maple syrup
1 tablespoon powdered sugar

In a medium bowl, combine rice, fruit cocktail and maple syrup. Mix well. Spoon into sauce dishes or small parfait glasses. Sprinkle with powdered sugar and serve.

NUTRIENT ANALYSIS	
Calories	118 kcal
Protein	1 g
Carbohydrate	29 g
Total Fat	0 g
Saturated	0 g
Polyunsaturated	0 g
Monounsaturated	0 g
Cholesterol	0 mg
Sodium	4 mg
Potassium	74 mg
Calcium	21 mg

SPICED FRUIT

SERVES 8

1 cup firmly packed brown sugar
½ cup sauterne table wine
¼ cup cider vinegar
15 whole cloves
2 sticks cinnamon
⅛ teaspoon curry powder
8 canned peach halves, drained
8 canned pear halves, drained
16 or more honeydew melon balls, fresh or frozen, or 2 kiwi fruit, pared and sliced
8 fresh pineapple spears or 1 20-ounce can pineapple chunks, drained

In a medium saucepan over medium heat, combine brown sugar, wine, vinegar, cloves, cinnamon and curry powder. Stir frequently until thoroughly heated. Place fruits in a large bowl. Pour hot spiced syrup over fruit. Cool, then chill overnight. Remove cloves and cinnamon sticks. Serve cold.

SPICED FRUIT
NUTRIENT ANALYSIS

Calories	283 kcal
Protein	1 g
Carbohydrate	74 g
Total Fat	0 g
Saturated	0 g
Polyunsaturated	0 g
Monounsaturated	0 g
Cholesterol	0 mg
Sodium	23 mg
Potassium	404 mg
Calcium	43 mg

Spiced Fruit with Ice Milk

For a simple but delicious variation, spoon ½ cup ice milk into each of 8 dessert bowls. Top with equal portions of Spiced Fruit.

SPICED FRUIT WITH ICE MILK NUTRIENT ANALYSIS	
Calories	367 kcal
Protein	4 g
Carbohydrate	86 g
Total Fat	3 g
Saturated	2 g
Polyunsaturated	0 g
Monounsaturated	1 g
Cholesterol	9 mg
Sodium	75 mg
Potassium	528 mg
Calcium	126 mg

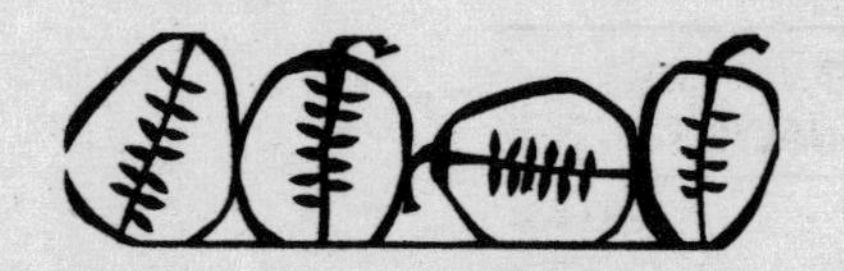

BROWNIES

SERVES 12;
1 BROWNIE PER SERVING

Vegetable oil spray
¾ cup all-purpose flour
1 cup sugar
⅓ cup cocoa
½ teaspoon baking powder
½ cup acceptable margarine, melted
3 egg whites
1 teaspoon vanilla
½ cup chopped walnuts

Preheat oven to 350° F. Lightly spray an 8-inch square baking pan with vegetable oil spray.

Sift dry ingredients together into a medium bowl. Add margarine, egg whites and vanilla and beat. Stir in nuts. Pour into prepared baking pan. Bake 30 to 35 minutes. Cool and cut into 12 equal portions.

NUTRIENT ANALYSIS

Calories	201 kcal
Protein	3 g
Carbohydrate	24 g
Total Fat	11 g
Saturated	2 g
Polyunsaturated	5 g
Monounsaturated	4 g
Cholesterol	0 mg
Sodium	29 mg
Potassium	96 mg
Calcium	21 mg

FUDGE

SERVES 48; 1 PIECE PER SERVING

Vegetable oil spray
1 cup firmly packed brown sugar
1 cup sugar
⅓ cup cocoa
⅔ cup skim milk
3 tablespoons acceptable margarine
1 teaspoon vanilla

FUDGE NUTRIENT ANALYSIS	
Calories	42 kcal
Protein	0 g
Carbohydrate	9 g
Total Fat	1 g
Saturated	0 g
Polyunsaturated	0 g
Monounsaturated	0 g
Cholesterol	0 mg
Sodium	3 mg
Potassium	34 mg
Calcium	9 mg

Lightly spray an 8-inch square baking pan with vegetable oil spray. Set aside.

Place brown sugar, sugar and cocoa in a 3-quart saucepan. Add milk and mix.

Cook over medium heat until mixture reaches 236° F. on a candy thermometer, or until a small amount of syrup dropped in cold water forms a soft ball. Remove from heat.

Add margarine but do not stir. Cool until bottom of pan is lukewarm. Add vanilla and beat with an electric mixer 5 to 10 minutes or until fudge is thick and no longer glossy. Spread in prepared pan. Cool until firm. Cut into 48 equal portions.

Nut Fudge

After beating, stir in ½ cup chopped walnuts.

NUT FUDGE NUTRIENT ANALYSIS	
Calories	50 kcal
Protein	0 g
Carbohydrate	9 g
Total Fat	2 g
Saturated	0 g
Polyunsaturated	1 g
Monounsaturated	1 g
Cholesterol	0 mg
Sodium	4 mg
Potassium	40 mg
Calcium	11 mg

Peanut Butter Fudge

After beating, add ½ cup peanut butter. Run a table knife through the fudge to form streaks.

PEANUT BUTTER FUDGE NUTRIENT ANALYSIS	
Calories	58 kcal
Protein	1 g
Carbohydrate	10 g
Total Fat	2 g
Saturated	0 g
Polyunsaturated	1 g
Monounsaturated	1 g
Cholesterol	0 mg
Sodium	16 mg
Potassium	53 mg
Calcium	10 mg

APPETIZERS AND SNACKS

Fresh Vegetable Platter

Stuffed Mushrooms

Sautéed Mushrooms on Toast

Dill Pickles

Bread-and-Butter Pickles

Sugared Peanuts

Spiced Nuts

Fruit-Nut Snack Mix

Party Mix

Mock Cream Cheese

California Onion Dip

Chili Dip

Snacking is an all-American pastime, whether it's munching at the movies, noshing after school or raiding the refrigerator at midnight.

Unfortunately, commercial snack foods like chips, cookies, chocolate candy, pizza and ice cream are often loaded with fat and salt. If you want nutritious snacks without all those "extras," look for fresh fruits and vegetables and snacks you can make using less fat and salt. Try a Fresh Vegetable Platter with California Onion Dip or Chili Dip.

Nuts and seeds are wonderful, crunchy treats, as the Sugared Peanuts and Spiced Nuts recipes should convince you. Since these are a little higher in fat than most of the recipes in this book, you'll want to eat them only occasionally. Eat them when you aren't concerned with calories or you need a quick, high-energy snack.

With a little ingenuity, you can create delicious snacks that are low in fat and salt. Here's a starter list, but use your imagination and add to it!

- Fruit and juices
- Raw vegetables with dips
- Home-fried tortilla shells served with salsa
- Soda crackers with unsalted tops
- Skim milk, low-fat yogurt, low-fat frozen yogurt, sherbet or ice milk
- Low-sodium cereal
- Bread sticks, unsalted pretzels, nuts and seeds
- Unsalted popcorn with acceptable margarine
- Specially prepared homemade cookies and cakes
- Sandwiches, canapés or tea sandwiches
- Plain hard candies

Even snacks can fit into a healthful low-sodium diet. The trick is to find the *right* snacks. These recipes will help you do just that.

FRESH VEGETABLE PLATTER

Green, red or yellow bell peppers
Carrots
Cucumbers
Zucchini
Fresh mushrooms
Radishes
Green onions
Asparagus spears
Whole green beans
Cauliflower florets
Broccoli florets
Cherry tomatoes

Rinse and dry vegetables.

Remove core and seeds from bell peppers and cut into strips. Scrub or peel carrots, cucumbers and zucchini and cut into slices or sticks. Slice mushrooms. Prepare radish roses.

Arrange these and remaining vegetables on a platter.

Serve with Mock Sour Cream, Yogurt-Dill Sauce, California Onion Dip or Chili Dip (see recipes, pages 194, 207, 287 and 288).

(Because vegetables and amounts used will vary widely according to individual preference, no nutrient analysis has been provided.)

STUFFED MUSHROOMS

SERVES 4;
4 MUSHROOMS PER SERVING

16 medium-size fresh mushrooms
1 tablespoon acceptable margarine
1 small onion, chopped
1 slice bread, torn into small pieces
½ cup diced cooked chicken, unsalted, skinned, all visible fat removed
2 tablespoons table sherry
¼ teaspoon marjoram
⅛ teaspoon freshly ground black pepper
⅛ teaspoon oregano
1 tablespoon acceptable margarine, melted

NUTRIENT ANALYSIS	
Calories	122 kcal
Protein	7 g
Carbohydrate	8 g
Total Fat	7 g
Saturated	1 g
Polyunsaturated	2 g
Monounsaturated	3 g
Cholesterol	15 mg
Sodium	50 mg
Potassium	260 mg
Calcium	19 mg

Preheat broiler.

Clean mushrooms with a vegetable brush or wipe with a damp cloth. Remove and finely chop stems. Heat 1 tablespoon margarine in a nonstick skillet over medium-high heat. Sauté chopped mushroom stems and onion until tender. Add all ingredients except remaining margarine.

Place mushroom caps, round side up, on a baking sheet. Brush with half of melted margarine. Broil 2 minutes. Remove from broiler. Invert caps and fill with chicken mixture. Brush with remaining melted margarine. Broil 3 minutes, or until mushrooms are tender and lightly browned on top. Serve as an appetizer.

SAUTÉED MUSHROOMS ON TOAST

SERVES 4; 1 SLICE PER SERVING

1 medium onion, finely chopped
2 tablespoons acceptable margarine
1 pound fresh mushrooms, sliced
2 teaspoons fresh lemon juice
Dash freshly ground black pepper
4 slices bread, toasted

Sauté onion in margarine until tender. Add mushrooms, cover and cook over low heat 8 to 10 minutes or until mushrooms are tender. Sprinkle with lemon juice and pepper. Serve over toast. This delicious snack is good anytime.

NUTRIENT ANALYSIS

Calories	146 kcal
Protein	4 g
Carbohydrate	18 g
Total Fat	7 g
Saturated	1 g
Polyunsaturated	2 g
Monounsaturated	3 g
Cholesterol	1 mg
Sodium	133 mg
Potassium	346 mg
Calcium	34 mg

DILL PICKLES

MAKES 1 QUART
SERVES 12; 1 PICKLE PER SERVING

12 small cucumbers
1 tablespoon dill seed or 3 heads fresh dill
1 tablespoon whole pickling spice
2 cloves garlic
1/8 teaspoon alum
2 grape leaves (optional)
2 1/4 cups water
1 1/2 cups cider vinegar
1 tablespoon sugar

NUTRIENT ANALYSIS

Calories	29 kcal
Protein	1 g
Carbohydrate	7 g
Total Fat	0 g
Saturated	0 g
Polyunsaturated	0 g
Monounsaturated	0 g
Cholesterol	0 mg
Sodium	4 mg
Potassium	265 mg
Calcium	25 mg

Rinse cucumbers thoroughly. Soak overnight in cold water. Dry cucumbers and place in a clean, hot quart jar. Add dill, pickling spice, garlic, alum and grape leaves to the jar.

In a small saucepan, heat water, vinegar and sugar over medium-high heat. Bring to a boil. Pour boiling liquid into a jar, filling jar to within 1/2 inch of the top. Wipe rim of jar, screw lid on tightly and place in a Dutch oven or other deep pan.

Cover jar completely with water. Bring to a boil and cook 20 minutes. (At higher altitudes, longer processing is necessary.)

Store pickles 2 weeks before using.

BREAD-AND-BUTTER PICKLES

MAKES 1 QUART
SERVES 16; APPROXIMATELY ¼ CUP PER SERVING

8 medium, crisp cucumbers (approximately 4 cups when sliced)
2 medium onions
1¼ cups cider vinegar
1¼ cups sugar
½ teaspoon turmeric
½ teaspoon mustard seed
¼ teaspoon celery seed

BREAD-AND-BUTTER PICKLES NUTRIENT ANALYSIS

Calories	78 kcal
Protein	1 g
Carbohydrate	20 g
Total Fat	0 g
Saturated	0 g
Polyunsaturated	0 g
Monounsaturated	0 g
Cholesterol	0 mg
Sodium	4 mg
Potassium	203 mg
Calcium	20 mg

Slice thoroughly chilled cucumbers and onions, cover and place in refrigerator.

In a medium saucepan over medium-high heat, combine vinegar, sugar and spices. Heat just to boiling. Add cucumber mixture and heat 2 to 3 minutes.

Chill and serve. May be stored in a covered container in refrigerator for 1 month.

For storage without refrigeration, sterilize 2 pint jars and immediately pack hot pickles loosely to within ½ inch of top. Wipe rim of jar, screw lid on tightly and place in a Dutch oven or other deep pan. Cover jars completely with water. Bring to a boil and cook 5 minutes. (At higher altitudes, longer processing is necessary.)

Pickle Relish
Finely chop the cucumbers and onions and add 1 finely chopped green or red bell pepper. Cook until liquid in mixture is nearly gone and relish is thickened. Storage is the same as for Bread-and-Butter Pickles.

PICKLE RELISH
NUTRIENT ANALYSIS

Calories	80 kcal
Protein	1 g
Carbohydrate	20 g
Total Fat	0 g
Saturated	0 g
Polyunsaturated	0 g
Monounsaturated	0 g
Cholesterol	0 mg
Sodium	4 mg
Potassium	210 mg
Calcium	21 mg

SUGARED PEANUTS

SERVES 10

Vegetable oil spray
2 cups unsalted, dry-roasted peanuts
1 cup sugar
½ cup water

Preheat oven to 350° F. Lightly spray a cookie sheet with vegetable oil spray.

Mix peanuts, sugar and water together in a medium saucepan over medium heat, stirring occasionally. Cook until mixture crystallizes and coats peanuts, approximately 10 to 12 minutes. Spread on cookie sheet and bake 20 to 25 minutes, mixing occasionally. Cool and store in tightly covered container.

Because of the high fat and sugar content of this recipe, these nuts should be used only as an occasional snack. They should not be eaten in large quantities.

NUTRIENT ANALYSIS

Calories	241 kcal
Protein	8 g
Carbohydrate	25 g
Total Fat	14 g
Saturated	2 g
Polyunsaturated	4 g
Monounsaturated	7 g
Cholesterol	0 mg
Sodium	2 mg
Potassium	197 mg
Calcium	26 mg

SPICED NUTS

SERVES 10

Vegetable oil spray
1 egg white
⅔ cup sugar
1 teaspoon ground cinnamon
2 cups pecan halves

Preheat oven to 325° F. Lightly spray a cookie sheet with vegetable oil spray. Set aside.

Beat egg white until foamy. Gradually add sugar and cinnamon, and beat until egg white forms stiff peaks. Add pecans and stir until coated with mixture. Pour coated nuts onto prepared cookie sheet. Using a fork, arrange nuts so they are not touching. Bake 15 to 20 minutes, or until egg white is dry and slightly browned. Cool and store in a tightly covered container.

Because of the high fat and sugar content of this recipe, these nuts should be used only as an occasional snack. They should not be eaten in large quantities.

NUTRIENT ANALYSIS

Calories	196 kcal
Protein	2 g
Carbohydrate	17 g
Total Fat	15 g
Saturated	1 g
Polyunsaturated	4 g
Monounsaturated	9 g
Cholesterol	0 mg
Sodium	6 mg
Potassium	91 mg
Calcium	11 mg

FRUIT-NUT SNACK MIX

SERVES 12; ¼ CUP PER SERVING

½ cup dried apricots, cut in quarters
½ cup dates, cut in half
¼ cup raisins
½ cup whole almonds
½ cup walnut halves
½ cup unsalted peanuts
¼ cup unsalted sunflower seeds

In a large bowl, toss ingredients together. Store in tightly covered container.

This high-energy mix is great to take on hikes and camping trips.

Note: You may substitute your favorite dried fruits or nuts in place of those listed.

NUTRIENT ANALYSIS*

Calories	155 kcal
Protein	4 g
Carbohydrate	15 g
Total Fat	10 g
Saturated	1 g
Polyunsaturated	4 g
Monounsaturated	4 g
Cholesterol	0 mg
Sodium	3 mg
Potassium	274 mg
Calcium	34 mg

* Based on ingredients listed.

PARTY MIX

SERVES 14

¼ cup acceptable margarine
½ teaspoon garlic powder
½ cup small unsalted pretzel sticks
½ cup puffed rice
1 cup spoon-size shredded wheat
½ cup unsalted peanuts

Melt margarine in a nonstick skillet over medium heat. Add garlic powder and mix well. Add remaining ingredients and toss together. Serve warm.

For a slightly different taste, use walnuts, pecans or a mixture of nuts in place of peanuts. For a sweeter taste, use ¼ cup raisins in place of the garlic powder.

NUTRIENT ANALYSIS*

Calories	78 kcal
Protein	2 g
Carbohydrate	5 g
Total Fat	6 g
Saturated	1 g
Polyunsaturated	2 g
Monounsaturated	3 g
Cholesterol	0 mg
Sodium	3 mg
Potassium	51 mg
Calcium	7 mg

* Based on ingredients listed.

MOCK CREAM CHEESE

MAKES 1¼ CUPS
SERVES 5; ¼ CUP PER SERVING

1 cup (8 ounces) unsalted dry-curd cottage cheese
¼ cup acceptable margarine, softened
Skim milk, if needed

In a blender or the work bowl of a food processor fitted with a metal blade, combine cottage cheese and margarine. Process until thoroughly blended.

If mixture appears too thick to spread, add skim milk, 1 teaspoon at a time, until the desired consistency is reached.

Cover tightly and store in refrigerator. Use as a sandwich spread topped with marmalade, jam or honey.

NUTRIENT ANALYSIS

Calories	105 kcal
Protein	5 g
Carbohydrate	1 g
Total Fat	9 g
Saturated	2 g
Polyunsaturated	3 g
Monounsaturated	4 g
Cholesterol	2 mg
Sodium	7 mg
Potassium	14 mg
Calcium	12 mg

CALIFORNIA ONION DIP

SERVES 20;
1 TABLESPOON PER SERVING

¼ cup skim milk
2 tablespoons low-sodium beef broth
1 cup (8 ounces) unsalted dry-curd cottage cheese
2 teaspoons fresh lemon juice
2 teaspoons vermouth or dry white table wine
1 teaspoon onion powder
½ teaspoon garlic powder
2 tablespoons onion flakes or ¼ cup chopped green onion

Place milk and beef broth in a blender or the work bowl of a food processor fitted with a metal blade. Process until mixed. Add remaining ingredients except onion flakes and process at high speed until smooth. Stir in onion.

Use as a dip for raw vegetables or toast strips.

NUTRIENT ANALYSIS

Calories	10 kcal
Protein	1 g
Carbohydrate	1 g
Total Fat	0 g
Saturated	0 g
Polyunsaturated	0 g
Monounsaturated	0 g
Cholesterol	1 mg
Sodium	3 mg
Potassium	17 mg
Calcium	8 mg

CHILI DIP

SERVES 20;
1 TABLESPOON PER SERVING

1 cup Chili Sauce (see recipe, page 200)
2 tablespoons fresh lemon juice
4 drops hot pepper sauce
2 tablespoons grated fresh horseradish
½ teaspoon onion powder

Place all ingredients in a blender or the work bowl of a food processor fitted with a metal blade. Process until blended. Chill.

Use as a sauce for crabmeat or clams or as a dip for raw vegetables.

NUTRIENT ANALYSIS

Calories	17 kcal
Protein	0 g
Carbohydrate	3 g
Total Fat	0 g
Saturated	0 g
Polyunsaturated	0 g
Monounsaturated	0 g
Cholesterol	0 mg
Sodium	8 mg
Potassium	72 mg
Calcium	5 mg

APPENDIX

APPENDIX A

The Low-Sodium Diet

The principal source of sodium in the American diet is salt, otherwise known as sodium chloride. For this reason, we entitled this book *The American Heart Association Low-Salt Cookbook*. We are, however, concerned with *all* the sodium in the diet—whether it comes from salt, monosodium glutamate, sodium bicarbonate or any other source—so we have developed a diet that we call a low-sodium diet. It is low in salt and all other forms of sodium. This diet is designed for those of you who have high blood pressure (and may also have high blood cholesterol and/or excessive weight). The recommendations in this section will help you decrease the amount of sodium in your diet, control your calorie intake and limit the amount of total fat, saturated fatty acids and dietary cholesterol you eat.

RISK FACTORS FOR HEART AND BLOOD VESSEL DISEASES

Certain risk factors increase the chance that you may develop cardiovascular disease, especially coronary heart disease and stroke. You have no control over some of them, such as a history of heart disease in the family, or being male. However, other risk factors can be controlled. Three of the most important risk factors you can control are high blood pressure, high blood cholesterol and cigarette smoking. Obesity and diabetes also increase the risk of heart disease. But no matter what your history, you may still be able to reduce your personal risk of heart disease by making healthful choices in the foods you eat, by deciding not to smoke, by maintaining a desirable body weight and by being generally active.

This section not only provides dietary treatment for high blood pressure but also includes information about dietary measures to decrease blood cholesterol levels and control body weight. Before you begin, you should know both your blood pressure and blood cholesterol levels. If you don't, have a physician measure them for you and ask him or her to explain the readings to you. If someone other than your physician takes the measurements, be sure to consult your own physician for an interpretation of the results. If your blood cholesterol levels and/or weight are high, use the information here to help lower them. If your blood cholesterol and weight are normal, use the information to help you maintain these desirable levels.

HIGH BLOOD PRESSURE (HYPERTENSION)

Blood pressure is a ratio measurement of the pressure that blood exerts against the inside of the artery wall when the heart beats, and when it is at rest. A device measures blood pressure in millimeters of mercury (mm Hg). The measurement is written as systolic blood pressure (taken while the heart is beating) over diastolic blood pressure (taken in between heartbeats). An example is 120/80 (read as "one-twenty over eighty"). Blood pressure is considered high when systolic blood pressure is 140 mm Hg or greater and/or diastolic blood pressure is 90 mm Hg or greater.

Normal Blood Pressure for
Persons 18 Years of Age or Older
Less than 140/90 mm Hg

Doctors have identified two kinds of high blood pressure. The cause of *essential* or *primary hypertension*, which accounts for 90 percent of all cases, is unknown. *Secondary hypertension* occurs because of another disease or a condition such as pregnancy. It is estimated that one-fourth of all Americans have some degree of high blood pressure. Uncontrolled high blood pressure increases the risk not only for heart attack and stroke but also for kidney damage and an enlarged heart. The primary dietary factors that help lower blood pressure for many people are discussed on pages 294–299.

HIGH BLOOD CHOLESTEROL (HYPERCHOLESTEROLEMIA)

A high level of cholesterol in the blood (hypercholesterolemia) is a risk factor for heart disease. Cholesterol is measured in milligrams per deciliter of blood (mg/dl). Elevated blood cholesterol contributes to a disease process called atherosclerosis. In atherosclerosis, cholesterol and other elements in blood are deposited along the smooth inner linings of arteries to form plaque. Over time, plaque builds up and narrows the inside of the artery. If this narrowed artery becomes entirely blocked, blood cannot carry oxygen the body needs to sustain life to its cells and tissues. If the blocked artery is in the heart itself—a coronary artery—the result is a heart attack. If the blocked artery is in the neck or head, the result is a stroke.

BLOOD CHOLESTEROL CATEGORIES FOR PERSONS 20 YEARS OF AGE OR OLDER

Desirable Blood Cholesterol	Borderline-High Blood Cholesterol	High Blood Cholesterol
Less than 200 mg/dl	200 to 239 mg/dl	240 mg/dl and above

Research shows that lowering elevated blood cholesterol levels helps reduce the risk of heart disease. The primary dietary factors that help lower blood cholesterol in most people are given for your reference below.

Dietary Factors That Help Lower Blood Cholesterol

Saturated Fatty Acids—Less than 10% of calories

Dietary Cholesterol—Less than 300 mg per day

Weight Control—Achieving and maintaining desirable body weight

Several dietary factors affect both elevated blood cholesterol and high blood pressure. These are discussed in detail in the following sections.

DIETARY FACTORS AFFECTING BLOOD PRESSURE

Making the right food choices can help lower blood pressure in many people.
The three major dietary factors are:

- Restricting sodium intake
- Controlling weight
- Restricting alcohol intake

Each one can be used alone or in combination with the others to lower blood pressure in many people. Some research indicates that eating foods high in potassium helps control high blood pressure, too. Other studies are investigating the effects of other minerals (such as calcium) on blood pressure.

SODIUM

A diet high in sodium may contribute to the development of high blood pressure in some people and cause blood pressure to stay high in others. It also can limit how well certain blood pressure medications work. Some people can control their high blood pressure by reducing the amount of sodium in their diet. Other people may need medication in addition. The food plans we have developed (see pages 331–338 and 355–361) provide about 2,000 milligrams (mg) of sodium per day. If your physician recommends a higher or lower level of sodium, a registered dietitian can make the necessary changes in the eating plans for you.

Salt is the most common source of sodium. Salt, or sodium chloride, is 40 percent sodium and 60 percent chloride. Americans typically consume from 4,000 to 5,800 milligrams of sodium per day. One teaspoon of salt has 2,196 milligrams of sodium. Each of the following sources provides a portion of the sodium found in the typical American diet:

- Sodium added to food during preparation or at the table (about 18 percent)
- Sodium added to food during processing (about 67 percent)
- Sodium occurring naturally in food and water (about 15 percent)

Food Preparation. One source of sodium is salt added during food preparation (at home or in restaurants) and at the table. You were not born with the taste for salt—you acquired it. It usually takes about a month of eating less salt and high-sodium foods to reduce your desire to salt your food. You can decrease your taste for salt (and sodium) by using little or none in food preparation, by not adding it at the table and by avoiding processed foods containing large amounts of sodium. Replace salt with herbs and spices or some of the salt-free seasoning mixes on the market. Add pepper, garlic, onion and/or lemon to foods to give them a more distinct flavor and help replace the taste of salt. We've listed some of the best seasonings for various foods in our "Herb, Spice and Seasoning Guide" on pages 362–364.

Most salt substitutes are potassium chloride. Adding a small amount of salt substitute to food after cooking will make the food taste "salted." Before using any salt substitute, check with your doctor to see if it is all right for you. Products labeled "lite" salt are usually part sodium chloride (salt) and part potassium chloride. We don't recommend using "lite" salt because it adds sodium to food.

In fact, any seasoning that uses "salt" as part of the name is high in sodium. Examples are "garlic salt," "celery salt" and "onion salt." However, plain "garlic powder," "celery powder" and "onion powder" are low in sodium and make an easy substitution possible if these are flavors you love.

COMMON FOODS HIGH IN SODIUM

Anchovies	Ham, cured	Pizza
Bacon	Ketchup	Salami
Barbecue sauce	Kosher processed meat	Salt
Bologna	Meat, canned or frozen in sauce	Sauerkraut
Buttermilk	Monosodium glutamate (MSG)	Sausage
Celery salt	Mustard	Seasoned salt
Cereal, dry	Nuts, salted	Seeds, salted
Cheese	Olives, green	Soup, canned
Chips, potato * and corn *	Pastrami	Soy sauce
Crackers *	Pepperoni	Steak sauce
Cured meat	Pickles	Wieners—beef, pork and turkey
Frankfurters		Worcestershire sauce
Garlic salt		

* Unsalted varieties are available.

Note: A list of sodium-containing compounds often added to processed foods is included in the information about reading food labels (see page 305).

Sodium in Processed Foods. Processed foods, such as ham, bacon, pickles, cheese and luncheon meat, are very high in sodium. Convenience foods, including most frozen dinners and entrées, shelf-stable dinners and ready-to-eat cereals, are also high in sodium because of salt and sodium compounds used to prepare and preserve them. Ingredients used in food preparation, such as baking powder and baking soda, add to the sodium content of bakery products as well. Obviously, adding salt to any food increases its sodium content.

Sodium Naturally Occurring in Food. Sodium is present in all foods of plant and animal origin: It occurs naturally in meat, fish, poultry, dairy products, grain products, fruits and vegetables. However, the amount of sodium found in most of these foods is small.

The water supply is another source of sodium. Most adults use 2 to 2½ quarts (8 to 10 glasses) of water each day in beverages and in cooking. The sodium content of water varies, according to the supply, from 1 to 1,500 milligrams per quart. Ten glasses (2½ quarts) of water containing 1,500 milligrams of sodium per quart could total as much as 3,750 milligrams. Chemicals used in the "softening" process of most water softeners increase the sodium content of water. Your local health department can analyze your water for sodium content. If it contains more than 80 parts per million (approximately 200 milligrams sodium in 10 glasses of water), you should use distilled water or bottled water without sodium for drinking and cooking.

Be aware of all the sources of sodium you consume. The foods listed in the diets (pages 314–361) are primarily unsalted. Since the amount of sodium naturally occurring in food is low, your diet may contain less than 2,000 milligrams of sodium per day if you eat your meals at home and all the foods you eat are unsalted. For more variety, you may add a specified amount of salt or high-sodium foods to bring your level of sodium up to 2,000 milligrams. (For example, you may wish to use regular margarine instead of low-sodium margarine.) The amount of sodium you may add, based on the calorie level of your diet, is shown on pages 331 and 355. A list of typical restaurant foods and other high-sodium foods is shown on pages 311–312. It is very important that you take into account the generally high amount of sodium usually present in restaurant food.

ALCOHOL

Research shows that people who drink too much alcohol tend to have high blood pressure. To help control blood pressure, it's best to drink only in moderation or not at all. If you drink, we recommend that all alcoholic beverages provide no more than 1 to 2 fluid ounces of ethanol per day. The amounts of beer, wine and spirits equal to ½ fluid ounce of ethanol are listed on pages 329 and 352. Remember that alcohol is also a major source of calories and can contribute to obesity.

POTASSIUM

People with high blood pressure are often advised to include good sources of potassium in their diet. Some major sources of potassium are listed below.

POTASSIUM SOURCES*

Potassium	Foods
400 mg or more	Banana, 1 medium
	Cantaloupe, 1 cup, cubed
	Honeydew melon, 1 cup, cubed
	Milk, skim, 1 cup
	Nectarine, 1 large
	Orange juice, 1 cup
	Potato, 1 medium
	Prunes, 10 medium
	Prune juice, ¾ cup
	Red beans, cooked, ½ cup
	Tomato juice, salt-free, 1 cup
200 to 399 mg	Apple juice, 1 cup
	Beef, lean, cooked, 3 oz.
	Beets, cooked, ½ cup
	Blackberries, 1 cup

* For more information on potassium, see the American Heart Association's booklet "Facts About Potassium," available from your local American Heart Association.

Potassium	Foods
200 to 399 mg	Brussels sprouts, fresh, ½ cup
	Carrot, raw, 1 large
	Celery, 3 (5-in.) stalks
	Cherries, raw, 15
	Chicken, cooked, 3 oz.
	Flounder, cooked, 3 oz.
	Grapefruit, ½
	Grapefruit juice, 1 cup
	Lentils, cooked, ½ cup
	Lima beans, green, ½ cup
	Orange, 1 medium
	Pork, fresh, lean, cooked, 3 oz.
	Salmon, pink, unsalted, canned, 3 oz.
	Spinach, cooked, ½ cup
	Strawberries, sliced, 1 cup
	Tomatoes, unsalted, canned, ½ cup
	Tuna, water-packed, unsalted, ½ cup
	Turkey, unprocessed, 3 oz.
	Watermelon, 2 cups, cubed

CALCIUM

Calcium is an important nutrient for healthy bones. For the best sources of calcium, choose from the dairy products group listed on pages 320 and 344.

WEIGHT CONTROL

Reducing excess weight is associated with lowering high blood pressure. Details on weight control are on pages 304–305.

DIETARY FACTORS AFFECTING BLOOD CHOLESTEROL

The foods you eat can affect your blood cholesterol levels. If you choose foods low in saturated fatty acids, most will also be low in total fat. Research shows that a diet lower in total fat, saturated fat and dietary cholesterol will help lower blood cholesterol; so will reducing to achieve and maintain your ideal body weight. Some research studies suggest that soluble fiber in the diet also may help lower the blood cholesterol level.

FAT

The fat in food is made up of two major types of fatty acids: saturated and unsaturated. Unsaturated fatty acids may be either polyunsaturated or monounsaturated. Some fats are a concentrated source of saturated fatty acids, while others are high in polyunsaturated or monounsaturated fatty acids. All fats, however, are a mixture of saturated, polyunsaturated and monounsaturated fatty acids.

Saturated Fatty Acids. Eating foods high in saturated fatty acids tends to raise your blood cholesterol level. Saturated fatty acids are found in animal products and in some plant products.

Animal fats high in saturated fatty acids include butterfat (in butter, cheese, whole milk, cream and ice cream); fat on beef, pork and lamb; fat in chicken skin; and lard. Plant sources of saturated fatty acids are cocoa butter, coconut oil, palm kernel oil and palm oil. Commercial foods containing coconut, palm or palm kernel oil may be advertised as "cholesterol-free" if all the ingredients are from plant sources. However, if coconut, palm kernel or palm oil is a major ingredient, the product may be high in saturated fatty acids. This is important to know if you are trying to lower blood cholesterol levels. Read the nutrition section of the label and try to select foods that contain more polyunsaturated fatty acids than saturated fatty acids (monounsaturated fatty acids are not listed on food labels).

Unsaturated Fatty Acids. You can use unsaturated fatty acids to replace some of the saturated fatty acids in your diet. The two main types of unsaturated fatty acids are: polyunsaturated and monounsaturated. Polyunsaturated fats and oils help lower the level of blood cholesterol. Safflower oil is the most polyunsaturated vegetable oil, followed by sunflower oil, corn oil and soybean oil. Foods high in monounsaturated fatty acids include canola oil, olive oil, peanut oil, avocados, olives and some nuts. Some research indicates that they may be as effective as polyunsaturated oils in lowering blood cholesterol when consumed in a diet low in saturated fats.

Fish is also a source of polyunsaturated fatty acids. Some fish, including cold-water fish such as salmon, mackerel and herring, are rich in fat (fish oil), while fish from warm waters, such as red snapper and flounder, are generally low in total fat. The fat in either high- or low-fat fish is low in saturated fatty acids.

When you are reading food labels, you may find hydrogenated fats and oils listed. Hydrogenation is a process that changes oils from their liquid form to a solid or semisolid form. This process makes them more saturated than they were in their original form. The greater the degree of hydrogenation, the more saturated the fat becomes. Hydrogenation is used in manufacturing margarines and shortenings. These products may be partially or almost completely hydrogenated. Some types of margarine and shortening made with partially hydrogenated unsaturated oils are acceptable to include in eating plans to lower high blood cholesterol.

The unsaturated fatty acid content of selected foods is listed in the chart below. Foods with the highest level of polyunsaturated fatty acids are listed first.

UNSATURATED FATTY ACID CONTENT OF SELECTED FOODS

(Listed in Order of Polyunsaturation)

1 Tablespoon	Polyunsaturated Fatty Acid (Grams)	Saturated Fatty Acid (Grams)	Monounsaturated Fatty Acid (Grams)
POLYUNSATURATED OILS			
Safflower oil	10.1	1.2	1.6
Sunflower oil	8.9	1.4	2.7
Corn oil	8.0	1.7	3.3
Soybean oil	7.9	2.0	3.2
MONOUNSATURATED OILS			
Canola oil	4.6	0.8	8.2
Peanut oil	4.3	2.3	6.2
Olive oil	1.1	1.8	9.9
MARGARINES, UNSALTED			
Safflower oil margarine (tub)	6.3	1.2	3.3
Corn oil margarine (tub)	4.5	2.1	4.5
Corn oil margarine (stick)	3.3	2.1	5.4
Soybean oil margarine (tub)	3.9	1.8	5.1
Soybean oil margarine (stick)	3.6	1.8	5.4
NUTS, UNSALTED			
Walnuts, black	2.9	0.3	1.0
Brazil nuts	2.1	1.4	2.0
Peanuts	1.4	0.6	2.2
Pecans	1.1	0.4	2.8
Almonds	1.0	0.4	3.0
Cashews	0.7	0.8	2.3
Pistachios	0.6	0.5	2.6
Macadamias	0.1	0.9	4.9
SEEDS, UNSALTED			
Sunflower seeds	2.9	0.5	0.9

1 Tablespoon	Poly-unsaturated Fatty Acid (Grams)	Saturated Fatty Acid (Grams)	Mono-unsaturated Fatty Acid (Grams)
Sesame seeds	2.0	0.6	1.7
Pumpkin/Squash seeds	1.8	0.7	1.2
SHORTENING			
Soybean and cottonseed oil	3.3	3.2	5.7

DIETARY CHOLESTEROL

Dietary cholesterol is found only in foods of animal origin, including meat, poultry, seafood and dairy products. Foods such as fruits, vegetables, grains, cereals, nuts and seeds do not contain cholesterol. Egg yolks and organ meats are very high in cholesterol. Some shellfish, such as shrimp, that are relatively high in cholesterol can be eaten occasionally within the recommended guidelines.

FIBER

Fiber is the indigestible part of food. There are two types of fiber—soluble and insoluble. Limited evidence shows that large amounts of soluble fiber can help lower blood cholesterol levels by an additional 2 percent when combined with the effects of a diet low in total fat, saturated fatty acids and dietary cholesterol as described in this section. Good sources of soluble fiber include oatmeal, oat bran and beans. Many so-called oat bran products (muffins, chips, waffles), however, actually contain very little oat bran and are high in sodium, total fat and saturated fatty acids.

Insoluble fiber, such as wheat bran, adds bulk to stools and helps with normal bowel function. Large amounts of insoluble fiber may interfere with the body's ability to absorb certain nutrients, such as calcium. Insoluble fiber does not appear to lower blood cholesterol.

WEIGHT CONTROL

Losing weight can help lower both blood pressure and blood cholesterol. To lose weight, consume fewer calories and increase your physical activity on a regular basis. Although this sounds simple, weight loss is not easy, and keeping weight off can be even more difficult than losing it.

One of the most effective methods for weight loss is reducing the amount of fat you eat. Since fat (saturated and unsaturated) is the most concentrated source of calories in your diet, reducing fat automatically decreases calories. Fat has more than twice the calories of the same amount of protein and carbohydrate. Protein and carbohydrate both have about 4 calories per gram; alcohol has 7 calories per gram; and all fats have 9 calories per gram. For example, 1 teaspoon of sugar (carbohydrate) provides 15 calories; 1 teaspoon of oil provides 40 calories—over 2½ times as many calories.

To maintain your ideal weight, eat no more calories than your body needs. As a guideline, typical calorie levels for men are 2,000 to 2,500 calories a day to maintain weight and 1,600 to 2,000 calories to lose weight. For women, typical calorie levels are 1,600 to 2,000 calories a day to maintain weight and 1,200 to 1,600 calories to lose weight.

Tips to Help You Prevent Overeating

- Select foods low in fat or fat-free.
- Eat slowly.
- Take small portions.
- Avoid second helpings.

For most people who decide to lose weight, a steady loss of 1 to 2 pounds a week is safe until the goal weight is reached. At the beginning of a weight-reduction eating plan, much of the "weight loss" is due to loss of water. Long-term success depends on two things: adopting an eating plan sufficiently low in calories to maintain the desirable lower weight; and taking part in regular physical activity. Such life-style changes help people who have lost weight keep it off.

FOOD LABELS

One of the greatest challenges of following a special eating plan is finding foods that fit your needs. You can obtain useful information by learning to read and compare food labels when you go shopping. Now that many product labels list sodium, fat and cholesterol content, shopping for low-sodium, low-fat foods is easier.

All food labels list the product's ingredients in order by weight. The ingredient present in the greatest amount is listed first. The ingredient contained in the least amount is listed last. Most packaged or prepared foods are high in sodium because their ingredients include high-sodium foods (see page 296) and/or sodium compounds (see below). The table on pages 305–306 will help you identify ingredients high in sodium, saturated fatty acids and/or cholesterol. To avoid getting too much of these, limit your use of products that list one or more of the ingredients or compounds found in this table.

SODIUM, SATURATED FATTY ACIDS AND CHOLESTEROL ON FOOD LABELS

Sodium Compounds		
Baking powder	Salt	Sodium hydroxide
Baking soda	Sodium alginate	Sodium nitrite
Disodium phosphate	Sodium benzoate	Sodium propionate
Monosodium glutamate (MSG)	Sodium caseinate	Sodium sulfite

Foods High in Saturated Fatty Acids and Cholesterol

Animal fat	Cream	Palm oil *
Bacon fat	Ham fat	Pork fat
Beef fat	Hardened fat or oil	Turkey fat
Butter	Hydrogenated vegetable oil *	Vegetable oil **
Chicken fat	Lamb fat	Vegetable shortening (some types) *
Cocoa butter *	Lard	Whole-milk solids
Coconut *	Palm kernel oil *	
Coconut oil *		

* Source of saturated fat only.

** Could contain coconut, palm or palm kernel oil.

SODIUM LABELING

Food labels use certain terms to describe the sodium content of those products. Each has a specific meaning. Knowing what each means can help you select low-sodium food.

Food Label Terms That Indicate Reduced Sodium

Term	Meaning
• "Sodium Free"	5 mg or less per serving
• "Low Sodium"	35 mg or less per serving
• "Moderately Low Sodium"	140 mg or less per serving
• "Reduced Sodium"	Usual sodium level is reduced by 75%
• "Unsalted" or "No Salt Added"	No salt added during processing

These terms refer only to sodium content and do not mean the product has less fat or saturated fatty acids. It's important to read labels carefully, since some foods low in sodium are high in fat. The following sample of nutritional information shows how to compare labels to identify a product lower in sodium, saturated fatty acids and cholesterol.

NUTRITIONAL INFORMATION: A COMPARISON OF LABELS

Nutrition Information Per Serving	Butter, Stick	Margarine, Tub	Unsalted Margarine, Tub
Serving size	1 Tbsp.	1 Tbsp.	1 Tbsp.
Calories	101	100	100
Protein, grams	0	0	0
Carbohydrate, grams	0	0	0
Fat, grams	11	11	11
Polyunsaturated, grams	1	5	5
Saturated, grams	8	2	2
Cholesterol, milligrams	33	0	0
Sodium, milligrams	120	95	4

Note: The amount of monounsaturated fat is not listed.

You can see that "unsalted" margarine has less sodium than regular margarine. Both types of margarine have less saturated fatty acid and dietary cholesterol than butter.

DINING OUT

Not surprisingly, you are more likely to find foods lower in sodium in restaurants that offer a wide variety of foods than in those that offer only a limited selection. Most restaurant food has salt and often monosodium glutamate (MSG) added to it. This is especially true if it is prepared ahead of time, frozen and reheated before serving. When you choose a restaurant that prepares food as it is ordered, you can tell the waiter to leave salt and MSG out of your portion. Naturally, you'll want to avoid using salt at the table. Also remember to avoid high-sodium condiments such as ketchup, mustard, soy sauce, steak sauce and salad dressing. A single restaurant meal may have anywhere from 1,000 to 4,000 milligrams of sodium.

The examples on pages 308 and 309 compare "typical"

restaurant and cafeteria menus with those that have been "modified" to be lower in fat and sodium. They illustrate how much you can decrease the sodium you are likely to consume when you dine out. Footnotes explain how the changes were made.

SAMPLE MENU—RESTAURANT MENU

Typical Menu	**Sodium (mg)**	**Low-Fat, Low-Sodium Menu***	**Sodium (mg)**
Rib steak cooked with salt (6 oz.)	650	Lean steak cooked without salt (6 oz.)	120
Baked potato with butter, cheese, sour cream, bacon bits	325	Baked potato with margarine, chives	60
Tossed salad with	20	Tossed salad with oil and vinegar	20
blue cheese dressing (1/4 cup)	670	dressing (1 Tbsp.)	0
Hot roll (1)	120	Hot roll (1)	120
Butter (1 pat)	40	Margarine (1 pat)	50
Apple pie (1 slice)	400	Sherbet (1 cup)	90
Total	2,225	Total	460

* The waiter was asked to have the steak cooked "without salt or fat" and to serve margarine and chives on the side for the potato. Oil and vinegar (in separate bottles, not Italian dressing) were used as salad dressing. Sherbet was selected because piecrust has salt and fat.

SAMPLE MENU—CAFETERIA MENU

Typical Menu	Sodium (mg)	Low-Fat, Low-Sodium Menu*	Sodium (mg)
Baked fish with topping (5 oz.)	1,002	Baked fish, topping removed (5 oz.)	575
Mashed potatoes (½ cup)	350	No potatoes	
Green beans (½ cup)	400	Green beans (½ cup)	400
Gelatin salad with cottage cheese (½ cup)	100	Gelatin salad with fruit (½ cup)	35
Chocolate cake with frosting (1 slice)	300	Melon wedge (1)	10
Total	2,152	Total	1,020

* The topping on baked fish was removed at the table and not eaten, to decrease sodium and fat. Only one vegetable was selected, since all choices were seasoned with salt and margarine. A gelatin salad with fruit contains less sodium than one containing cottage cheese. Fruit was selected for dessert because the cake was prepared with salt and baking powder (high in sodium) and was high in fat.

If you eat out very often, you'll need to keep track of the sodium in restaurant food. This means adding up the milligrams of sodium in each food to be sure that your total does not go over 2,000 milligrams for the day. Approximate sodium values for some common restaurant foods are listed on pages 311–312.

If you do *not* eat away from home on a regular basis, you may be getting less sodium than the amount recommended by your physician. If so, you may use regular margarine instead of unsalted margarine at home. You may also be able to add other high-sodium foods, such as those listed on pages 311–312, to increase your sodium to 2,000 milligrams. A registered dietitian can help you plan your meals.

When Dining Out

- Select a restaurant where food is cooked to order.
- Request that food be prepared without salt or fat.
- Be aware of those foods that have salt added during preparation; either avoid them or select only one.

- If an entrée is served with breading, topping or sauce, remove it before eating.
- Avoid table salt and high-sodium condiments and garnishes (pickles and olives).
- Avoid salads and other foods containing cheese and cottage cheese.
- Use lemon or oil and vinegar (in separate bottles, not Italian dressing) on salad.
- Request that sauces and salad dressings be served on the side.
- Fresh or canned fruit may be eaten as an appetizer, salad or dessert.
- If fruit pie is served, decrease sodium and fat by eating only the filling and leaving the crust.
- Compensate at home for high-sodium foods eaten out by using very low-sodium foods, such as unsalted margarine, unsalted bread and unsalted cereal.

When Choosing Deli Food

- Request "fresh-cooked" turkey or lean roast beef. Most precooked deli meats have salt and sodium-containing preservatives added.
- Skip the mayonnaise, mustard and ketchup on your sandwich.
- Order lettuce, tomato and/or onion for your sandwich.
- Use thinly sliced bread or one slice of regular bread for your sandwich to decrease the sodium.
- Avoid pasta salads, which usually have salt and Italian-type dressing added.

- "Dress" a tossed green salad with oil and vinegar from separate bottles (not Italian dressing).
- Choose fruit, sherbet or frozen yogurt for dessert.

SODIUM VALUES IN RESTAURANT AND OTHER COMMERCIAL FOODS

Foods	Approximate* Sodium (mg)
ENTRÉES, SALTED WHILE COOKING	
Chicken, breast or thigh and drumstick, grilled, skin removed after cooking** (1 med.)	250
Chicken, breast or thigh and drumstick, skin removed before cooking** (1 med.)	400
Chinese stir-fried entrées (2½ cups)	1,800
Fish, broiled or grilled (5 oz.)	600
Ham, lean (fat trimmed) (5 oz.)	1,700
Spaghetti with tomato and meat sauce (2½ cups)	1,050
Spaghetti with tomato sauce (2½ cups)	1,525
Steak, grilled (fat trimmed) (6 oz.)	650
Turkey, processed, from delicatessen (1 oz.)	120
Turkey, processed and commercially packaged (1 oz.)	400
SIDE DISHES, SEASONED WITH SALT AND MARGARINE	
Mashed potatoes (no gravy) (½ cup)	350
Rice, white (½ cup)	300
Sauerkraut (½ cup)	1,000
Vegetables, canned (½ cup)	400
Vegetables, frozen or fresh (½ cup)	250
SALADS	
Chicken salad (½ cup)	500
Coleslaw with vinaigrette dressing (½ cup)	450
Cottage cheese (½ cup)	425
Pasta salad (½ cup)	400

* Values rounded off for ease in use.

** In a restaurant, removing skin after cooking removes part of the salt used in cooking.

Foods	Approximate* Sodium (mg)
Potato salad (½ cup)	600
Tuna salad (½ cup)	400
SALAD DRESSINGS, REGULAR OR LOW-CALORIE	
French dressing (1 Tbsp.)	225
Italian dressing (1 Tbsp.)	125
Ranch dressing (1 Tbsp.)	125
Thousand Island dressing (1 Tbsp.)	125
SOUPS	
Beef bouillon (1 cup)	650
Chicken with noodles (1 cup)	950
Split pea (1 cup)	1,000
CRACKERS	
Bread sticks (2 sticks, 4 x ½ in.)	120
Melba toast, rectangular (5)	250
Saltines, regular (6)	200
CEREALS	
Bran, bud type (⅓ cup)	175
Oatmeal, cooked in unsalted water (½ cup)	1
Oatmeal, instant or cooked in salted water, prepared (1 packet or approx. ¾ cup cooked)	285
Ready-to-eat flake cereals, regular (1 individual serving box)	225
CONDIMENTS	
Cocktail sauce (1 Tbsp.)	175
Ketchup (1 Tbsp.)	175
Margarine (1 pat or 1 tsp.)	35
Mayonnaise-type salad dressing (1 Tbsp.)	100
Mustard (1 Tbsp.)	200
Olives, green (10 small)	800
Olives, black or ripe (5 extra-large)	250
Pickles, dill (1 spear, 6 x ½ in.)	450
Soy sauce (1 Tbsp.)	1,025
Steak sauce (1 Tbsp.)	300
Taco sauce (1 Tbsp.)	150

* Values rounded off for ease in use.

Step-One and Step-Two Diets

The American Heart Association has two eating plans for lowering blood cholesterol: the Step-One Diet and the Step-Two Diet.

The Step-One Diet (pages 314–338) moderately decreases your intake of total fat, saturated fatty acids and cholesterol. The Step-Two Diet (pages 339–361) further restricts your intake of saturated fatty acids and cholesterol. Use it when your doctor says you need additional lowering of your blood cholesterol. The Step-One and Step-Two diets provide no more than 2,000 milligrams of sodium per day. These eating patterns can help lower blood pressure and blood cholesterol levels.

Eating plans that are reduced in calories often do not meet the Recommended Dietary Allowance (1989) for calcium and iron. When you select foods you should take special care to ensure adequate calcium and iron intake. If you follow a low-calorie eating plan for a long time, you may wish to consult your dietitian or physician about supplementing calcium and iron in your diet.

The Step-One Diet

FOOD GROUPS

In the Step-One eating plan, foods are separated into seven groups based on the amount of fat, carbohydrate, protein and calories they provide. All foods listed as appropriate are prepared without added salt. The food groups are:

1. meat, poultry and seafood
2. eggs
3. dairy products
4. fats and oils
5. breads, cereals, pasta and starchy vegetables
6. vegetables and fruits
7. optional foods—desserts, sweets and alcohol

The foods within each group contain similar amounts of nutrients (carbohydrates, protein and fat). While you're getting started, use a food scale, measuring cups and measuring spoons to help determine portion sizes.

MEAT, POULTRY AND SEAFOOD

Foods in this group average, per ounce cooked, about 22 milligrams sodium, 60 calories, 3 grams fat, 1 gram saturated fatty acids and 25 milligrams dietary cholesterol. They provide protein, phosphorus, vitamins B_6, B_{12} and other vitamins and minerals. Lean red meats in addition are good sources of iron and zinc.

We recommend eating no more than 6 ounces of cooked meat, fish or poultry each day. This will limit your intake of saturated fatty acids, dietary cholesterol and sodium. Choose from the following list.

APPROPRIATE FOODS

SEAFOOD
All fresh and frozen fish
Crab, lobster, scallops, clams and oysters
Shrimp and crayfish (moderately high in cholesterol)
Tuna and salmon (canned in water, unsalted)
Sardines (canned, unsalted—rinsed)

POULTRY (without skin)
Chicken
Cornish hen
Turkey, unprocessed or fresh-cooked (not pre-basted)

VEAL (trimmed of visible fat)
All cuts are lean except for veal cutlets (ground or cubed); examples of lean veal are chops and roasts

BEEF (trimmed of visible fat)
USDA Select or Choice grades of lean beaf, such as round steak, sirloin tip, tenderloin and extra-lean ground beef

PORK (trimmed of visible fat)
Fresh pork, such as tenderloin and loin chops

LAMB (trimmed of visible fat)
Lamb chops
Lamb cubes for stew

WILD GAME
Venison
Rabbit
Squirrel
Pheasant (without skin)
Wild duck (without skin)

SODIUM, FAT AND CHOLESTEROL INFORMATION

When selecting meat, poultry and seafood, be careful to choose those most appropriate for your dietary plan. These hints will help you do just that.

- Cured, processed and pickled foods are high in sodium. Examples include ham, Canadian bacon, turkey ham, pickled herring, processed turkey, processed beef and processed chicken.
- Many processed meats, such as luncheon meat, wieners and sausage, are high in sodium and saturated fatty acids.
- Pre-basted turkeys have fat and salt added. Ask your butcher to special-order an "unbasted" or fresh turkey for you.
- Most deli-type precooked turkey and roast beef have salt or sodium compounds added.
- Most canned meats, such as tuna, salmon and chicken, are packed with broth or added salt. Purchase unsalted canned meats or rinse regular canned meats with cold water to help decrease the sodium.
- Many precooked frozen and canned entrées are prepared with salt.
- "Prime" grade, heavily marbled and fatty meats are high in saturated fatty acids.
- Liver, brains, heart, kidney and sweetbreads are high in cholesterol and should be limited.
- Shellfish contains less fat than does meat or poultry. Although shrimp and crayfish are relatively high in cholesterol, they can be eaten occasionally. Imitation shellfish (surimi) is high in sodium.

PORTION SIZE (COOKED MEAT)*

CHICKEN	
½ breast	3 oz.
1 leg and thigh	3 oz.
FRESH PORK	
1 medium chop	3 oz.

* Meat loses about 25% of its weight during cooking (for example, 4 oz. raw will be about 3 oz. cooked). Eat no more than 6 oz. cooked weight daily.

LAMB	
2 small chops	3 oz.
BEEF	
1 small hamburger patty	3 oz.
1 piece cooked lean meat, about the size of a deck of cards	3 oz.
¾ cup diced meat	3 oz.
FISH	
¾ cup flaked	3 oz.

ABOUT FOOD PREPARATION

The way you prepare your food is important to the success of your eating plan. Use this information to learn the best ways possible.

- Rinse frozen fish packed in a salt or brine solution with water before using.
- Trim all visible fat from meat and remove skin from poultry before cooking.
- Buy only the leanest ground beef, pork and turkey (no more than 15 percent fat). Pour off fat after browning. Ground meat is generally higher in fat than nonground meat.
- After cooking meat for a stew or soup, allow it to cool so the fat can rise to the top. Then remove the fat before adding vegetables and other ingredients.
- Preparing meat, poultry or seafood by frying, basting or sautéing adds extra fat. Remember to count this in your daily fat allowance.
- Dried beans, peas, lentils and soybean curd (tofu) are good sources of protein when eaten with low-fat dairy products. Small amounts of meat, fish or poultry can be combined with rice or pasta for a hearty entrée.

EGGS

Eggs are a good source of protein, phosphorus, vitamins A, D, B_6, B_{12} and other vitamins and minerals. Egg yolks are high in cholesterol, whereas egg whites contain no cholesterol. The Step-One Diet allows up to 3 egg yolks per week. One large whole egg has about 70 milligrams sodium, 79 calories, 6 grams fat, 2 grams saturated fatty acids and 213 to 220 milligrams cholesterol. You may supplement your diet with cholesterol-free egg substitutes. Check the label to see if salt has been added and how much sodium is provided by one serving. The chart at the bottom of the opposite page shows how much egg you normally get in various foods. It's easy to underestimate the amount you eat, especially when eggs are "hidden" in cakes, cookies or baked goods.

WHEN USING EGGS

Eggs can be part of a low-sodium, low-modified-fat, low-cholesterol diet. Just remember to eat no more than 3 yolks per week. Here are some tips to help you meet that goal.

- Prepare scrambled eggs, omelettes and the like so that only one or two egg yolks per serving are used. Add a few egg whites to the mixing bowl to make more generous portions.
- Many recipes contain egg yolk. Use the chart on page 319 to find out the approximate whole-egg content of various prepared foods.
- Substitute egg whites in recipes calling for whole eggs. For example, you may use two egg whites instead of each whole egg in muffins, cookies, puddings and pie fillings.
- The following chart shows that egg substitutes without added salt, egg whites and whole eggs have similar sodium content:

Food	Amount	Sodium
Whole egg	1 egg	70 mg
Egg substitute	¼ cup	80 to 120 mg
Egg whites	2	100 mg

- Egg substitute with cheese is high in sodium and fat.
- To prepare omelettes with egg substitute or egg, use low-sodium ingredients such as green onions, mushrooms, fresh tomatoes or green bell pepper to add flavor.

HOW EGGS ADD UP

Egg-Containing Foods	Approx. Portion of Whole Egg
BEVERAGES	
Eggnog (approximately ½ cup)	¼
BREADS	
Cornbread (1/9 of 9-in. square pan)	¼
Muffin (1)	1/10
Pancakes, 4-in. (2)	¼
DESSERTS	
Baked custard or crème brûlée (6-oz. custard cup)	½
Chocolate, lemon meringue or pumpkin pie (⅛ of 9-in. pie)	⅓
Pound cake (1/12 of loaf)	¼
Sponge cake (1/12 of 9-in. square cake)	½
Tapioca pudding (½ cup)	⅓
Yellow or chocolate 2-layer cake (1/16 of 9-in. cake)	⅛
MAIN DISHES	
Cheese soufflé (1 cup)	½
Chicken salad (½ cup)	⅓
Corn pudding (½ cup)	½
Egg salad	1 to 2
Omelette (depends on size)	1 to 3
SALAD DRESSINGS	
Mayonnaise (¼ cup)	¼
Thousand Island (¼ cup)	⅓

DAIRY PRODUCTS

The low-fat dairy products listed below average about 115 milligrams sodium, 90 calories, 3 grams fat, 2 grams saturated fatty acids and 11 milligrams cholesterol per portion. Milk and milk products are the major source of calcium in the American diet. They also provide riboflavin, protein and vitamins A, B_6 and B_{12}. Low-fat or skim-milk products that have been fortified with vitamins A and D have essentially the same nutrients as whole-milk products, but they have less fat and fewer calories. Skim milk and nonfat yogurt, however, actually have more protein and calcium than do whole milk and whole-milk yogurt.

PORTION SIZE

MILK AND YOGURT	
Skim or 1% milk	1 cup
Nonfat or low-fat plain yogurt	1 cup
CHEESE	
Unsalted low-fat or dry-curd cottage cheese	½ cup
Mozzarella cheese, part-skim	1 oz.
Ricotta cheese, part-skim	1 oz.
Low-fat cheese; no more than 150 mg sodium and 5 grams fat per oz. (¼ cup, diced)	1 oz.
Dry, grated cheese, such as dry Parmesan (1 Tbsp.)	¼ oz.
FROZEN DESSERTS	
Frozen low-fat yogurt	½ cup
Ice milk	½ cup
Sherbet (See "Optional Foods," pages 328–329)	

SODIUM, FAT AND CHOLESTEROL INFORMATION

Because of the wide variation among the many dairy products available, reading labels on these items is very important. These tips will help you select foods appropriate for your diet.

- Regular cheese, low-fat cheese and cottage cheese are high in sodium.
- Natural cheese is lower in sodium than processed cheese.

- Some supermarkets carry cheese reduced in both fat and sodium.
- Select low-fat cheese with no more than 5 grams fat per ounce and no more than 150 milligrams sodium per ounce.
- Cream substitutes—nondairy coffee creamers, sour cream substitutes and whipped toppings—often contain coconut, palm or palm kernel oil and are therefore high in saturated fatty acids. Read labels carefully.

ADDITIONAL FACTS ABOUT CALCIUM

(The recommended amount of calcium is 800 milligrams or more per day for adults.)

		Calcium mg
1 cup	Skim milk	302
	1%, low-fat milk	300
	2%, low-fat milk	297
	3.3%, whole milk	291
	Yogurt, plain, skim	452
	Yogurt, plain, low-fat	414
	Yogurt, fruit flavor, low-fat	344
	Yogurt, plain, whole	274
½ cup	Cottage cheese, low-fat, 1% fat, unsalted	69
	Cottage cheese, low-fat, 2% fat, unsalted	78
	Cottage cheese, creamed, unsalted	63
	Ice milk, vanilla, soft serve, 2.6% fat	137
	Ice milk, vanilla, hard, 4.3% fat	88
	Sherbet, orange, 2% fat	52
	Frozen yogurt, fruit varieties	162
1 oz.	Cheese, mozzarella, part-skim	183
	Cheese, low-fat (low-sodium)	186

FATS AND OILS

All the foods in the "Fats and Oils" food group are high in fat and calories. Some are high in vitamins A or E. One portion of the "Fats and Oils" group averages about 1 milligram sodium, 5 grams fat, 1 gram saturated fatty acids, 45 calories and negligible cholesterol.

SODIUM, FAT AND CHOLESTEROL INFORMATION

Cocoa butter, coconut, coconut oil, palm kernel oil and palm oil contain more saturated than unsaturated fatty acids. Look for the listing of these fats when you read package labels. Select only those foods that contain 2 grams or less of saturated fat per tablespoon. (You might wish to refer to the list on pages 305–306 for review.) Currently, information about monounsaturated fatty acids is not listed on the nutrition label.

PORTION SIZE	
VEGETABLE OILS	
Safflower, corn, sunflower, soybean, olive, canola, peanut	1 tsp.
MARGARINE, UNSALTED	
Margarine containing 2 grams or less of saturated fat per tablespoon	1 tsp.
Diet margarine	2 tsp.
NUTS AND SEEDS, UNSALTED	
Chopped nuts, except coconut	1 Tbsp.
Seeds, any variety (without shells)	1 Tbsp.
SALAD DRESSINGS	
French, Italian, Thousand Island or mayonnaise-type salad dressing, unsalted	1 Tbsp.
Mayonnaise	2 tsp.
SHORTENING	
Soybean and cottonseed oil	1 tsp.
OTHER FATS	
Peanut butter, unsalted	2 tsp.
Avocado	⅛ medium

ABOUT USING FATS AND OILS

Follow these guidelines for selecting appropriate fats and oils for this diet.

- Use unsalted margarine at home if you eat one or more meals away from home daily. This will help make up for the high sodium content of restaurant food. If you don't eat out regularly, you may use regular margarine instead of unsalted margarine at home.
- To help you select appropriate margarines and shortenings, read the labels. As a general guide, select margarine that has 2 grams or less of saturated fat per tablespoon. Limit your use of shortening because it's higher in saturated fatty acids than are margarine and oil.
- Diet margarine has about twice as much sodium as does regular tub margarine.
- Many oil-free salad dressings are high in sodium, but oil-free, low-sodium varieties are available. Some low-sodium, low-fat salad dressings can be purchased in individual packets to use when eating out.

BREADS, CEREALS, PASTA AND STARCHY VEGETABLES

Foods in this group contain an average of 92 milligrams sodium, 80 calories, 1 gram of fat and negligible saturated fatty acids and cholesterol per portion. We have included low-fat, unsalted soups in this group. Whole-grain or enriched breads and cereals provide B vitamins and iron. They also provide protein, and they are a major source of this nutrient in vegetarian diets. Whole-grain products also contribute magnesium, folacin and fiber.

SODIUM, FAT AND CHOLESTEROL INFORMATION

The following information will help you select and prepare appropriate foods from this group.

- If you eat more than one meal away from home daily, use unsalted bread with your meals at home. This helps make up for the high sodium content of restaurant food. If you do not eat out regularly, you can use regular bread instead of unsalted bread.

- Regular canned or dehydrated varieties of soup are high in sodium. A low-sodium soup should have no more than 2 grams of fat per cup.
- If you use skim or 1 percent milk to prepare soup, count ½ cup milk per 1 cup soup as part of the dairy allowance.
- Cream soup in restaurants is usually prepared with salt and whole milk or cream.
- Most ready-to-eat cereals are high in sodium. Read the labels to find low-sodium varieties, such as shredded wheat, puffed rice and puffed wheat.
- Cook hot cereal, pasta, rice and vegetables without salt added to the water.
- Individually portioned instant hot cereals, rice mixes and pasta mixes are high in sodium.

PORTION SIZE

BREADS	
Bagel	½
Bread sticks, unsalted, 4 in. long, ½ in. diameter	2
Bread, white, whole wheat, rye, oatmeal, pumpernickel	1 slice
Croutons, plain bread crumbs	1 cup
English muffin	½
Hamburger or hot dog bun	½
Pita, 6 in. diameter	½
Roll, plain (1 oz.)	1
Tortilla, corn, 6 in. diameter	1
CEREALS, PASTA AND RICE	
Shredded wheat	1 biscuit or ½ cup
Flake-type cereal, ready-to-eat, unsalted	1 cup
Puffed cereal, unsalted	1½ cups
Cooked cereal, bulgur, grits (cooked in unsalted water)	½ cup
Pasta (cooked in unsalted water)	½ cup
Rice (cooked in unsalted water)	⅓ cup

CRACKERS	
Animal crackers	8
Graham crackers, 2½ in. square	3
Matzo, 4 x 6 in.	¾ oz.
Melba toast, unsalted	5 slices
Popcorn (popped, no salt or fat added)	3 cups
Pretzels, unsalted	¾ oz.
Saltine-type crackers, unsalted tops	6
STARCHY VEGETABLES (fresh, frozen or canned without salt)	
Baked beans	¼ cup
Corn	½ cup
Corn on cob, 6 in. long	1
Dried beans, peas, lentils	⅓ cup
Green peas	½ cup
Lima beans	½ cup
Potato, baked (3 oz.)	1
Potato, mashed, no salt added	½ cup
Squash, acorn or butternut	¾ cup
Sweet potato or yam	⅓ cup
COMMERCIAL SOUPS (unsalted, prepared with water)*	
Bouillon, broth, consommé	As desired
Chicken noodle, gazpacho, minestrone, onion, tomato, vegetarian	1 cup
Beef noodle, chicken rice, chunky-style turkey noodle, oyster stew, split pea (may use milk allowance)	¾ cup
QUICK BREADS (1 serving = 1 Bread + 1 Fat)**	
Banana bread (16 slices per loaf)	1 slice
Biscuit (2 in. diameter)	1
Cornbread muffin	1
Pancake (4 in. diameter)	1
Waffle (9 in. diameter)	¼

* Homemade soups low in fat may be counted as the same amount of a similar commercial soup.

** Prepared with low-sodium baking powder, skim milk, unsaturated oil, unsalted margarine, egg substitute or egg white. Omit salt from the recipe. If you use a whole egg, count it as part of the egg allowance.

Note: Most commercial biscuits, muffins, pancakes and croissants are high in sodium and are not made with the recommended fats.

ABOUT FOOD PREPARATION

The following tips will help you prepare foods in this group.

- Homemade biscuits, muffins, cornbread, banana bread, soft rolls, pancakes, French toast and waffles should be prepared with the egg yolk allowance (no more than 3 per week), egg substitute or egg whites; skim or 1 percent milk; and unsaturated oil or unsalted margarine. Omit salt, baking powder and baking soda from the recipe and replace them with low-sodium baking powder. You may need to use more of the low-sodium baking powder than the regular to get the same effect in a recipe; read the label.
- Check the dietetic or "special" foods section of your supermarket for low-sodium mixes for pancakes and other products.
- You can stretch your meat allowance by combining meat, poultry or seafood with rice, pasta or vegetables.

VEGETABLES AND FRUITS

An average portion of vegetables has about 13 milligrams sodium and 25 calories. An average portion of fruit has about 1 milligram sodium and 60 calories. Nearly all vegetables and fruits are low in fat, and none contain cholesterol.

Vegetables and fruits are important sources of vitamins A and C and fiber. Dark green and deep yellow vegetables are good sources of vitamin A. Most dark green vegetables, if not overcooked, are important sources of vitamin C, as are citrus fruits (oranges, grapefruit, tangerines and lemons), melons, berries and tomatoes. Dark green vegetables are also valued for riboflavin, folacin, iron and magnesium. Certain greens—collards, kale, mustard, turnip and dandelion—provide calcium.

PORTION SIZE

VEGETABLES	
Most vegetables	½ cup raw or cooked
Raw cabbage, Chinese cabbage, celery, cucumbers, mushrooms, green onions, peppers, radishes and zucchini	Quantities as desired (negligible fat and calories)
SALAD GREENS	
Endive, escarole, lettuce, romaine and spinach	Quantities as desired (negligible fat and calories)
FRUIT AND JUICE	
Fruit	½ cup or 1 medium-size piece of fruit
Fruit juice	½ cup

WHEN USING VEGETABLES AND FRUITS

When selecting and preparing foods from this group, use this information to help you get the nutrition you want without the extra sodium and fat.

- Fresh, frozen and unsalted canned vegetables are low in sodium. Select those that don't have seasoning or sauce added.
- Regular canned vegetables, tomato sauce, tomato paste, tomato juice and vegetable juice cocktail are high in sodium. Use the unsalted variety.
- Sauerkraut, pickles and pickled vegetables are high in sodium.
- Vegetables and fruits have no fat, except for avocados and olives. (You'll find these listed under "Fats and Oils—Portion Size" on page 322.)
- Vegetables prepared with butter, cream or cheese are high in fat.
- Fried vegetables have several times more fat and calories than vegetables prepared without fat.

- Fresh fruits and fruits canned in water are lower in calories than fruits canned in juice or in syrup. To reduce calories, drain fruits canned in syrup.

OPTIONAL FOODS—DESSERTS, SWEETS AND ALCOHOL

Each of the homemade desserts (cakes, cookies and pies) listed below has about 22 milligrams sodium, 285 calories and 6 to 10 grams fat. The amounts listed count as *two* portions of Optional Foods.

Each of the "sweets" on this list contains about 22 milligrams sodium, 75 calories and 0 to 1 grams fat. Each counts as *one* portion of Optional Foods.

One portion of any alcoholic beverage listed below contains 9 milligrams sodium, ½ ounce ethanol and 90 to 150 calories. Count each one as *one* portion of Optional Foods.

	PORTION SIZE
DESSERTS*	
2-layer cake, frosted (1/12 of cake)	1 slice
Sheet cake, frosted (2¼ × 2½ × 1½-in. piece or 1/20 of 9 × 13-in. cake)	1 piece
Cupcake, frosted (average size)	1
Oatmeal raisin cookies	4
Double-crust fruit pie (⅛ of 9-in. pie)	1 slice
SWEETS	
Carbonated beverage (sweetened)**	6 fl. oz.
Lemonade (sweetened)	6 fl. oz.
Candy made primarily with sugar (e.g., candy corn, gum drops, mints and hard candy)	¾ oz.
Angel food cake (1/24 of cake)	1 slice
Gingersnaps	2
Fruit ice	⅓ cup

* Homemade, prepared according to the first tip listed on page 329.

** Be sure the beverage is low in sodium—read the label.

Sherbet	1/3 cup
Fruit-flavored gelatin (sweetened)	1/2 cup
Sugar, syrup, honey, jam, preserves or marmalade	1 1/2 Tbsp.
Fig bar	1
ALCOHOLIC BEVERAGES	
Beer	12 fl. oz.
80-proof spirits (bourbon, gin, rum, Scotch, tequila, vodka, whiskey)	1 1/2 fl. oz.
Wine, red or white	4 fl. oz.

ABOUT DESSERTS, SWEETS AND SNACKS

Use the following information to help you select and prepare foods appropriate for your dietary plan.

- Desserts (cakes, pies, cookies and puddings) may be made with low-sodium baking powder, unsalted margarine or unsaturated oil, skim or 1 percent milk, allowed eggs, egg substitute or egg whites. Omit salt from recipe. If you use a whole egg, count it as part of the egg allowance.
- Many snack products, such as chips and rich crackers, are high in sodium and saturated fatty acids. However, some chips are cooked in unsaturated oil and are not salted. Choose only those labeled as "no salt added" and that contain more polyunsaturated than saturated fatty acids.
- A few kinds of cookies are low in fat, such as fig bars and gingersnaps. Plain angel food cake has no fat. If you are uncertain, read the label and choose only those with 2 grams of fat or less per portion.

FREE FOODS

One portion of these foods and drinks contains fewer than 20 calories and no fat. You don't need to limit those items that have no portion size specified.

PORTION SIZE

	PORTION SIZE
DRINKS	
Bouillon or broth without fat, low-sodium	
Diet carbonated drinks *	1 per day
Carbonated water	
Cocoa powder, unsweetened	1 Tbsp.
Coffee/tea	
Drink mixes, sugar-free	
Tonic water, sugar-free	
SWEET SUBSTITUTES *	
Candy, hard, sugar-free	
Gelatin, sugar-free	
Gum, sugar-free	
Jam/jelly, sugar-free	2 tsp.
Pancake syrup, sugar-free	
Sugar substitutes (saccharin or aspartame)	
FRUITS	
Cranberries, unsweetened	½ cup
Rhubarb, unsweetened	½ cup
CONDIMENTS	
Ketchup, low-sodium	1 Tbsp.
Horseradish, freshly grated	
Mustard, low-sodium	
Pickles, dill, unsweetened, low-sodium	
Salad dressing, oil-free, low-sodium	
Vinegar	

* Sweet substitutes are listed for the benefit of those following diabetic diets.

SAMPLE EATING PLANS: STEP-ONE DIET*

	Daily Portions			
Food Group	**2,500 Calories**	**2,000 Calories**	**1,600 Calories**	**1,200 Calories**
Meat, Poultry and Seafood (unsalted)	6 oz.	6 oz.	6 oz.	6 oz.
Eggs, whole (unsalted)	3/week	3/week	3/week	3/week
Dairy Products (unsalted)	4	3	3	2
Fats and Oils (unsalted)	8	6	3	3
Breads, Cereals, Pasta and Starchy Vegetables (unsalted)	10	7	4	3
Vegetables (unsalted)	4	4	4	4
Fruits	5	3	3	3
Optional Foods (unsalted)	2	2	2	0
Sodium from Food Groups, mg	1,639	1,244	965	731
Sodium from Water, mg	200	200	200	200
Additional Sodium,** mg	+150	+550	+800	+1,050
Total sodium	1,989 mg	1,994 mg	1,965 mg	1,981 mg

* Your physician or dietitian can recommend an appropriate calorie plan. Sample eating plans for the Step-Two Diet are on pages 355–361.

**Additional Sodium: A specific amount of sodium can be added to each of the eating plans. This "additional sodium" can be in the form of:

- Salt added at the table or in food preparation (home only)
  1/4 tsp. salt = 500 mg sodium
  1/2 tsp. salt = 1,000 mg sodium
- Restaurant foods, see pages 311–312.

EATING PLANS FOR CALORIE LEVELS HIGHER THAN 2,500 CALORIES

If you eat more than 2,500 calories a day, you can easily get more than 2,000 milligrams of sodium daily. If so, limit your intake of sodium by using all unsalted products, including unsalted bread and bread products. Be careful also to limit the sodium in the food you eat away from home.

YOUR DAILY EATING PLAN IN PORTIONS

Planning your meals to lower total fat, saturated fatty acids, dietary cholesterol and sodium will be easier if you plot them on a chart. The chart on page 333 shows a sample eating plan for a person on the Step-One Diet at 2,000 calories per day and about 2,000 milligrams of sodium. Spreading the allowable portions listed on page 331 over all meals and snacks during the day, the chart reflects the daily number of portions allowed for each food group. Use the blank form on page 334 to chart your daily eating plan.

The sample menus that follow the chart are examples of how the Step-One eating plan may be used. They include a variety of foods that can be eaten at home or in restaurants.

YOUR DAILY EATING PLAN IN PORTIONS*—STEP-ONE DIET

Calories 2,000 **Fat <30%** **Saturated fat <10%** **Cholesterol <300 mg** **Sodium 2,000 mg**

	Meat, Poultry & Seafood	Eggs	Dairy Products	Fats & Oils	Bread, Cereal & Starchy Vegetables	Vegetables	Fruit	Optional
Breakfast			1	1	2		1	
Snack								
Lunch	2 oz.		1	2	2	2	1	
Snack								
Dinner	4 oz.		1	3	2	2		2
Bedtime Snack					1		1	

* A blank form is provided on page 334 for your use. < = Less than.

YOUR DAILY EATING PLAN IN PORTIONS—STEP-ONE DIET

Calories ______ Fat ______ Saturated fat ______ Cholesterol ______ Sodium ______

	Meat, Poultry & Seafood	Eggs	Dairy Products	Fats & Oils	Bread, Cereal & Starchy Vegetables	Vegetables	Fruit	Optional
Breakfast								
Snack								
Lunch								
Snack								
Dinner								
Bedtime Snack								

SAMPLE MENU FOR THE STEP-ONE DIET—2,500 CALORIES

	Food Group Portions
BREAKFAST	
Orange Juice (1 cup)	2 Fruits
Shredded Wheat Cereal (1 cup) with	2 Breads
Sliced Banana (1/2)	1 Fruit
Milk, 1% (1 cup)	1 Dairy
Whole-Wheat Toast (2 slices)	2 Breads
Margarine, unsalted (2 tsp.)	2 Fats
LUNCH	
Hamburger Sandwich	
Lean Ground Beef, broiled (3 oz.)	3 Meats
Mozzarella Cheese, part-skim (1 oz.)	1 Dairy
Hamburger Bun (1)	2 Breads
Lettuce (1 leaf)	Free
Tomato (2 slices)	Free
Ketchup, regular* (1 Tbsp.)	Free
Tossed Salad	
Lettuce (1 cup)	Free
Tomato Wedges (1 tomato)	1 Vegetable
Grated Carrots (1/2 cup)	1 Vegetable
French Dressing, unsalted (2 Tbsp.)	2 Fats
Fresh Grapes (15)	1 Fruit
Milk, 1% (1 cup)	1 Dairy
DINNER	
Broiled Salmon (3 oz.) with	3 Meats
Margarine, unsalted (1 tsp.), and	1 Fat
Lemon (2 wedges)	Free
Steamed White Rice (2/3 cup) with	2 Breads
Margarine, unsalted (1 tsp.)	1 Fat
Steamed Snow Peas with Tomato Wedges and Onion (1 cup)	2 Vegetables
Cantaloupe, cubed (1 cup)	1 Fruit
French Bread (2 slices)	2 Breads
Margarine, unsalted (2 tsp.)	2 Fats
Milk, 1% (1 cup)	1 Dairy
Chocolate Cake with Quick Frosting (1/16 of cake)	2 Optional

* *Additional Sodium:* 150 mg allowed
Added: 1 Tbsp. regular Ketchup (175 mg sodium)

Nutrient Analysis:
1,979 mg Sodium (includes 200 mg sodium from water)
2,512 Calories, distributed as follows:

19% Protein	28% Fat	210 mg Cholesterol
55% Carbohydrate	8% Saturated Fatty Acids	

(The amount of cholesterol is less than 300 mg because no eggs were included in this menu.)

SAMPLE MENU FOR THE STEP-ONE DIET—2,000 CALORIES

	Food Group Portions
BREAKFAST	
Cranberry Juice Cocktail (1 cup)	3 Fruits
Poached Egg (1)	1 Egg
Bagel (1)	2 Breads
Margarine, unsalted (2 tsp.)	2 Fats
Milk, 1% (1 cup)	1 Dairy
LUNCH	
Roast Beef Sandwich	
Roast Beef (3 oz.)	3 Meats
Whole-Wheat Bread (2 slices)	2 Breads
Mayonnaise (2 tsp.)	1 Fat
Lettuce (1 leaf)	Free
Split Pea Soup, unsalted (3/4 cup)	1 Bread
Relishes	
Sliced Tomato (1 tomato)	1 Vegetable
Cauliflower Florets (3)	1 Vegetable
Milk, 1% (1 cup)	1 Dairy
Chocolate Ice Milk (1/2 cup)	1 Dairy
DINNER (at restaurant)	
Grilled Chicken Breast * (3 oz.)	3 Meats
Baked Potato (1 medium) with	1 Bread
Margarine, regular * (1 tsp.), and	1 Fat
Chives (1 Tbsp.)	Free
Broccoli and Carrots * (1/2 cup)	1 Vegetable
Margarine, regular (1 tsp.), used in preparation of vegetables	1 Fat
Tossed Salad	
Lettuce (1 cup)	Free
Tomato Wedges (1 tomato)	1 Vegetable
Vinegar	Free
Dinner Roll (1)	1 Bread
Margarine, regular * (1 tsp.)	1 Fat
Orange Sherbet (2/3 cup)	2 Optional

* *Additional Sodium:* 550 mg allowed

Added: 3 oz. Chicken Breast prepared with salt, skin removed after cooking (250 mg sodium)
2 tsp. regular Margarine (70 mg sodium)
1/2 cup frozen Broccoli and Carrots prepared with salt (250 mg sodium)

Nutrient Analysis:

1,997 mg Sodium (includes 200 mg sodium from water)
1,990 Calories, distributed as follows:

21% Protein	27% Fat	451 mg Cholesterol
53% Carbohydrate	9% Saturated Fatty Acids	

(The amount of cholesterol is greater than 300 mg because an egg is included in this menu.)

SAMPLE MENU FOR THE STEP-ONE DIET—1,600 CALORIES

	Food Group Portions
BREAKFAST	
Fresh Grapefruit (½)	1 Fruit
Corn Flakes, regular* (1 cup) with	1 Bread
Sliced Nectarine (1)	1 Fruit
Milk, 1% (1 cup)	1 Dairy
LUNCH	
Broiled Chicken Thigh (2 oz.)	2 Meats
Corn on the Cob (6 in.)	1 Bread
Margarine, regular* (1 tsp.), on corn	1 Fat
Tossed Salad	
Lettuce (1 cup)	Free
Tomato Wedges (1 tomato)	1 Vegetable
Cucumber Slices (6)	Free
Vinegar	Free
Melba Toast, unsalted (5 slices)	1 Bread
Strawberry Frozen Yogurt (½ cup)	1 Dairy
DINNER	
Swiss Steak	
Round Steak (4 oz.)	4 Meats
Tomatoes, canned, unsalted (½ cup)	1 Vegetable
Green Pepper Strips (½ pepper)	Free
Onion, diced (2 Tbsp.)	Free
Steamed Broccoli (2 spears)	1 Vegetable
Carrot-Raisin Salad	
Raw Carrots, grated (½ cup)	1 Vegetable
Raisins (2 Tbsp.)	1 Fruit
Mayonnaise (2 tsp.)	1 Fat
Whole-Wheat Dinner Roll (1)	1 Bread
Margarine, regular* (1 tsp.)	1 Fat
Milk, 1% (1 cup)	1 Dairy
Angel Food Cake (1/12 of cake)	2 Optional

* *Additional Sodium:* 800 mg allowed
Added: 1 cup regular Corn Flakes (225 mg sodium)
2 tsp. regular Margarine (70 mg sodium)
¼ tsp. salt (500 mg sodium) in food preparation or at the table

Nutrient Analysis:
2,003 mg Sodium (includes 200 mg sodium from water)
1,576 Calories, distributed as follows:
23% Protein 26% Fat 177 mg Cholesterol
54% Carbohydrate 9% Saturated Fatty Acids
(The amount of cholesterol is less than 300 mg because no eggs were included in this menu.)

SAMPLE MENU FOR THE STEP-ONE DIET—1,200 CALORIES

	Food Group Portions
BREAKFAST	
Fresh Strawberries (1¼ cup)	1 Fruit
Plain Low-fat Yogurt (1 cup)	1 Dairy
Raisin Bread Toast (1 slice)	1 Bread
Margarine, regular * (1 tsp.)	1 Fat
LUNCH (at delicatessen)	
Turkey Sandwich	
Turkey Breast, processed * (2 oz.)	2 Meats
Whole-Wheat Bread (2 slices)	2 Breads
Mayonnaise (2 tsp.)	1 Fat
Lettuce (1 leaf)	Free
Tomato (2 slices)	Free
Relishes	
Cherry Tomatoes (4)	1 Vegetable
Carrot Sticks (4)	1 Vegetable
Dill Pickle Spear * (6 in.)	Free
Fresh Bartlett Pear (1)	1 Fruit
DINNER	
Broiled Sirloin Steak (4 oz.)	4 Meats
Steak Sauce * (1 Tbsp.)	Free
Steamed Asparagus (6 spears)	1 Vegetable
Steamed Yellow Squash (½ cup)	1 Vegetable
Margarine, regular * (1 tsp.), on vegetables	1 Fat
Fresh Fruit Salad (Apples, Oranges, Grapes) (1 cup)	1 Fruit
Vanilla Frozen Yogurt (½ cup)	1 Dairy

* *Additional Sodium:* 1,050 mg allowed
Added: 2 tsp. regular Margarine (70 mg sodium)
2 oz. processed Turkey Breast (450 mg sodium)
1 6-in. long Dill Pickle Spear (450 mg sodium)
1 Tbsp. Steak Sauce (300 mg sodium)

Nutrient Analysis:
2,016 mg Sodium (includes 200 mg sodium from water)
1,229 Calories, distributed as follows:

25% Protein	29% Fat	142 mg Cholesterol
49% Carbohydrate	10% Saturated Fatty Acids	

(The amount of cholesterol is less than 300 mg because no eggs were included in this menu.)

The Step-Two Diet

The Step-Two Diet is usually recommended for people who need to make additional changes in their eating plan to reach the blood cholesterol goal recommended by their physician. Since all of the foods suggested are prepared without salt, the Step-Two Diet is also low in sodium.

FOOD GROUPS

In this eating plan, as in the Step-One Diet, foods are grouped into seven categories according to the fat, carbohydrate, protein and calories they provide. The food groups are:

1. meat, poultry and seafood
2. eggs
3. dairy products
4. fats and oils
5. breads, cereals, pasta and starchy vegetables
6. vegetables and fruits
7. optional foods—desserts, sweets and alcohol

In three of these food groups (numbered above as 5, 6 and 7) the information is basically the same as it is in the Step-One Diet. The general changes you'll need to make in the other four food groups in the Step-Two Diet are:

1. meat, poultry and seafood: Choose the very leanest.
2. eggs: Limit egg yolks to one per week.
3. dairy products: Select nonfat products, skim milk and cheese with 2 grams of fat or less per ounce.
4. fats and oils: Use margarine and oils instead of shortening.

MEAT, POULTRY AND SEAFOOD

Since only the leanest foods in this group are included, 1-ounce portions average 22 milligrams sodium, 55 calories, 2 grams fat, 0.8 gram saturated fatty acids and 25 milligrams dietary cholesterol. To reduce the amount of saturated fatty acids and cholesterol in the meat group, this eating plan allows only the leanest cuts. Limit or avoid shrimp and organ meats because of their cholesterol content.

Eat no more than 6 ounces of very lean cooked meat, fish or poultry each day.

APPROPRIATE FOODS

SEAFOOD
All fresh and frozen fish
Crab, lobster, scallops, clams and oysters
Tuna or salmon (canned in water, unsalted)

POULTRY (without skin)
Chicken
Cornish hen
Turkey, unprocessed or fresh-cooked (not pre-basted)

VEAL (trimmed of visible fat)
All cuts are lean except for veal cutlets.

BEEF (trimmed of visible fat)
USDA Select or Choice grades of lean beef,* such as round steak, sirloin tip and tenderloin

PORK (trimmed of visible fat)
Fresh pork, such as tenderloin and loin chops

LAMB (trimmed of visible fat)
Lamb chops
Lamb cubes for stew

WILD GAME
Venison
Rabbit
Squirrel
Pheasant (without skin)
Wild duck (without skin)

* To assure the leanest ground meat, select a lean cut such as round steak and have it ground.

SODIUM, FAT AND CHOLESTEROL INFORMATION

When selecting meat, poultry, and seafood, be careful to choose those most appropriate for your dietary plan. These hints will help you.

- Cured, processed and pickled foods are high in sodium. Examples include ham, Canadian bacon, turkey ham, pickled herring, processed turkey, processed beef and processed chicken.
- Many processed meats, such as luncheon meat, wieners and sausage, are high in sodium and saturated fatty acids.
- Pre-basted turkeys have fat and salt added. Ask your butcher to special-order an "unbasted" or fresh turkey for you.
- Most deli-type precooked turkey and roast beef have salt or sodium compounds added.
- Most canned meats, such as tuna, salmon and chicken, are packed with broth or added salt. Purchase unsalted canned meats or rinse regular canned meats with cold water to help decrease the sodium.
- Many precooked frozen and canned entrées are prepared with salt.
- "Prime" grade, heavily marbled and fatty meats are high in saturated fatty acids.
- Regular ground meat (even extra lean) has more fat than allowed in the Step-Two Diet. Select a lean meat cut, such as round steak, and have it trimmed and ground.
- Avoid all organ meats, since they are high in cholesterol.
- Shrimp and crayfish have about twice as much cholesterol as beef and chicken and should be avoided in the Step-Two Diet. Imitation shellfish (surimi) is high in sodium.

PORTION SIZE (COOKED MEAT)*

CHICKEN	
½ breast	3 oz.
1 leg and thigh	3 oz.
FRESH PORK	
1 medium chop	3 oz.
LAMB	
2 small chops	3 oz.
BEEF	
1 piece cooked lean meat, about the size of a deck of cards	3 oz.
¾ cup diced meat	3 oz.
FISH	
¾ cup flaked	3 oz.

* Meat loses about 25% of its weight during cooking (for example, 4 oz. raw will be about 3 oz. cooked). Eat no more than 6 oz. cooked daily.

ABOUT FOOD PREPARATION

The way you prepare your food is important to the success of your eating plan. Use this information to learn the best ways possible.

- Rinse frozen fish packed in a salt or brine solution with water before using.
- Trim all visible fat from meat and remove skin from poultry before cooking.
- After cooking meat for a stew or soup, allow it to cool so the fat can rise to the top. Then remove the fat before adding vegetables and other ingredients.
- Preparing meat, poultry or seafood by frying, basting or sautéing adds extra fat. Remember to count this in your daily fat allowance.
- Dried beans, peas, lentils and soybean curd (tofu) are good sources of protein when eaten with low-fat dairy products. Small amounts of meat, fish or poultry can be combined with rice or pasta for a hearty entrée.

EGGS

To further reduce the amount of cholesterol and saturated fatty acids in your diet, limit egg yolks to 3 per week. One large whole egg contains 70 milligrams sodium, 79 calories, 5 grams fat, 2 grams saturated fatty acids and 213 to 220 milligrams cholesterol. If you like, supplement your diet with cholesterol-free egg substitutes. However, be sure to read the egg-substitute label to see if salt has been added to the product.

WHEN USING EGGS

Eggs can be part of a low-sodium, low-modified-fat, low-cholesterol diet. Just remember to eat no more than 3 yolks per week. Here are some tips to help you meet that goal.

- Prepare scrambled eggs, omelettes and the like so that only one egg yolk per portion is used. Add a few egg whites to the mixing bowl to make more generous servings.
- Many recipes contain egg yolk. To find out the approximate whole egg content of various prepared foods, see the chart on page 319.
- Substitute egg whites in recipes calling for whole eggs. For example, you may use two egg whites instead of each whole egg in muffins, cookies, puddings and pie fillings.
- The following chart shows that egg substitutes without added salt, egg whites and whole eggs have similar sodium content.

Food	Amount	Sodium
Whole egg	1 egg	70 mg
Egg substitute	¼ cup	80 to 120 mg
Egg whites	2	100 mg

- Egg substitute with cheese is high in sodium and fat.
- To prepare omelettes with egg substitute or egg, use low-sodium ingredients such as green onions, mushrooms, fresh tomatoes or green bell pepper to add flavor.

DAIRY PRODUCTS

The dairy products in the Step-Two Diet contain less fat than those in Step-One, since the allowed amounts of fat and saturated fatty acids are lower. An average portion from this group has 117 milligrams sodium, 80 calories, 2 grams fat, 1 gram saturated fatty acids and 9 milligrams cholesterol. To further reduce the amount of saturated fatty acids you get from this food group, choose only skim milk, nonfat dairy products and cheese with 2 grams of fat or less per ounce.

	PORTION SIZE
MILK AND YOGURT	
Skim milk *	1 cup
Nonfat or low-fat plain yogurt	1 cup
CHEESE	
Unsalted low-fat or dry-curd cottage cheese	½ cup
Low-fat cheese; no more than 200 mg sodium and 2 grams fat per oz.	1 oz.
FROZEN DESSERTS	
Frozen low-fat yogurt	½ cup
Sherbet (See "Optional Foods," pages 351–352)	

* 1% milk has 2.2 grams fat per cup more than skim milk. If skim milk is unacceptable to you, adjust the eating plan to allow 1% milk.

SODIUM, FAT AND CHOLESTEROL INFORMATION

Because of the wide variation among the many dairy products available, reading labels on these items is very important. These tips will help you select foods appropriate for your diet.

- Regular cheese, low-fat cheese and cottage cheese are high in sodium. Natural cheese is lower in sodium than processed cheese. Some supermarkets carry cheese reduced in both fat and sodium.
- Read the labels carefully because some low-fat dairy products are high in sodium, and some low-sodium products are high in fat.
- Select low-fat cheese with no more than 2 grams fat per ounce and no more than 150 milligrams sodium per ounce.
- Cream substitutes—nondairy coffee creamers, sour cream substitutes and whipped toppings—often contain coconut, palm or palm kernel oil and are therefore high in saturated fatty acids. Read labels carefully.

FATS AND OILS

An average portion from this group contains about 1 milligram sodium, 45 calories, 5 grams fat and less than 1 gram saturated fatty acids. To reduce saturated fatty acids, substitute margarine (stick or tub) for shortening.

SODIUM, FAT AND CHOLESTEROL INFORMATION

Cocoa butter, coconut, coconut oil, palm oil and palm kernel oil contain more saturated than unsaturated fatty acids. Look for these fats when you read package labels. Select only foods that contain 2 grams or less of saturated fat per tablespoon. (You might wish to refer to the list on pages 305–306 for review.) Currently, information about monounsaturated fatty acids is not listed on the nutrition label.

ABOUT USING FATS AND OILS

Follow these guidelines for selecting appropriate fats and oils for this diet.

- If you eat one or more meals in restaurants every day, use unsalted margarine at home. This will help compensate for the high sodium content of restaurant food. If you don't eat out regularly, you may use regular margarine instead of unsalted margarine at home.

- To help you select appropriate margarines, read the labels. Try to select margarine that contains 2 grams or less of saturated fat per tablespoon. On the Step-Two Diet, avoid shortening, since it's higher in saturated fatty acids than are margarine and oil.
- Diet margarine has about twice as much sodium as does regular tub margarine.
- Many oil-free salad dressings are high in sodium, but oil-free, low-sodium varieties are available. Some low-sodium, low-fat salad dressings can be purchased in individual packets to use when eating out.

	PORTION SIZE
VEGETABLE OILS	
Safflower, corn, sunflower, soybean, olive, canola, peanut	1 tsp.
MARGARINES, UNSALTED	
Margarine containing 2 grams or less of saturated fat per tablespoon	1 tsp.
Diet margarine	2 tsp.
NUTS AND SEEDS, UNSALTED	
Chopped nuts, except coconut	1 Tbsp.
Seeds, any variety (without shells)	1 Tbsp.
SALAD DRESSINGS	
French, Italian, Thousand Island or mayonnaise-type salad dressing, unsalted	1 Tbsp.
Mayonnaise	2 tsp.
OTHER FATS	
Peanut butter, unsalted	2 tsp.
Avocado	⅛ medium

BREAD, CEREALS, PASTA AND STARCHY VEGETABLES

Foods in this group contain an average of 92 milligrams sodium, 80 calories, 1 gram of fat and negligible saturated fatty acid and cholesterol per portion. We have included low-fat, unsalted soups in this group. Whole-grain or enriched breads and cereals provide B vitamins and iron. They also provide protein and are a major source of this nutrient in vegetarian diets. Whole-grain products also contribute magnesium, folacin and fiber.

	PORTION SIZE
BREADS	
Bagel	½
Bread sticks, unsalted, 4 in. long, ½ in. diameter	2
Bread, white, whole-wheat, rye, oatmeal, pumpernickel	1 slice
Croutons, plain bread cubes	1 cup
English muffin	½
Hamburger or hot dog bun	½
Pita, 6 in. diameter	½
Roll, plain (1 oz.)	1
Tortilla, corn, 6 in. diameter	1
CEREALS, PASTA AND RICE	
Shredded wheat	1 biscuit or ½ cup
Flake-type cereal, ready-to-eat, unsalted	1 cup
Puffed cereal, unsalted	1½ cups
Cooked cereal, bulgur, grits (cooked in unsalted water)	½ cup
Pasta (cooked in unsalted water)	½ cup
Rice (cooked in unsalted water)	⅓ cup
CRACKERS	
Animal crackers	8
Graham crackers, 2½ in. square	3
Matzo, 4 x 6 in.	¾ oz.
Melba toast, unsalted	5 slices
Popcorn (popped, no salt or fat added)	3 cups

	PORTION SIZE
Pretzels, unsalted	3/4 oz.
Saltine-type crackers, unsalted tops	6
STARCHY VEGETABLES (fresh, frozen or canned without salt)	
Baked beans	1/4 cup
Corn	1/2 cup
Corn on cob, 6 in. long	1
Dried beans, peas, lentils	1/3 cup
Green peas	1/2 cup
Lima beans	1/2 cup
Potato, baked (3 oz.)	1
Potato, mashed, no salt added	1/2 cup
Squash, acorn or butternut	3/4 cup
Sweet potato or yam	1/3 cup
COMMERCIAL SOUPS (unsalted, prepared with water*)	
Bouillon, broth, consommé	As desired
Chicken noodle, gazpacho, minestrone, onion, tomato, vegetarian	1 cup
Beef noodle, chicken rice, chunky-style turkey noodle, oyster stew, split pea (may use milk allowance)	3/4 cup
QUICK BREADS (1 serving = 1 Bread + 1 Fat)**	
Banana bread (16 slices per loaf)	1 slice
Biscuit (2 in. diameter)	1
Cornbread muffin	1
Pancake (4 in. diameter)	1
Waffle (9 in. diameter)	1/4

* Homemade soups low in fat may be counted as the same amount of a similar commercial soup.

** Prepared with low-sodium baking powder, skim milk, unsaturated oil, unsalted margarine, egg substitute or egg white. Omit salt from the recipe. If you use a whole egg, count it as part of the egg allowance.

Note: Most commercial biscuits, muffins, pancakes and croissants are high in sodium and are not made with the recommended fats.

SODIUM, FAT AND CHOLESTEROL INFORMATION

The following information will help you select and prepare appropriate foods from this group.

- If you eat more than one meal away from home daily, use unsalted bread at home. This helps make up for the high sodium content of restaurant food.
- Regular canned or dehydrated varieties of soup are high in sodium. A low-sodium soup should have no more than 2 grams of fat per cup.
- If you use skim milk to prepare soup, count ½ cup milk per 1 cup soup as part of the dairy allowance.
- Cream soup in restaurants is usually prepared with salt and whole milk or cream.
- Most ready-to-eat cereals are high in sodium. Read the labels to find low-sodium varieties, such as shredded wheat, puffed rice and puffed wheat.
- Cook hot cereal, pasta, rice and vegetables without salt added to the water.
- Individually portioned instant hot cereals, rice mixes and pasta mixes are high in sodium.

ABOUT FOOD PREPARATION

The following tips will help you prepare foods in this group.

- Homemade biscuits, muffins, cornbread, banana bread, soft rolls, pancakes, French toast and waffles should be prepared with the egg yolk allowance (3 per week), egg substitute or egg whites; skim milk; and unsaturated oil or unsalted margarine. Omit salt, baking powder and baking soda from the recipe and replace them with low-sodium baking powder. You may need to use more of the low-sodium baking powder than the regular to get the same effect in a recipe; read the label.
- Check the dietetic or "special" foods section of your supermarket for low-sodium mixes for pancakes and other products.
- You can stretch your meat allowance by combining meat, poultry or seafood with rice, pasta or vegetables.

VEGETABLES AND FRUITS

An average portion of vegetables has about 13 milligrams sodium and 25 calories. An average portion of fruit has about 1 milligram sodium and 60 calories. Nearly all vegetables and fruits are low in fat, and none contain cholesterol.

Vegetables and fruits are important sources of vitamins A and C and fiber. Dark green and deep yellow vegetables are good sources of vitamin A. Most dark green vegetables, if not overcooked, are important sources of vitamin C, as are citrus fruits (oranges, grapefruit, tangerines and lemons), melons, berries and tomatoes. Dark green vegetables are also valued for riboflavin, folacin, iron and magnesium. Certain greens—collards, kale, mustard, turnip and dandelion —provide calcium.

PORTION SIZE

VEGETABLES	
Most vegetables	½ cup raw or cooked
Raw cabbage, Chinese cabbage, celery, cucumbers, mushrooms, green onions, peppers, radishes and zucchini	Quantities as desired (negligible fat and calories)
SALAD GREENS	
Endive, escarole, lettuce, romaine and spinach	Quantities as desired (negligible fat and calories)
FRUIT AND JUICE	
Fruit	½ cup or 1 medium-size piece of fresh fruit
Fruit juice	½ cup

WHEN USING VEGETABLES AND FRUITS

When selecting and preparing foods from this group, use this information to help you get the nutrition you want.

- Fresh, frozen and unsalted canned vegetables are low in sodium. Select those that don't have seasoning or sauce added.
- Regular canned vegetables, tomato sauce, tomato paste, tomato juice and vegetable juice cocktail are high in sodium. Use the unsalted variety.
- Sauerkraut, pickles and pickled vegetables are high in sodium.
- Vegetables and fruits have no fat, except for avocados and olives. (These are listed under "Fats and Oils—Portion Size" on page 346.)
- Vegetables prepared with butter, cream or cheese are high in fat.
- Fried vegetables have several times more fat and calories than vegetables prepared without fat.
- Fresh fruits and fruits canned in water are lower in calories than fruits canned in juice or in syrup. Drain fruits canned in syrup.

OPTIONAL FOODS—DESSERTS, SWEETS AND ALCOHOL

Each homemade dessert (cakes, cookies and pies) listed on pages 328 and 352 has about 22 milligrams sodium, 285 calories and 6 to 10 grams fat. The amounts listed count as *two* portions of Optional Foods.

Each of the "sweets" on this list contains about 22 milligrams of sodium, 75 calories and 0 to 1 gram of fat. Each count as *one* portion of Optional Foods.

One portion of any alcoholic beverage listed on the following page contains 9 milligrams sodium, ½ ounce ethanol and 90 to 150 calories. Count each as *one* portion of Optional Foods.

ABOUT DESSERTS, SWEETS AND SNACKS

This information can help you select and prepare these foods.

- Desserts (cakes, pies, cookies and puddings) may be made with low-sodium baking powder, unsalted margarine or unsaturated oil, skim milk, allowed eggs, egg substitute or egg whites. Omit salt from recipe. If you use a whole egg, count it as part of the egg allowance.

PORTION SIZE	
DESSERTS*	
2-layer cake, frosted (1/12 of cake)	1 slice
Sheet cake, frosted (2¼ × 2½ × 1½-in. piece or 1/20 of 9 × 13-in. cake)	1 piece
Cupcake, frosted (average size)	1
Oatmeal raisin cookies	4
Double-crust fruit pie (⅛ of 9-in. pie)	1 slice
SWEETS	
Carbonated beverage (sweetened)**	6 fl. oz.
Lemonade (sweetened)	6 fl. oz.
Candy made primarily with sugar (e.g., candy corn, gum drops, mints and hard candy)	¾ oz.
Angel food cake (1/24 of cake)	1 slice
Gingersnaps	2
Fruit ice	⅓ cup
Sherbet	⅓ cup
Fruit-flavored gelatin (sweetened)	½ cup
Sugar, syrup, honey, jam, preserves or marmalade	1½ Tbsp.
Fig bar	1
ALCOHOLIC BEVERAGES	
Beer	12 fl. oz.
80-proof spirits (bourbon, gin, rum, Scotch, tequila, vodka, whiskey)	1½ fl. oz.
Wine, red or white	4 fl. oz.

* Homemade, prepared according to the first tip listed above.

** Be sure the beverage is low in sodium—read the label.

- Many snack products, such as chips and rich crackers, are high in sodium and saturated fatty acids. However, some chips are cooked in unsaturated oil and are not salted. Choose only those labeled as "no salt added" and that contain more polyunsaturated than saturated fatty acids.
- A few types of cookies are low in fat, such as fig bars and gingersnaps. Plain angel food cake has no fat. If you are uncertain, read the label and choose only those with 2 grams of fat or less per portion.

FREE FOODS

	PORTION SIZE
DRINKS	
Bouillon or broth without fat, low-sodium	
Diet carbonated drinks *	1 per day
Carbonated water	
Cocoa powder, unsweetened	1 Tbsp.
Coffee/tea	
Drink mixes, sugar-free	
Tonic water, sugar-free	
SWEET SUBSTITUTES *	
Candy, hard, sugar-free	
Gelatin, sugar-free	
Gum, sugar-free	
Jam/jelly, sugar-free	2 tsp.
Pancake syrup, sugar-free	
Sugar substitutes (saccharin or aspartame)	
FRUITS	
Cranberries, unsweetened	½ cup
Rhubarb, unsweetened	½ cup
CONDIMENTS	
Ketchup, low-sodium	1 Tbsp.
Horseradish, freshly grated	
Mustard, low-sodium	
Pickles, dill, unsweetened, low-sodium	
Salad dressing, oil-free, low-sodium	
Vinegar	

* Sweet substitutes are listed for the benefit of those following diabetic diets.

One portion of the foods and drinks listed on the previous page contains less than 20 calories and no fat. You don't need to limit those items that have no portion size specified.

EATING PLANS FOR CALORIE LEVELS HIGHER THAN 2,500 CALORIES

If you eat more than 2,500 calories a day, you can easily get more than 2,000 milligrams of sodium daily. If so, limit your intake of sodium by using all unsalted products, including unsalted bread and bread products. Be careful also to limit the sodium in the food you eat away from home.

YOUR DAILY EATING PLAN IN PORTIONS

Planning your meals to lower total fat, saturated fatty acids, dietary cholesterol and sodium will be easier if you plot them on a chart. The chart on page 356 shows a sample eating plan for a person on the Step-Two Diet at 2,000 calories per day. Spreading the allowable portions listed below over all meals and snacks during the day, the chart reflects the daily numbers of portions allowed for each food group. Use the blank form on page 357 to chart your daily eating plan.

The sample menus that follow the chart are examples of how the Step-Two eating plan may be used. They include a variety of foods that can be eaten at home or in restaurants.

SAMPLE EATING PLANS: STEP-TWO DIET*

Food Group	Daily Portions: 2,500 Calories	2,000 Calories	1,600 Calories	1,200 Calories
Meat, Poultry and Seafood (unsalted)	6 oz.	6 oz.	6 oz.	6 oz.
Eggs, whole (unsalted)	1/week	1/week	1/week	1/week
Dairy Products (unsalted)	3	2	2	3
Fats and Oils (unsalted)	8	7	5	2
Breads, Cereals, Pasta and Starchy Vegetables (unsalted)	10	8	5	4
Vegetables (unsalted)	5	4	4	4
Fruits	7	4	3	3
Optional Foods (unsalted)	2	2	2	0
Sodium from Food Groups, mg	1,520	1,201	922	798
Sodium from Water, mg	200	200	200	200
Additional Sodium,** mg	+250	+550	+850	+1,000
Total Sodium	1,970 mg	1,951 mg	1,972 mg	1,998 mg

* Your physician or dietitian can recommend an appropriate calorie plan. Sample eating plans for the Step-One Diet are on pages 331–338.

**Additional Sodium: A specific amount of sodium can be added to each of the eating plans. This "additional sodium" can be in the form of:

- Salt added at the table or in food preparation (home only)
  1/4 tsp. salt = 500 mg sodium
  1/2 tsp. salt = 1,000 mg sodium
- Restaurant foods, see pages 311–312.

YOUR DAILY EATING PLAN IN PORTIONS*—STEP-TWO DIET

Calories 2,000 | Fat <30% | Saturated fat <7% | Cholesterol <200 mg | Sodium 2,000 mg

	Meat, Poultry & Seafood	Eggs	Dairy Products	Fats & Oils	Bread, Cereal & Starchy Vegetables	Vegetables	Fruit	Optional
Breakfast			1	1	2		1	
Snack								
Lunch	2 oz.			3	2	2	1	
Snack								
Dinner	4 oz.		1	3	3	2	1	2
Bedtime Snack					1		1	

* A blank form is provided on page 357 for your use. < = Less than.

YOUR DAILY EATING PLAN IN PORTIONS—STEP-TWO DIET

Calories ______ Fat ______ Saturated fat ______ Cholesterol ______ Sodium ______

	Meat, Poultry & Seafood	Eggs	Dairy Products	Fats & Oils	Bread, Cereal & Starchy Vegetables	Vegetables	Fruit	Optional
Breakfast								
Snack								
Lunch								
Snack								
Dinner								
Bedtime Snack								

SAMPLE MENU FOR THE STEP-TWO DIET—2,500 CALORIES

	Food Group Portions
BREAKFAST	
Apple Juice (1 cup)	2 Fruits
Shredded Wheat (1 cup) with	2 Breads
Sliced Banana (1)	2 Fruits
Milk, skim (1 cup)	1 Dairy
Whole-Wheat Toast (2 slices)	2 Breads
Margarine, unsalted (2 tsp.)	2 Fats
LUNCH	
Grilled Chicken Sandwich	
Grilled Chicken Breast (3 oz.)	3 Meats
Kaiser Roll (1 medium)	2 Breads
Mayonnaise (2 tsp.)	1 Fat
Lettuce (1 leaf), Tomato (2 slices)	Free
Corn on the Cob (6 in.)	1 Bread
Margarine, unsalted (1 tsp.), on corn	1 Fat
Tomato Wedges (1 tomato) and	1 Vegetable
Green Pepper Strips (1/2 pepper) in	Free
French Salad Dressing, unsalted (1 Tbsp.)	1 Fat
Fresh Bartlett Pear (1)	1 Fruit
Milk, skim (1 cup)	1 Dairy
DINNER	
Beef Shish Kabob	
Sirloin Steak (3 oz.)	3 Meats
Cherry Tomatoes (4)	1 Vegetable
Onion Wedges (1 small onion)	1 Vegetable
Mushrooms, fresh (4)	Free
White Rice, unsalted (2/3 cup) with	2 Breads
Margarine, unsalted (1 tsp.)	1 Fat
Steamed Green Beans (1 cup)	2 Vegetables
Margarine, unsalted (1 tsp.), on Green Beans	1 Fat
Fresh Strawberries (1 1/4 cups) and Pineapple Chunks, canned in juice (1/3 cup)	2 Fruits
Pumpernickel Bread (1 slice)	1 Bread
Margarine, unsalted (1 tsp.)	1 Fat
Milk, skim (1 cup)	1 Dairy
Oatmeal Cookies (4 cookies)	2 Optional

Additional Sodium: 250 mg allowed
Added: 1/8 teaspoon salt (250 mg sodium) in food preparation or at the table.

Nutrient Analysis:
1,941 mg Sodium (includes 200 mg sodium from water)
2,530 Calories, distributed as follows:

18% Protein	25% Fat	163 mg Cholesterol
60% Carbohydrate	5% Saturated Fatty Acids	

(The amount of cholesterol is less than 200 mg because no eggs were included in this menu.)

SAMPLE MENU FOR THE STEP-TWO DIET—2,000 CALORIES

	Food Group Portions
BREAKFAST	
Orange Juice (1/2 cup)	1 Fruit
Egg Substitute (equivalent to 1 egg) with Margarine, unsalted (1 tsp.)	1 Fat
Bagel (1 medium)	2 Breads
Margarine, unsalted (1 tsp.)	1 Fat
Cream of Wheat, unsalted (1/2 cup), with	1 Bread
Raisins (2 Tbsp.)	1 Fruit
Milk, skim (1 cup)	1 Dairy
LUNCH	
Roast Beef Pita Sandwich	
Roast Beef (2 oz.)	2 Meats
Pita Bread (1 medium)	2 Breads
Mayonnaise (2 tsp.)	1 Fat
Lettuce (1 leaf)	Free
Tomato (2 slices)	Free
Tossed Salad	
Lettuce (1 cup)	Free
Tomato Wedges (1 tomato)	1 Vegetable
Grated Carrots (1/2 cup)	1 Vegetable
French Salad Dressing, unsalted (2 Tbsp.)	2 Fats
Bread Sticks, unsalted (2)	1 Bread
Fresh Peach (1)	1 Fruit
Vanilla Frozen Yogurt (1/2 cup)	1 Dairy
DINNER	
Broiled Salmon (4 oz.) with Dill and	4 Meats
Margarine, unsalted (1 tsp.)	1 Fat
Steamed Broccoli and Cauliflower (1 cup)	2 Vegetables
Steamed Corn (1/2 cup)	1 Bread
Watermelon, cubed (1 1/4 cups)	1 Fruit
Whole-Wheat Dinner Roll (1)	1 Bread
Margarine, unsalted (1 tsp.)	1 Fat
Apple Pie (1/8 of 9-in. pie)	2 Optional

* *Additional Sodium:* 550 mg allowed
Added: 1/4 teaspoon salt (500 mg sodium) in food preparation or at the table

Nutrient Analysis:
1,929 mg Sodium (includes 200 mg sodium from water)
2,008 Calories, distributed as follows:

19% Protein	29% Fat	167 mg Cholesterol
54% Carbohydrate	6% Saturated Fatty Acids	

(The amount of cholesterol is less than 200 mg because no eggs were included in this menu.)

SAMPLE MENU FOR THE STEP-TWO DIET—1,600 CALORIES

	Food Group Portions
BREAKFAST	
Canteloupe, cubed (1 cup)	1 Fruit
Corn Flakes, unsalted (1 cup) with	1 Bread
Fresh Strawberries (1 1/4 cups)	1 Fruit
Milk, skim (1 cup)	1 Dairy
Whole-Wheat Toast (1 slice)	1 Bread
Margarine, unsalted (1 tsp.)	1 Fat
LUNCH (at delicatessen)	
Turkey Sandwich	
Turkey Breast, processed * (3 oz.)	3 Meats
Whole-Wheat Bread (2 slices)	2 Breads
Mayonnaise (2 tsp.)	1 Fat
Lettuce (1 leaf)	Free
Tomato (2 slices)	Free
Tossed Salad	
Lettuce (1 cup)	Free
Tomato Wedges (1 tomato)	1 Vegetable
French Salad Dressing * (2 Tbsp.)	2 Fats
Fresh Apple (1)	1 Fruit
DINNER	
Roast beef (3 oz.)	3 Meats
New Potatoes (1/2 cup) with Parsley and	1 Bread
Margarine, unsalted (1 tsp.)	1 Fat
Steamed Green Beans (1/2 cup)	1 Vegetable
Steamed Carrots (1/2 cup)	1 Vegetable
Green Salad	
Romaine Lettuce (1 cup)	Free
Tomato Wedges (1 tomato)	1 Vegetable
Vinegar	Free
Milk, skim (1 cup)	1 Dairy
Orange Sherbet (2/3 cup)	2 Optional

* *Additional Sodium:* 850 mg allowed
Added: 3 oz. processed Turkey Breast (360 mg sodium)
2 Tbsp. regular French Dressing (450 mg sodium)

Nutrient Analysis:
1,954 mg Sodium
1,592 Calories, distributed as follows:

21% Protein	25% Fat	152 mg Cholesterol
57% Carbohydrate	6% Saturated Fatty Acids	

(The amount of cholesterol is less than 200 mg because no eggs were included in this menu.)

SAMPLE MENU FOR THE STEP-TWO DIET—1,200 CALORIES

	Food Group Portions
BREAKFAST	
Fresh Blueberries (1 cup)	1 Fruit
Plain Nonfat Yogurt (1 cup)	1 Dairy
English Muffin (1)	2 Breads
Margarine, unsalted (1 tsp.)	1 Fat
LUNCH	
Tossed Salad	
Lettuce (2 cups)	Free
Tomato Wedges (1 tomato)	1 Vegetable
Grated Carrots (½ cup)	1 Vegetable
Vinegar	Free
Bread Sticks, unsalted (2)	1 Bread
Fresh Grapes (15)	1 Fruit
Milk, skim (1 cup)	1 Dairy
DINNER (at restaurant)	
Grilled Half Chicken * (6 oz.)	6 Meats
Broccoli Spears * (3)	1 Vegetable
Margarine (1 tp.), used in preparation of broccoli	1 Fat
Tossed Salad	
Lettuce (1 cup)	Free
Tomato Wedges (1 tomato)	1 Vegetable
French Salad Dressing * (1 Tbsp.)	1 Fat
White Roll (1)	1 Bread
Fresh Strawberries (1¼ cups)	1 Fruit

* *Additional Sodium:* 1,000 mg allowed

Added: 6 oz. Chicken (breast, thigh and drumstick) prepared with salt, skin removed after cooking (500 mg sodium)

½ cup frozen Broccoli prepared with salt (250 mg sodium)

1 Tbsp. regular French Dressing (225 mg sodium)

Nutrient Analysis:

1,945 mg Sodium

1,226 Calories, distributed as follows:

29% Protein	22% Fat	165 mg Cholesterol
51% Carbohydrate	6% Saturated Fatty Acids	

(The amount of cholesterol is less than 200 mg because no eggs were included in this menu.)

APPENDIX B

Herb, Spice and Seasoning Guide

DIPS	Caraway, dill, garlic, oregano, parsley, freshly ground black pepper
SOUPS AND STEWS	
Bean soup	Dry mustard powder
Vegetable soup	Sugar, vinegar
Skim milk chowders	Bay leaf,* peppercorns
Pea soup	Bay leaf,* coriander, fresh parsley
Stews	Basil, bay leaf,* cayenne, chervil, chili powder, cinnamon, cumin, curry, fennel, garlic, ginger, marjoram, nutmeg, onion, parsley, saffron
Various	Basil, bay leaf,* burnet, cayenne, chervil, chili powder, cloves, curry, dill, garlic, ginger, marjoram, mint, mustard, nutmeg, onion, oregano, parsley, freshly ground black pepper, rosemary, sage, savory, sesame, tarragon, thyme, watercress
SALADS	Basil, burnet, chervil, coriander, dill, fresh lemon juice, mint, fresh mushrooms, mustard, oregano, parsley, freshly ground black pepper, rosemary, sage, savory, sesame seeds, turmeric, vinegar, watercress

* Always remove bay leaf from dish before serving.

MEAT, FISH AND POULTRY	
Fish and seafood	Allspice, basil, bay leaf,* cayenne, curry powder, cumin, fennel, garlic, green bell pepper, fresh lemon juice, mace, marjoram, mint, fresh mushrooms, Dijon mustard, dry mustard powder, green onion, paprika, saffron, sage, sesame, tarragon, thyme, turmeric, white wine
Poultry	Basil, bay leaf,* cinnamon, curry powder, garlic, green bell pepper, fresh lemon juice, mace, marjoram, fresh mushrooms, onion, paprika, fresh parsley, lemon pepper, poultry seasoning, rosemary, saffron, sage, savory, sesame, thyme, tarragon, white wine
Game	Bay leaf,* garlic, fresh lemon juice, fresh mushrooms, onion, rosemary, sage, savory, tarragon, thyme, vinegar
Beef	Allspice, bay leaf,* cayenne, cumin, curry powder, garlic, green bell pepper, marjoram, fresh mushrooms, dry mustard, nutmeg, onion, freshly ground black pepper, rosemary, sage, thyme, red wine
Pork	Apple, applesauce, cinnamon, cloves, fennel, garlic, mint, onion, sage, savory, red wine
Lamb	Curry powder, garlic, mint, mint jelly, onion, pineapple, rosemary, sage, savory, sesame, red wine
Veal	Apricot, bay leaf,* curry powder, ginger, fresh lemon juice, marjoram, mint, fresh mushrooms, oregano, saffron, sage, savory, tarragon, white wine
Various	Cayenne, chervil, chili powder, coriander, curry powder, dill, garlic, ginger, marjoram, onion, oregano, parsley, freshly ground black pepper

VEGETABLES	
Asparagus	Garlic, fresh lemon juice, onion, vinegar
Beans	Caraway, cloves, cumin, mint, savory, tarragon, thyme
Beets	Anise, caraway, fennel, ginger, savory
Carrots	Anise, cinnamon, cloves, mint, sage, tarragon
Corn	Allspice, green bell pepper, pimiento, fresh tomato

* Always remove bay leaf from dish before serving.

Cucumbers	Chives, dill, garlic, vinegar
Green beans	Dill, fresh lemon juice, marjoram, nutmeg, pimiento
Greens	Garlic, fresh lemon juice, onion, vinegar
Peas	Allspice, green bell pepper, mint, fresh mushrooms, onions, fresh parsley, sage, savory
Potatoes	Chives, dill, green bell pepper, onion, pimiento, saffron
Squash	Allspice, brown sugar, cinnamon, cloves, fennel, ginger, mace, nutmeg, onion, savory
Tomatoes	Allspice, basil, garlic, marjoram, onion, oregano, sage, savory, tarragon, thyme
Various	Basil, burnet, cayenne, chervil, dill, marjoram, mint, fresh mushrooms, nutmeg, oregano, parsley, freshly ground black pepper, poppy seeds, rosemary, sage, sesame seeds, sunflower seeds, tarragon, thyme, turmeric, watercress
BAKED GOODS	
Breads	Anise, caraway, cardamom, fennel, poppy seeds, sesame seeds
Desserts	Anise, caraway, cardamom, cinnamon, cloves, coriander, fennel, ginger, mace, mint, nutmeg, poppy seeds, sesame seeds
Fruits	Allspice, anise, basil, cardamom, cinnamon, cloves, cumin, curry, ginger, mint, nutmeg, poppy seeds, rosemary, watercress
Eggs	Basil, chervil, chili powder, cumin, curry, fennel, marjoram, mustard, oregano, parsley, freshly ground black pepper, poppy seeds, rosemary, saffron, savory, sesame seeds, tarragon, thyme, turmeric, watercress

APPENDIX C

American Heart Association Affiliates

American Heart Association
National Center
Dallas, TX

American Heart Association
Alabama Affiliate, Inc.
Birmingham, AL

American Heart Association
Alaska Affiliate, Inc.
Anchorage, AK

American Heart Association
Arizona Affiliate, Inc.
Phoenix, AZ

American Heart Association
Arkansas Affiliate, Inc.
Little Rock, AR

American Heart Association
California Affiliate, Inc.
Burlingame, CA

American Heart Association of
Metropolitan Chicago, Inc.
Chicago, IL

American Heart Association of
Colorado/Wyoming, Inc.
Denver, CO

American Heart Association
Connecticut Affiliate, Inc.
Wallingford, CT

American Heart Association
Dakota Affiliate, Inc.
Jamestown, ND

American Heart Association
Delaware Affiliate, Inc.
Newark, DE

American Heart Association
Florida Affiliate, Inc.
St. Petersburg, FL

American Heart Association
Georgia Affiliate, Inc.
Marietta, GA

American Heart Association
Hawaii Affiliate, Inc.
Honolulu, HI

American Heart Association of Idaho/Montana, Inc.
Boise, ID

American Heart Association
Illinois Affiliate, Inc.
Springfield, IL

American Heart Association
Indiana Affiliate, Inc.
Indianapolis, IN

American Heart Association
Iowa Affiliate, Inc.
Des Moines, IA

American Heart Association
Kansas Affiliate, Inc.
Topeka, KS

American Heart Association
Kentucky Affiliate, Inc.
Louisville, KY

American Heart Association
Greater Los Angeles Affiliate, Inc.
Los Angeles, CA

American Heart Association
Louisiana Affiliate, Inc.
Destrehan, LA

American Heart Association
Maine Affiliate, Inc.
Augusta, ME

American Heart Association
Maryland Affiliate, Inc.
Baltimore, MD

American Heart Association
Massachusetts Affiliate, Inc.
Framingham, MA

American Heart Association of Michigan, Inc.
Lathrup Village, MI

American Heart Association
Minnesota Affiliate, Inc.
Minneapolis, MN

American Heart Association
Mississippi Affiliate, Inc.
Jackson, MS

American Heart Association
Missouri Affiliate, Inc.
St. Louis, MO

American Heart Association
Nation's Capital Affiliate, Inc.
Washington, DC

American Heart Association
Nebraska Affiliate, Inc.
Omaha, NE

American Heart Association
Nevada Affiliate, Inc.
Las Vegas, NV

American Heart Association
New Hampshire Affiliate, Inc.
Manchester, NH

American Heart Association
New Jersey Affiliate, Inc.
North Brunswick, NJ

American Heart Association
New Mexico Affiliate, Inc.
Albuquerque, NM

American Heart Association
New York City Affiliate, Inc.
New York City, NY

American Heart Association
New York State Affiliate, Inc.
North Syracuse, NY

American Heart Association
North Carolina Affiliate, Inc.
Chapel Hill, NC

American Heart Association
Northeast Ohio Affiliate, Inc.
Cleveland, OH

American Heart Association
Ohio Affiliate, Inc.
Columbus, OH

American Heart Association
Oklahoma Affiliate, Inc.
Oklahoma City, OK

American Heart Association
Oregon Affiliate, Inc.
Portland, OR

American Heart Association
Pennsylvania Affiliate, Inc.
Camp Hill, PA

Puerto Rico Heart Association, Inc.
Hato Rey, Puerto Rico

American Heart Association
Rhode Island Affiliate, Inc.
Pawtucket, RI

American Heart Association
South Carolina Affiliate, Inc.
Columbia, SC

American Heart Association
Southeastern Pennsylvania Affiliate, Inc.
Conshohocken, PA

American Heart Association
Tennessee Affiliate, Inc.
Nashville, TN

American Heart Association
Texas Affiliate, Inc.
Austin, TX

American Heart Association
Utah Affiliate, Inc.
Salt Lake City, UT

American Heart Association
Vermont Affiliate, Inc.
Williston, VT

American Heart Association
Virginia Affiliate, Inc.
Glen Allen, VA

American Heart Association
Washington Affiliate, Inc.
Seattle, WA

American Heart Association
West Virginia Affiliate, Inc.
Charleston, WV

American Heart Association
Wisconsin Affiliate, Inc.
Milwaukee, WI

APPENDIX D

For More Information

American Heart Association
National Center
7272 Greenville Avenue
Dallas, TX 75231-4596
(800) AHA-USA1
(800) AHA-8721

The following American Heart Association brochures may be of interest to you:

"About High Blood Pressure"

"About High Blood Pressure in African-Americans"

"About High Blood Pressure in Children: What Parents Should Know"

"Dietary Treatment of High Blood Pressure and High Blood Cholesterol: A Manual for Patients"

"Dining Out: A Guide to Restaurant Dining"

"High Blood Pressure"

"High Blood Pressure Fact Sheet"

"High Blood Pressure in Teenagers"

"How You Can Help Your Doctor Treat Your High Blood Pressure"

"Salt, Sodium and Blood Pressure: Piecing Together the Puzzle"

"The American Heart Association Diet: An Eating Plan for Healthy Americans"

"What Every Woman Should Know About High Blood Pressure"

"What to Ask About High Blood Pressure"

Index